The Protestant Reformation

DOCUMENTARY HISTORY OF WESTERN CIVILIZATION
edited by Eugene C. Black and Leonard W. Levy

ANCIENT AND MEDIEVAL HISTORY OF THE WEST

Morton Smith: ANCIENT GREECE

A. H. M. Jones: A HISTORY OF ROME THROUGH THE FIFTH CENTURY
Vol. I: The Republic
Vol. II: The Empire

Deno Geanakopolos: BYZANTINE EMPIRE

Marshall W. Baldwin: CHRISTIANITY THROUGH THE CRUSADES

Bernard Lewis: ISLAM THROUGH SULEIMAN THE MAGNIFICENT

David Herlihy: HISTORY OF FEUDALISM

William M. Bowsky: RISE OF COMMERCE AND TOWNS

David Herlihy: MEDIEVAL CULTURE AND SOCIETY

EARLY MODERN HISTORY

Hannah Gray: CULTURAL HISTORY OF THE RENAISSANCE

Florence Edler De Roover: MONEY, BANKING & COMMERCE, 13TH-16TH CENTURIES

V. J. Parry: THE OTTOMAN EMPIRE

Ralph E. Giesey: EVOLUTION OF THE DYNASTIC STATE

J. H. Parry: THE EUROPEAN RECONNAISSANCE

Hans J. Hillerbrand: THE PROTESTANT REFORMATION

John C. Olin: THE CATHOLIC COUNTER-REFORMATION

Orest Ranum: THE CENTURY OF LOUIS XIV

Thomas Hegarty: RUSSIAN HISTORY THROUGH PETER THE GREAT

Marie Boas-Hall: THE SCIENTIFIC REVOLUTION

Barry E. Supple: HISTORY OF MERCANTILISM

_____: IMPERIALISM, WAR & DIPLOMACY,1550-1763

Herbert H. Rowen: THE LOW COUNTRIES

C. A. Macartney: THE EVOLUTION OF THE HABSBURG & HOHENZOLLERN DYNASTIES

Lester G. Crocker: THE ENLIGHTENMENT

Robert Forster: EIGHTEENTH CENTURY EUROPEAN SOCIETY

A volume
in
DOCUMENTARY HISTORY
of
WESTERN CIVILIZATION

THE PROTESTANT REFORMATION

edited by
HANS J. HILLERBRAND

WALKER AND COMPANY
New York

THE PROTESTANT REFORMATION
Copyright © 1968 by Hans J. Hillerbrand.

Library of Congress Catalog Card Number: 68-13328.

Printed in the United States of America.

Published in the United States of America in 1968 by Walker and Company, a division of Walker Publishing Company, Inc.

Published simultaneously in Canada by The Ryerson Press, Toronto.

Volumes in this series are published in association with Harper & Row, Publishers, Inc., from whom paperback editions are available in Harper Torchbooks.

Contents

ௐௐௐௐௐௐௐௐௐௐௐௐௐௐௐௐௐௐௐௐ

IV. John Calvin

V. The English Reformation

Preface

According to the proverb fools step boldly where angels fear to tread. Perhaps this wise word should be applied to my attempt to compress the abundant literature of the Protestant Reformation into a modest volume. After all, Luther's writings fill nearly one hundred folio volumes and Calvin's hardly less. Most of the Protestant reformers were verbal exhibitionists who eagerly committed their thoughts to print. This was, indeed, the secret of their success.

Thus, the task of editing was a painful one, especially since it became apparent that the rigorous restriction to a few major documents (in keeping with the format of the series) meant that only the old stand-bys survived the repeated process of selection. Many interesting and lesser-known materials (admittedly, however, not of primary importance) had to fall by the wayside. The selections are to illustrate the various facets, both geographic and theological, of the Protestant Reformation. In almost every instance documents are to be more than illustrative, however. They are meant to allow reflection and discussion of the issues raised. Still, I trust that the volume is both competent and useful.

The various bibliographical aids in both the introductory essay and the introductions to the documents are designed to direct the reader to further literature; they concentrate on publications in English.

Duke University, 1967   HANS J. HILLERBRAND

Chronology

<table>
<tr><td>1509</td><td>Accession of Henry VIII of England
Erasmus' The Praise of Folly</td></tr>
<tr><td>1515</td><td>Accession of Francis I of France</td></tr>
<tr><td>1517</td><td>Publication of Luther's Ninety-five Theses</td></tr>
<tr><td>1519</td><td>Charles V elected German Emperor
Zwingli Leutpriester in Zürich
Leipzig disputation between Luther and Eck; Luther's repudiation of councils</td></tr>
<tr><td>1520</td><td>Bull Exsurge Domine threatens Luther with excommunication
Revolt of the Communeros in Spain</td></tr>
<tr><td>1521</td><td>Luther's excommunication. His appearance before the Diet at Worms.
The Edict of Worms</td></tr>
<tr><td>1522</td><td>The Turks occupy Belgrade
Luther's translation of the New Testament</td></tr>
<tr><td>1523</td><td>Beginnings of ecclesiastical transformation in Zürich</td></tr>
<tr><td>1524</td><td>Peasants' uprising in Germany
War between Charles V and Francis I</td></tr>
<tr><td>1525</td><td>Battle of Pavia
Tyndale's English New Testament</td></tr>
<tr><td>1526</td><td>Battle of Mohács
League of Cognac
Diet of Speyer allows German territorial rulers to decide on administration of Edict of Worms</td></tr>
<tr><td>1527</td><td>Sacco di Roma
Henry VIII begins to seek annulment of his marriage with Catherine of Aragon</td></tr>
</table>

Introduction

⎍⎍⎍⎍⎍⎍⎍⎍⎍⎍⎍⎍⎍⎍⎍⎍⎍⎍⎍⎍⎍⎍⎍⎍⎍⎍

I

Few would deny that the Reformation of the sixteenth century marks one of the great epochs in the history of Western civilization. To be sure, modern narratives seldom praise it as the time of the restoration of the gospel or denounce it as the time of fatal religious perversion. That it was an occasion of dramatic change, however, can hardly be contested.[1]

For the better part of a century Europe was variously influenced by the events precipitated by the Protestant reformers. Needless

---

[1] There are basic bibliographical aids for Reformation studies in the volumes of two journals: the *Revue d'Histoire Ecclésiastique* and the *Archiv für Reformationsgeschichte*. See also the *Bibliographie de la Réforme, 1450–1648* (5 vols. Leyden, 1961–1965); E. Schottenloher, *Bibliographie zur deutschen Geschichte im Zeitalter der Glaubensspaltung* (7 vols. Stuttgart, 1962 ff.). The following Reformation histories also include extensive bibliographical surveys: E. Hassinger, *Das Werden des neuzeitlichen Europas* (Braunschweig, 1959); H. J. Grimm, *The Reformation Era* (New York, 1965); E. Leonard, *History of Protestantism* (London, 1965).

The following are standard reference works: F. L. Cross (ed.), *The Oxford Dictionary of the Christian Church* (New York and London, 1957); K. Galling (ed.), *Die Religion in Geschichte und Gegenwart* (3rd ed., 5 vols., Tübingen, 1957–1962); H. S. Bender & C. H. Smith (eds.), *The Mennonite Encyclopedia* (4 vols. Scottdale, Pennsylvania, 1955–1959).

Note the following standard monographs on the Reformation: L. v. Ranke, *History of the Reformation in Germany* (New York, 1905); P. Smith, *The Age of the Reformation* (New York, 1920); R. H. Bainton, *The Reformation of the Sixteenth Century* (Boston, 1953); H. J. Grimm, *op. cit.*; G. R. Elton (ed.), *The New Cambridge Modern History. The Reformation, 1520–1559* (Cambridge, 1958); G. R. Elton, *Reformation Europe, 1517–1559* (London, 1963, New York: Harper Torchbooks, 1966); O. Chadwick, *The Reformation* (London, 1964); H. J. Hillerbrand, *The Reformation. A Narrative History* (New York, 1965); A. G. Dickens, *Reformation and Society in Sixteenth-Century Europe* (New York, 1966).

to say, some of these, such as the struggle between Spain and France that began in the last decade of the fifteenth century and stretched well into the sixteenth, or the steadily widening horizon of the discoveries across the seas, had nothing to do with the religious controversy. Other events, outwardly religious in character, were primarily oriented by different factors, or at the least by a conflux of religious and political considerations. One must be wary of pious oversimplifications. Still, in its main features the Protestant Reformation affected the course of Europe in countless different ways.

If the sixteenth century itself was an unending battle between Catholics and Protestants, subsequent centuries have battled over the proper interpretation of the epoch. A "history" of Reformation histories would make fascinating reading and would demonstrate persuasively that the past is by no means dead, but engages the historian's commitment.[2] The Reformation is a battleground *par excellence* of historical interpretation, and raises problems comparable to those of the Protectorate of seventeenth-century England, the revolution of eighteenth-century France, or the unification of nineteenth-century Germany. In recent years more sophisticated canons of historical research have excluded the grossest forms of parochial hagiography on both sides of the ecclesiastical fence—the Protestant Merle d'Aubigny and the Catholic John Cochläus are hardly acceptable today—but ecclesiastical labels are still important and, what is more, the widely divergent views of the "secular" historians preclude scholarly consensus.

Many basic questions surround the Reformation. What were its causes? Was it precipitated by the *Zeitgeist* prevailing in Europe, so that there would have been a religious upheaval even if Luther or Zwingli had died in their cradles? Was the Reformation an authentically religious phenomenon, or the result of certain political, social, or economic developments? Was it "medieval" or "modern" in its orientation? What was the teaching of the reformers? What was the significance of the Reformation? The measure

---

[2] Historiographical surveys are found in R. H. Bainton, "Interpretations of the Reformation," *American Historical Review*, 66 (1960); J. P. Dolan, *A History of the Reformation* (New York, 1964); W. A. Clebsch, "New Perspectives on the Reformation," *Religion in Life*, 35 (1965).

of scholarly agreement with respect to these questions differs; far from offering definitive answers, we can here only call attention to their persistent presence.[3]

II

In order to understand the Protestant Reformation it is necessary to recall that in the time before the storm people were intensely religious.[4] The intensity of religious commitment cannot easily be demonstrated, but all the evidence—the number of religious books, the gifts to religious causes, the frequency of pilgrimages, the membership of voluntary religious societies—suggests that people were as religious as they had always been, and that they took their religion seriously. There was some deviation from the ideal, and we can easily cite criticisms of the church in which two themes in particular constantly recur: the financial burden imposed by the church and the unspiritual demeanor of the clergy. One must be careful, however, not to generalize too freely. The picture of a church in a state of complete perversion on the eve of the Reformation has little historical basis. Nor is it correct to say that in the early sixteenth century every sensible person yearned for ecclesiastical reform. Abuses were in fact few and far between. More to the point is that this was a generally restless society in which dramatic changes were everywhere taking place. No doubt there was uneasiness about the church, a latent dissatisfaction and disquiet. None of these, however, were pronounced or intense enough to make a religious upheaval inescapable. The generation might well have passed from the scene without having witnessed any kind of ecclesiastical change. A proper admixture of factors was necessary to bring the latent dissatisfaction into the open. When this happened, probably no one was more astounded than the man who had precipitated it: Martin Luther, a youthful and unknown professor of theology of Wittenberg.

[3] A number of different perspectives are gathered together in L. W. Spitz, *The Reformation: Material or Spiritual?* (Boston, 1962).

[4] For an appraisal of the situation on the eve of the Reformation see J. Lortz, *How the Reformation Came* (New York, 1964).

III

Martin Luther and the publication of his Ninety-five Theses mark the beginning of the Reformation.[5] The theme of these Theses was the doctrine of indulgences, acknowledgedly a minor point of Catholic theology, which Luther meant to expound in a routine academic disputation. The immediate cause of Luther's step had been his disgust with the indulgence proclamation of John Tetzel. This proclamation was part and parcel of a grandiose political, financial and ecclesiastical scheme, and Luther had reached into a hornet's nest. Public excitement was engendered and knowledge of Luther's somewhat esoteric Theses was not restricted to a few theological experts. Since his pronouncement was taken to be directed against the hierarchy and the papacy (which it was not), he increasingly received support from those who were dissatisfied with the general state of ecclesiastical affairs. A controversy evolved which slowly but surely moved to more central issues. By the summer of 1519 the issue was that of religious authority; Luther

---

[5] On Luther's writings in English see G. S. Robbert, "A Checklist of Luther's Writings in English," *Concordia Theological Monthly*, 36 (1965), and the 55-volume edition presently in the process of publication: *Luther's Works. American Edition* (St. Louis–Philadelphia, 1955 ff.). Also to be noted are J. Dillenberger (ed.), *Martin Luther* (Chicago, 1961); *Martin Luther. Reformation Writings*, trans. B. L. Woolf (2 vols., London–New York, 1956); vols. 15–18 of the Library of Christian Classics (Philadelphia, 1953 ff.). Bibliographical surveys are found in H. J. Grimm, "Luther Research Since 1920," *Journal of Modern History*, 32 (1960); J. Dillenberger, "Major Volumes and Selected Periodical Literature in Luther-Studies, 1956–1959," *Church History*, 30 (1961).

The following biographies are standard: R. H. Bainton, *Here I Stand: A Life of Martin Luther* (New York, 1950); E. G. Schwiebert, *Luther and His Times* (St. Louis, 1950); E. G. Rupp, *Luther's Progress to the Diet of Worms* (Chicago, 1951, New York: Harper Torchbooks, 1964); R. H. Fife, *The Revolt of Martin Luther* (New York, 1957); E. H. Erikson, *Young Man Luther* (New York, 1958); G. Ritter, *Luther. His Life and Work* (New York, 1963).

Luther's theology is treated by P. S. Watson, *Let God be God* (Philadelphia, 1950); E. G. Rupp, *The Righteousness of God* (London, 1954); L. Pinomaa, *Faith Victorious* (Philadelphia, 1963); H. Bornkamm, *The Heart of the Reformation Faith* (New York, 1965).

repudiated the infallibility of both general councils and the pope, and replaced them with *sola scriptura*, Scripture alone.

Luther's proclamation was widely echoed and he became the hero of Germany. A host of disciples joined his cause, some because they had been genuinely touched by his religious message, others because they confused their own religious or even political aspirations with his.[6] While some may have been strange bedfellows—mistaking Luther for a German nationalist or an Erasmian Humanist—their support was real and vastly consequential. By 1521 Luther's "reformation" had become a popular movement.

It also had become heretical. Since the early months of 1518 the wheels of the curial machinery had turned, now slowly, now rapidly, to assess the orthodoxy of the Wittenberg professor. By the summer of 1520 the verdict was reached: the bull *Exsurge Domine* condemned some forty of Luther's teachings as heretical. This should have been the end of the matter. For many reasons, it was not. Thus Luther outlived his excommunication and died peacefully in bed. More than that, he witnessed the establishment of Protestant churches. Once the impossibility of achieving a conciliation with the Catholic church had become obvious, Luther and the other reformers decided to go their own way and their theological pronouncements were translated into ecclesiastical practice. Numerous different questions begged to be answered about such problems as the place of the church in society, the form of worship, or ministerial training.

By that time a host of reformers had appeared on the scene, all in their own way echoing Luther's repudiation of the Catholic church. Multiplicity meant strength, but it also meant diversity, for these reformers did not fully agree with one another's theological positions. Some of the disagreements were innocuous, as, for example, those between Luther and Melanchthon, while others were more consequential, particularly since they soon issued into open controversy and revealed that Protestantism was a house divided against itself.

The most spectacular example was Huldrych Zwingli, the reformer of Zürich. Akin to Luther in a variety of ways, including

---

[6] On the rise of variant forms of Protestantism see E. G. Rupp, "Luther and the Puritans," in *Luther Today* (Decorah, Iowa, 1957).

his basic understanding of the New Testament, he sought to transform the faith and life of the church in Zürich according to his
particular understanding of the gospel. He clashed with Luther
over the correct interpretation of the Lord's Supper, a controversy
that was to dominate the history of Protestantism for many years.[7]

Of equal importance was the emergence of a radical form of
Protestantism. Its spokesmen were erstwhile disciples of Luther
and Zwingli, men who had become impatient with what seemed
to them a slow and haphazard program of reform. They advocated
nothing less than a "reform" of the Reformation. In terms of their
own positive principles, they were a motley crew, holding to almost as many opinions as there were men. Most numerous among
them were the Anabaptists, who advocated the *imitatio Christi*,
to be evidenced by believer's baptism, pacifism, and a church
composed only of those who had freely and determinedly elected
to be Christ's disciples.[8] The story of Anabaptism in the sixteenth
century was one of bloody and ruthless persecution, practiced by
Catholics and Protestants alike with a grim determination worthy
of a better cause. It was a story of martyrdom and of suffering.
Since rebaptism was a crime, the legal situation was hopeless for
the Anabaptists. It was made worse by the disruption of the unity
of society through the Anabaptist postulate of a voluntary church.

The Reformation in England deserves a special word, for there
the ecclesiastical transformation followed its own distinct pattern.[9]

[7] On Zwingli see S. M. Jackson (ed.), *Selected Works of Huldreich
Zwingli* (Philadelphia, 1901); S. M. Jackson (ed.), *The Latin Works and
Correspondence of Huldreich Zwingli* (3 vols., New York–Philadelphia,
1912–1929); G. W. Bromiley (ed.), *Zwingli and Bullinger* (Philadelphia,
1953).

Bibliographical surveys are found in B. Thompson, "Zwingli Study Since
1918," *Church History*, 19 (1950); G. W. Locher, "The Change of the
Understanding of Zwingli in Recent Research," *Church History*, 34 (1965).
The following biographies are to be noted: S. M. Jackson, *Huldrych
Zwingli* (New York, 1901); O. Farner, *Huldrych Zwingli* (4 vols., Zürich,
1943–1960); J. H. Rilliet, *Zwingli, Third Man of the Reformation* (Phila-
delphia, 1964); O. Farner, *Zwingli, the Reformer* (New York, 1952);
J. Courvoisier, *Zwingli. A Reformed Theologian* (Richmond, 1963).

[8] On Anabaptism see H. J. Hillerbrand, "The Origin of Sixteenth-Century Anabaptism: Another Look," *Archiv für Reformationsgeschichte*, 53
(1962), and G. H. Williams, *The Radical Reformation* (Philadelphia,
1962).

[9] See P. Hughes, *The Reformation in England* (3 vols., New York,
1950–1954); A. G. Dickens, *The English Reformation* (London, 1954). A

England had its share of reforming spirits in the early years of the Reformation, men like Bilney, Barnes, or Tyndale, who propounded a theology that in many ways echoed the themes of Luther's proclamation. How successful these reformers would have been in altering the religious scene in England can only be conjectured, for before they could demonstrate their persuasiveness and vitality King Henry VIII utilized the existing anti-Roman sentiment and undertook to cut the English church from its Catholic matrix. The reason was his "great matter," Henry's effort to secure an ecclesiastical annulment of his marriage to Catherine of Aragon. For a combination of political and other reasons, the pope was unwilling to grant this annulment and, influenced by Thomas Cranmer and Thomas Cromwell, Henry decided that as king of England he could do as he pleased.[10] Declaring himself "supreme head of the church," he disputed the authority of the pope but otherwise altered little of Catholic theology. The theological temper of the English church until Henry's death in 1547 virtually remained Catholic.

Under Henry's son, Edward VI, who reigned from 1547–1553, England steered a more distinctly Protestant course, expressed especially in the second edition of the *Book of Common Prayer* of 1552. But Edward's reign was too brief to allow the firm establishment of the Protestant faith in the land. And the same comment must be made about Edward's half-sister, Mary, who succeeded him and desperately sought to re-Catholicize England, but died after a reign of only five years. She had vehemently persecuted the Protestants during this time, but making martyrs proved to be a terrible blunder for it only intensified the hatred of "popery" among the English people. Queen Elizabeth I, who ascended the English throne in 1558, enjoyed above all the blessing of longevity (she ruled until 1603), which allowed her religious settlement of 1559 to become permanent.[11] This settlement was characterized

---

full bibliography is found in C. Read (ed.), *Bibliography of British History*. Tudor Period (2nd ed., Oxford, 1959). W. Clebsch, *England's Earliest Protestants* (New Haven, 1965), stresses the religious factor in the earliest phase of the English Reformation.

[10] See here G. R. Elton, "King or Minister? The Man Behind the Henrician Reformation," *History*, 39 (1954).

[11] C. S. Meyer, *Elizabeth I and the Religious Settlement of 1559* (St. Louis, 1960).

by a moderate Protestantism, which was at once a virtue and a vice. It was vehemently attacked by Catholics, who thought that the settlement was too radical, and by some Protestants, who thought that it was too conservative. The Protestants, called "Puritans," who were so persuaded, battled endlessly with the church of England over the proper interpretation of ecclesiastical polity.[12] But the Elizabethan settlement survived these challenges, if for no other reason than that it never lost the support of the crown and found some highly competent apologetes.

John Calvin, the frail, modest, scholarly reformer of Geneva,[13] was of the second generation of reformers who succeeded in synthesizing a new kind of Protestantism; systematic and persuasive, it proved to be vastly influential in the Anglo-Saxon world. Calvin was one of the outstanding theologians of the century—since there was no dearth of theologians this statement must not be taken lightly—and the systematic exposition of his theological thought, the *Institutes of the Christian Religion*, is one of the major documents of the Christian tradition. A Frenchman by birth, a lawyer-Humanist by training, a practical reformer in Geneva almost by accident, Calvin conceived of his reformatory work in a broad political setting. Like Zwingli in this respect, he saw direct implications of the gospel for the public and social realm; he set out not only to reform the faith of the Genevan citizens but also to transform the city itself. Some contemporaries thought him eminently successful. In John Knox's well known encomium, Geneva was the "most perfect school of Jesus Christ since the days of the apostles."

Calvin is sometimes described as an ecclesiastical tyrant and

---

[12] The standard work on Puritanism is M. M. Knappen, *Tudor Puritanism* (Chicago, 1939).

[13] On Calvin see J. T. McNeill, "Thirty Years of Calvin Study," *Church History*, 17 (1948); E. A. Dowey, "Studies in Calvin and Calvinism Since 1948," *Church History*, 24 (1955), 29 (1960); W. Niesel, *Calvin-Bibliographie* (München, 1961). A good English edition of the *Institutes* is J. T. McNeill (ed.), *John Calvin: Institutes of the Christian Religion* (2 vols., Philadelphia, 1960). On the theology of the Genevan reformer, see E. A. Dowey, *The Knowledge of God in Calvin's Theology* (New York, 1952); W. Niesel, *The Theology of Calvin* (Philadelphia, 1956); J. T. McNeill, *The History and Character of Calvinism* (New York, 1954 and 1967); F. Wendel, *The Origin and Development of Calvin's Thought* (New York, 1963).

Geneva during his time as an ecclesiastical police state. There is some truth to this observation; like all half-truths, however, it is dangerously one-sided. Life was strict and regimented in Geneva; the consistory kept a careful eye on the demeanor of the citizens. But sixteenth-century society in general was circumscribed by numerous rules; in Geneva there was only slightly more regimentation and supervision than elsewhere. Far more important was the different ethos of the Genevan citizens who gladly shared, or at least tolerated, Calvin's vision of the Christian commonwealth. Calvin can hardly have been a tyrant; he faced staunch opposition during his first decade in Geneva and he always depended upon the good will of the Genevan authorities to carry out his program.

IV

These various streams of the Protestant Reformation arose from specific theological affirmations, which were expressed in differing ecclesiastical organizations—churches with pastors, people, and a definite polity and way of life. All the Protestant reformers were determined to translate their theological theories into ecclesiastical practice, and all were concerned that theirs should be the legally established religion of their respective commonwealths. Some were more successful than others. In England, as we have noted, the settlement decreed by Queen Elizabeth gave lasting success to Protestantism, and in similar fashion other countries such as Scotland, Scandinavia, and Holland saw the permanent establishment of the Protestant faith. In Germany, the Peace of Augsburg in 1555 brought legal recognition of Lutheranism for those territories whose ruler decided to accept it. The radical expressions of Protestantism never secured such legal recognition, except in isolated instances and on a modest scale. And at some places, such as France or Poland, the struggle for the recognition of the Protestant faith occupied the larger part of the century. Thus, success was varied. At the end of the century, however, the map of Europe was predominantly Protestant; Catholicism seemed to be at its nadir.

V

Several features characterized the Protestant Reformation of the sixteenth century.[14] First and perhaps foremost is the fact that it was a phenomenon of European dimensions. While the intensity of Protestant belief and the measure of eventual success differed from country to country, virtually all Europe was affected—Italy no less than Sweden, England no less than Poland. In this sense, this was an era with a common temper, affecting all of Europe simultaneously, in contrast to the Renaissance, for example, which never exerted such impact. Reformation scholarship is divided as to whether or not this European movement is to be traced to Martin Luther alone. Students of the Swiss or English Reformation have insisted on the autonomous character of the ecclesiastical transformation in their lands, suggesting that Luther only added further strength and impetus to basically indigenous developments. However, Luther's proclamation undoubtedly had an effect, even if only as a catalyst. It may be that his stand merely encouraged others to speak up boldly, but it was because of his encouragement that the Reformation spread beyond Germany.

A second feature of the Reformation (and it is not unnecessary to mention this) is that it was a religious phenomenon. The slogans of the reformers were religious slogans and their writings theological writings. This is external evidence, it is true, and does not refute the possible objection that religion provided a convenient rationalization for the pursuit of more tangible political or economic goals. But this admittedly attractive argument neglects several persuasive facts; in particular it overlooks the martyrs of the time. These men and women from all religious factions, Catholics, Lutherans, Calvinists, Anglicans, and Anabaptists, reveal intense religious commitment. Many went to the stake for their convictions, and many others who were not put to death suffered physical pain and economic hardship.

[14] Perceptive statements of Protestant thought are found in J. S. Whale, *The Protestant Tradition* (Cambridge, 1955); J. Dillenberger and C. Welch, *Protestant Christianity Interpreted Through Its Development* (New York, 1954).

Moreover, the acceptance of the Protestant faith was in some instances the least prudent political policy to pursue. This was certainly true in Germany between 1521 and 1525, when it was virtually political suicide to accept the new faith. The peasants' uprising of 1524–1525, with the support it seemed to draw from the Lutheran proclamation, dismayed those charged with the maintenance of law and order. No one knew how the matter would end. In the 1520's the Catholics in Germany possessed a formidable hold on political power that should have given second thoughts to anyone who sought to break with the Catholic church for other than religious reasons. Most rulers possessed as much authority in ecclesiastical affairs as they desired.

Still, it would be naive to suggest that political considerations were completely absent. Indeed, the great theme of the age was, as Ranke observed, the interaction of religion and politics. Religion alone does not suffice as a full explanation for events, for in many ways political considerations intruded upon the ecclesiastical course of events. Zwingli's quest for a Protestant alliance, the formation of the League of Schmalkald, and the ecclesiastical transformation in Poland or France, show that Protestantism was politically involved.

By the same token, however, politics alone is an insufficient guide to understanding these dramatic events: Zwingli's unwillingness to compromise his theological position at the Marburg colloquy on communion even though this meant the abject failure of his political plans, and Luther's unwillingness to become the spokesman for the German people in 1521, are evidence of this.

Religion and politics interacted in countless ways, determining the temper of the age. In their light some men appeared nobler than we are wont to acknowledge, while some lofty ecclesiastical ideals were exposed as being much shabbier than was claimed.

VI

Theologically, the Protestant reformers thought themselves in the authentic Catholic tradition from which, they argued, the papal church had departed. And they were in a sense good Catholics. They accepted the three ancient creeds, so common ground existed between the old and the new church. The trinitarian affirmation or the christological definitions of the early church were never questioned by the reformers. But the Protestant Reformation was not a "reform" movement in the sense of seeking only to clip off certain "abuses" in the church and otherwise accept the status quo. To be sure, Luther and his fellow-reformers now and then talked about the correction of ecclesiastical abuses and initially their efforts may have been so understood by the people. But the real thrust of the reformers was in a different direction—a reinterpretation of the gospel. The reformers propounded a different understanding of the New Testament, and while this understanding had connections with the theological tradition of the Fathers, especially St. Augustine, it can justly be called new. When the Protestants talked about "reform," therefore, they thought not so much about the practical life of the church as about a new theological understanding.

One slogan seemed to express this new understanding most profoundly: the righteousness of faith, or of justification *sola fide*, by faith alone. The reformers attributed man's reconciliation with God solely to the divine offer of forgiveness which was to be appropriated by man through faith: no merits here, no harmonious cooperation between divine grace and human effort. Man, the sinner, is freely accepted by God. This assertion had many ramifications. The notion of the priesthood of all believers stated that all believers have full access to God and do not require the aid of the intermediary priest. In principle this did away with the distinction between clergy and laity and emphasized the fellowship of the Christian congregation.

Equally important was the stress upon *sola scriptura*, Scripture alone, for it propounded a new norm of religious authority. Only the Bible was acknowledged as a true source of Christian truth. This meant the repudiation of the authority of the church—the decisions of church councils, the papal pronouncements, indeed all that the reformers called "human traditions." Only if these ecclesiastical statements agreed with Scripture were they to be accepted as authentic.

There were additional aspects of the Protestant evangel, such as the repudiation of the primacy of the papal office or the acknowledgment of only two sacraments, namely, communion and baptism. The latter affirmation resulted from the reinterpretation of the nature of the sacrament which related the spiritual benefits of the sacrament more intimately to the faith of the individual. The cultural consequences of the Reformation must also be noted.[15] The stress on the Bible as source of Christian truth and the corollary that each man must read it for himself meant that the religious responsibilities of the individual were vastly increased. A more sophisticated theological literacy was mandatory and this led to a determined pedagogical effort; schools were established, and language training was stressed. Behind it lay the Protestant notion of "vocation" which affirmed that all human endeavors, not only the clerical ones, are the fulfillment of a divine call. The swineherd was therefore as much called by God to his work as was the monk. The most menial work, performed in response to God's call, was endowed with religious significance; it was both important in its own right, and related to the divine purpose.

A further word must be said about what might be called the "Protestant spirit" for it was this "spirit" that caught the imagination of the people perhaps more than the theological doctrines expounded by the Protestant divines. The point of the Protestant proclamation was that religion was to be personal and creative. It called for personal involvement, not merely the affirmation of the dogma of the church or the external participation in its rites. It also called for the bold scrutiny of theological tradition and the willingness to reject it where it did not seem to be in harmony with the biblical message. At this point, one might well add, Catholics are most pronounced in their repudiation of the Reformation. The eminent Catholic historian Joseph Lortz chided Luther for not being "a full listener," that is, for making absolute his own understanding of the faith. Indeed, the reformers appear as the great destroyers—as tearing down the walls of the Romanists, as Luther put it in his tract on *The Babylonian Captivity of the Church:* tearing down the wall of five sacraments, the wall of transubstantiation, of the ecclesiastical superiority over the temporal power, of a celibate clergy. All ecclesiastical affirmations were to be examined creatively in the light of Scripture. Accordingly, an air of freedom surrounded the Protestant proclamation,

[15] See K. Holl, *The Cultural Significance of the Reformation* (New York, 1959).

for such a personal and creative religion left little room for regulations and regimentation. The Christian was a free lord over all things, Luther said, and a dutiful servant of all things.

Two generations ago the German sociologist Max Weber sought to relate the Protestant ethic, especially that of Calvinism, to the rise of capitalism.[16] Subsequent research has tended to be skeptical of his thesis, but about the general cultural significance of the Reformation there should be little doubt. The Reformation was hardly the cradle of the modern world—in a variety of ways its questions were medieval questions—Luther's plea at Worms was hardly a plea for religious tolerance of the autonomy of conscience, and Calvin's economic thought was hardly the paradigm for Adam Smith. This must not obscure the fact, however, that these and many other "modern" notions made their first appearance during the sixteenth century, and the Reformation did its share in stimulating them: Protestantism stressed the centrality of the individual; sought to reduce the intervention of political power in ecclesiastical affairs; cast the glow of "vocation" over formerly menial undertakings; and raised the spirit of free, personal, and creative inquiry. All this could not help but change the face of society.

VII

This religiously lively and exuberant age produced an enormous literature. The printing press was the handmaiden of the Protestant reformers who, without Gutenberg's invention, could not have made the impact they did. John Foxe, the English martyrologist, observed aptly, "We have great cause to give thanks to the providence of almighty God, for the excellent arte of Printing, most happily of late found out and now commonly practiced everywhere, to the singular benefite of Christes Church."[17] The

[16] See M. Weber, *The Protestant Ethic and the Spirit of Capitalism* (London, 1930), and R. W. Green, *Protestantism and Capitalism: The Weber Thesis and Its Critics* (Boston, 1959).

[17] John Foxe (ed.), *The whole Workes of W. Tyndall, John Frith, and doct. Barnes* (London, 1572–1573) as quoted in M. Aston, "Lollardy and the Reformation: Survival or Revival?" *History,* 49 (1964), 169.

printing press helped to make the Reformation a success.[18] The number of Protestant publications was legion. By 1523 some thirteen hundred different editions of tracts by Luther alone had been published; assuming that each edition involved between seven hundred and fifty and eight hundred copies, we reach a total of about one million copies. The first truly popular tract from Luther's pen, the *Sermon on Indulgence and Grace* written in German and printed in 1518, was reprinted fourteen times in 1518, five times in 1519, and four times in 1520.

We tend to overlook the dimensions of this flood of propaganda. Reformation scholarship has been preoccupied with the eminent figures of the time, titans such as Luther, Zwingli, or Calvin, who were astonishingly prolific: the Weimar edition of Luther's writings alone consists of almost one hundred volumes. We should remember that the minor reformers, in their turn, followed their precedent with enthusiasm. Men like Bucer, Schwenckfeld, Oecolampadius, Brenz, Melanchthon, or Carlstadt were indefatigable and highly productive when it came to putting their thoughts to print. Carlstadt published over fifty tracts and Schwenckfeld's writings comprise almost twenty volumes. They would not have been published had there not been a demand, and their publication in such quantities indicates the popular character of the Reformation.

But more must be said about the literature of the Reformation than its mere quantity. Most of it appeared in a new format, what we today would call "paperback size," and consisted of a few quarto or octavo pages, and a woodcut to characterize the content—a pamphlet, in other words. Naturally, Luther and the other reformers could also spin out lengthy and tedious prose. In the main, however, their tracts were brief (seldom more than forty pages in length), they could be read quickly, were inex-

---

[18] L. W. Holborn, "Printing and the Growth of a Protestant Movement in Germany," *Church History*, 11 (1942). See also K. Schottenloher, *Flugblatt und Zeitung* (Berlin, 1922); H. Maylan (ed.), *Aspects de la propaganda religieuse* (Geneva, 1957); M. Gravier, *Luther et l'opinion publique. Essai sur la littérature satirique et polémique en langue allemande pendant les années decisives de la Réforme* (Paris, 1943); O. Clemen, *Die lutherische Reformation und der Buchdruck* (Leipzig, 1939); H. Volz, "Flugschriften der Reformationszeit," in K. Galling (ed.), *Religion in Geschichte und Gegenwart* (Tübingen, 1958), II, 985; F. Betten, "The Cartoon in Luther's Warfare Against the Church," *Catholic Historical Review*, 5 (1925).

pensive, and were written in the vernacular. This last was, perhaps, their most incisive characteristic.[19] The Protestant reformers made a determined effort to speak to the common people. In so doing they broke with tradition, for theological tracts had never been published in the language of the people; even Erasmus, who waxed so eloquent about his hope that the farmer might sing of the gospel behind his plow, always wrote in Latin. Not so the Protestant divines.

Luther set the precedent here. A few of his theological pronouncements were in Latin, as, for example, his ninety-five Theses or his tract *The Babylonian Captivity of the Church*. Most of his tracts, however, were in German. The other reformers followed his example, at worst multiplying the number of vernacular Protestant tracts, at best spreading the message of the Reformation across Germany and Europe. No matter what the country and who the reformer, the characteristic feature was always the use of the vernacular. And even as Luther had aided the formation of the German language, so the reformers in other European countries contributed their share to the formation of their respective languages.[20] In all instances a preeminent achievement was the translation of the Bible, in Germany associated with the name of Luther, in England with that of William Tyndale, in Sweden with that of Olavus Petri. There was no dearth of men eager to translate the Holy Writ into the vernacular.

By repudiating Latin as the language of theological discourse the reformers also changed the character of theological writing. They abandoned the traditional forms of theological exposition and replaced them with a fresh style. Especially in the early years of the Reformation the Protestant writers used a great variety of literary forms—open letters, satires, dialogues, biblical expositions, sermonic exhortations, etc. It goes without saying that this creative use of literary forms contributed to the significance of these tracts. An eminent characteristic of Protestant literature was its simplicity; profound religious thoughts were expressed simply, though with zeal and determination. As the decades passed, however, Protestant

[19] See here the study by H. Bornkamm, *Luther als Schriftsteller* (Heidelberg, 1965).

[20] For Luther see H. Volz, *Bibel und Bibeldruck in Deutschland im 15. und 16. Jahrhundert* (Mainz, 1960).

theologians increasingly adopted the heavy style of the medieval scholastics and the precision of Latin recommended itself once again for theological exposition. By the end of the century, Protestant theological writing was as tedious as Catholic works had been at the beginning.

Another characteristic of Protestant literature was its biblical flavor. Biblical commentaries and homilies came from the pen of all reformers and even topical tracts contained an enormous number of biblical references. While the medieval scholastics had done their prooftexting from other scholastic authorities, the Protestant theologians, though occasionally referring to the early Fathers, most frequently cited Scripture. This, of course, was in line with the Protestant principle of *sola scriptura*, which became a distinct literary characteristic.

A good deal of the Protestant literature was polemical in character; that is, it was directed against specific men or issues and arose from controversy. Virtually all the writings had a specific *raison d'être* and only very few—Calvin's *Institutes of the Christian Religion* was a notable exception—were the result of unhurried reflection. The tone of the writings was thus at times vehement and even abusive.

VIII

When the reformers who had first ventured a new interpretation of the gospel had passed from the scene, the question which had haunted the Reformation from its very inception—where is truth? —was still contested by the proponents of the old and the new faith. But one fact was beyond dispute: Western Christendom was tragically divided not into two religious factions only but into no less than five—Catholic, Lutheran, Calvinist, Anglican, and Anabaptist. Though these divisions were the result of intense religious conviction, they could not help but lessen the intensity of religious belief in Europe. The Reformation of the sixteenth century was the last period in the history of Western civilization when men were preoccupied with religion, argued it, fought and even died for it. Its consequences are still with us.

I. *The German Reformation*

⎍⎍⎍⎍⎍⎍⎍⎍⎍⎍⎍⎍⎍⎍⎍⎍⎍⎍⎍⎍⎍⎍⎍⎍⎍⎍⎍

1. Martin Luther: Preface to the first volume of Latin writings (1545)*

In the pursuit of his academic responsibilities at Wittenberg Luther formulated a new theology which, since it diverged from the medieval theological consensus, eventually led to the Reformation. The starting point of this new theology was a basic insight into the nature of biblical religion. Though there is some uncertainty about the exact date of this insight, Luther surely had come to it well before the outbreak of the indulgences controversy in 1517. Luther commented on his theological development on several occasions, notably in the year before his death, when he wrote the Preface to the first volume of his Latin writings then in the process of publication.

The setting of Luther's recollection is a description of the *res indulgentiara*, the indulgences affair, to point out to the reader how the Reformation began. Luther meant to show both how deeply embedded he was in papal religion and also what brought him theological deliverance. Luther described his own spiritual state at the time, the nature of his problem, and his solution—a new understanding of the notion of "the righteousness of God." Faced with an exegetical problem, he found an exegetical answer.

LITERATURE
U. Saarnivaara, *Luther Discovers the Gospel* (St. Louis, 1951).

MEANWHILE, I had already during that year returned to interpret the Psalter anew. I had confidence in the fact that I was more skil-

---

* *Luther's Works*. Vol. 34. Career of the Reformer IV, ed. Lewis W. Spitz (Philadelphia, 1960), pp. 336–37.

ful, after I had lectured in the university on St. Paul's epistles to the Romans, to the Galatians, and the one to the Hebrews. I had indeed been captivated with an extraordinary ardor for understanding Paul in the Epistle to the Romans. But up till then it was not the cold blood about the heart, but a single word in chapter 1 [:17], "In it the righteousness of God is revealed," that had stood in my way. For I hated that word "righteousness of God," which, according to the use and custom of all the teachers, I had been taught to understand philosophically regarding the formal or active righteousness, as they called it, with which God is righteous and punishes the unrighteous sinner.

Though I lived as a monk without reproach, I felt that I was a sinner before God with an extremely disturbed conscience. I could not believe that He was placated by my satisfaction. I did not love, yes, I hated the righteous God who punishes sinners, and secretly, if not blasphemously, certainly murmuring greatly, I was angry with God, and said, "As if, indeed, it is not enough, that miserable sinners, eternally lost through original sin, are crushed by every kind of calamity by the law of the decalogue, without having God add pain to pain by the gospel and also by the gospel threatening us with his righteousness and wrath!" Thus I raged with a fierce and troubled conscience. Nevertheless, I beat importunately upon Paul at that place, most ardently desiring to know what St. Paul wanted.

At last, by the mercy of God, meditating day and night, I gave heed to the context of the words, namely, "In it the righteousness of God is revealed, as it is written, 'He who through faith is righteous shall live.'" There I began to understand that the righteousness of God is that by which the righteous lives by a gift of God, namely by faith. And this is the meaning: the righteousness of God is revealed by the gospel, namely, the passive righteousness with which merciful God justifies us by faith, as it is written, "He who through faith is righteous shall live." Here I felt that I was altogether born again and had entered paradise itself through open gates. There a totally other face of the entire Scripture showed itself to me. Thereupon I ran through the Scriptures from memory. I also found in other terms an analogy, as, the work of God, that is, what God does in us, the power of God, with which He makes us strong, the wisdom of God, with which He makes us wise, the strength of God, the salvation of God, the glory of God.

And I extolled my sweetest word with a love as great as the hatred with which I had before hated the word "righteousness of God." Thus that place in Paul was for me truly the gate to paradise. Later I read Augustine's *The Spirit and the Letter,* where contrary to hope I found that he, too, interpreted God's righteousness in a similar way, as the righteousness with which God clothes us when He justifies us. Although this was heretofore said imperfectly and he did not explain all things concerning imputation clearly, it nevertheless was pleasing that God's righteousness with which we are justified was taught.

2. Martin Luther: *The Freedom of a Christian Man* (1520)*

This pamphlet was one of the three treatises Luther wrote in 1520, the other two being the *Babylonian Captivity of the Church* and the *Open Letter to the Christian Nobility,* and is an incisive exposition of his thought. Luther wrote the tract in October of the year when there was great uncertainty about papal action against him. Published in both German and Latin, it quickly became popular and its title offered a slogan that was widely echoed.

Its theme was that of Christian freedom, but in a broader sense it delineated the principles of Luther's program of ecclesiastical reform. The other two tracts of the year had sought to do the same—the *Open Letter* by demanding a reform in the structure of the church, the *Babylonian Captivity* by questioning Catholic sacramental teaching. The pamphlet on Christian freedom discussed the principles of the new life in Christ as it grew out of a new understanding of the nature of the Christian gospel. What must a Christian do? On the basis of the "righteousness of faith," the cornerstone of this new gospel, Luther repudiated the rigidity of Catholic morality and offered his own reconstruction. The treatise opened with the assertion that "a Christian is a perfectly free lord of all, subject to none," only bound to his

* *Luther's Works.* Vol. 31. Career of the Reformer I, ed. Harold J. Grimm (Philadelphia, 1957), pp. 327–79.

neighbor in love. Luther repudiated what might be called the Aristotelian notion that good works make a good man and insisted a good man does good works, and does so freely and without legal regimentation. The burden of Luther's tract was to show how a vibrant and dynamic faith makes this possible. A slightly condensed version of the entire tract is reprinted below.

LITERATURE
G. W. Forell, *Faith Active in Love* (New York, 1954).

MANY people have considered Christian faith an easy thing, and not a few have given it a place among the virtues. They do this because they have not experienced it and have never tasted the great strength there is in faith. It is impossible to write well about it or to understand what has been written about it unless one has at one time or another experienced the courage which faith gives a man when trials oppress him. But he who has had even a faint taste of it can never write, speak, meditate, or hear enough concerning it. It is a living "spring of water welling up to eternal life," as Christ calls it in John 4 [:14].

As for me, although I have no wealth of faith to boast of and know how scant my supply is, I nevertheless hope that I have attained to a little faith, even though I have been assailed by great and various temptations; and I hope that I can discuss it, if not more elegantly, certainly more to the point, than those literalists and subtle disputants have previously done, who have not even understood what they have written.

To make the way smoother for the unlearned—for only them do I serve—I shall set down the following two propositions concerning the freedom and the bondage of the spirit:

A Christian is a perfectly free lord of all, subject to none.

A Christian is a perfectly dutiful servant of all, subject to all.

These two theses seem to contradict each other. If, however, they should be found to fit together they would serve our purpose beautifully. Both are Paul's own statements, who says in 1 Cor. 9 [:19], "For though I am free from all men, I have made myself a slave to all," and in Rom. 13 [:8], "Owe no one anything, except to love one another." Love by its very nature is ready to serve and be subject to him who is loved. So Christ, although He was Lord of all, was "born of woman, born under the law" [Gal. 4:4], and therefore was at the same time a free man and a servant, "in the form of God" and "of a servant" [Phil. 2:6–7].

Let us start, however, with something more remote from our subject, but more obvious. Man has a twofold nature, a spiritual and a bodily one. According to the spiritual nature, which men refer to as the soul, he is called a spiritual, inner, or new man. According to the bodily nature, which men refer to as flesh, he is called a carnal, outward, or old man, of whom the Apostle writes in 2 Cor. 4 [:16], "Though our outer nature is wasting away, our inner nature is being renewed every day." Because of this diversity of nature the Scriptures assert contradictory things concerning the same man, since these two men in the same man contradict each other, "for the desires of the flesh are against the Spirit, and the desires of the Spirit are against the flesh," according to Gal. 5 [:17].

First, let us consider the inner man to see how a righteous, free, and pious Christian, that is, a spiritual, new, and inner man, becomes what he is. It is evident that no external thing has any influence in producing Christian righteousness or freedom, or in producing unrighteousness or servitude. A simple argument will furnish the proof of this statement. What can it profit the soul if the body is well, free, and active, and eats, drinks, and does as it pleases? For in these respects even the most godless slaves of vice may prosper. On the other hand, how will poor health or imprisonment or hunger or thirst or any other external misfortune harm the soul? Even the most godly men, and those who are free because of clear consciences, are afflicted with these things. None of these things touch either the freedom or the servitude of the soul. It does not help the soul if the body is adorned with the sacred robes of priests or dwells in sacred places or is occupied with sacred duties or prays, fasts, abstains from certain kinds of food, or does any work than can be done by the body and in the body. The righteousness and the freedom of the soul require something far different since the things which have been mentioned could be done by any wicked person. Such works produce nothing but hypocrites. On the other hand, it will not harm the soul if the body is clothed in secular dress, dwells in unconsecrated places, eats and drinks as others do, does not pray aloud, and neglects to do all the above-mentioned things which hypocrites can do.

Furthermore, to put aside all kinds of works, even contemplation, meditation, and all that the soul can do, does not help. One
thing, and only one thing, is necessary for Christian life, righteousness, and freedom. That one thing is the most holy Word of God,
the gospel of Christ, as Christ says, John 11 [:25], "I am the resurrection and the life; he who believes in me, though he die, yet shall
he live"; and John 8 [:36], "So if the Son makes you free, you will
be free indeed"; and Matt. 4 [:4], "Man shall not live by bread
alone, but by every word that proceeds from the mouth of God."
Let us then consider it certain and firmly established that the soul
can do without anything except the word of God and that where
the word of God is missing there is no help at all for the soul. If
it has the word of God it is rich and lacks nothing since it is the
word of life, truth, light, peace, righteousness, salvation, joy, liberty, wisdom, power, grace, glory, and of every incalculable blessing. This is why the prophet in the entire Psalm [119] and in many
other places yearns and sighs for the word of God and uses so
many names to describe it.

On the other hand, there is no more terrible disaster with which
the wrath of God can afflict men than a famine of the hearing of
His word, as He says in Amos [8:11]. Likewise there is no greater
mercy than when He sends forth His word, as we read in Psalm
107 [:20]: "He sent forth His word, and healed them, and
delivered them from destruction." Nor was Christ sent into the
world for any other ministry except that of the word. Moreover,
the entire spiritual estate—all the apostles, bishops, and priests—
has been called and instituted only for the ministry of the word.

You may ask, "What then is the word of God, and how shall it
be used, since there are so many words of God?" I answer: The
Apostle explains this in Romans 1. The word is the gospel of God
concerning His Son, who was made flesh, suffered, rose from the
dead, and was glorified through the Spirit who sanctifies. To preach
Christ means to feed the soul, make it righteous, set it free, and
save it, provided it believes the preaching. Faith alone is the saving
and efficacious use of the word of God, according to Rom. 10
[:9]: "If you confess with your lips that Jesus is Lord and believe in your heart that God raised Him from the dead, you will
be saved." Furthermore, "Christ is the end of the law, that every
one who has faith may be justified" [Rom. 10:4]. Again, in Rom.

1 [:17], "He who through faith is righteous shall live." The word of God cannot be received and cherished by any works whatever but only by faith. Therefore it is clear that, as the soul needs only the word of God for its life and righteousness, so it is justified by faith alone and not any works; for if it could be justified by anything else, it would not need the word, and consequently it would not need faith.

This faith cannot exist in connection with works—that is to say, if you at the same time claim to be justified by works, whatever their character—for that would be the same as "limping with two different opinions" [1 Kings 18:21], as worshipping Baal and kissing one's own hand [Job 31:27-28], which, as Job says, is a very great iniquity. Therefore the moment you begin to have faith you learn that all things in you are altogether blameworthy, sinful, and damnable, as the Apostle says in Rom. 3 [:23], "Since all have sinned and fall short of the glory of God," and, "None is righteous, no, not one; . . . all have turned aside, together they have gone wrong," Rom. 3 [:10-12]. When you have learned this you will know that you need Christ, who suffered and rose again for you so that, if you believe in Him, you may through this faith become a new man in so far as your sins are forgiven and you are justified by the merits of another, namely, of Christ alone.

Since, therefore, this faith can rule only in the inner man, as Rom. 10 [:10] says, "For man believes with his heart and so is justified," and since faith alone justifies, it is clear that the inner man cannot be justified, freed, or saved by any outer work or action at all, and that these works, whatever their character, have nothing to do with this inner man. On the other hand, only ungodliness and unbelief of heart, and no outer work, make him guilty and a damnable servant of sin. Wherefore it ought to be the first concern of every Christian to lay aside all confidence in works and increasingly to strengthen faith alone and through faith to grow in the knowledge, not of works, but of Christ Jesus, who suffered and rose for him, as Peter teaches in the last chapter of his first epistle, 1 Pet. [5:10]. No other work makes a Christian. Thus when the Jews asked Christ, as related in John 6 [:28], what they must do "to be doing the work of God," He brushed aside the multitude of works which He saw they did in great profusion and suggested one work, saying, "This is the work of God, that you

believe in Him whom He has sent" [John 6:29]; "for on Him has
God the Father set His seal" [John 6:27].

Therefore true faith in Christ is a treasure beyond comparison
which brings with it complete salvation and saves man from every
evil, as Christ says in the last chapter of Mark [16:16]: "He who
believes and is baptized will be saved; but he who does not believe
will be condemned." Isaiah contemplated this treasure and foretold
it in chapter 10: "The Lord will make a small and consuming word
upon the land, and it will overflow with righteousness" [Cf. Is.
10:22]. This is as though he said, "Faith, which is a small and
perfect fulfilment of the law, will fill believers with so great a
righteousness that they will need nothing more to become righteous." So Paul says, Rom. 10 [:10], "For man believes with his
heart and so is justified."

Should you ask how it happens that faith alone justifies and
offers us such a treasure of great benefits without works in view
of the fact that so many works, ceremonies, and laws are prescribed
in the Scriptures, I answer: First of all, remember what has been
said, namely, that faith alone, without works, justifies, frees, and
saves; we shall make this clearer later on. Here we must point out
that the entire Scripture of God is divided into two parts: commandments and promises. Although the commandments teach
things that are good, the things taught are not done as soon as
they are taught, for the commandments show us what we ought
to do but do not give us the power to do it. They are intended to
teach man to know himself, that through them he may recognize
his inability to do good and may despair of his own ability. That
is why they are called the Old Testament and constitute the Old
Testament. For example, the commandment, "You shall not covet"
[Ex. 20:17], is a command which proves us all to be sinners, for
no one can avoid coveting no matter how much he may struggle
against it. Therefore, in order not to covet and to fulfil the commandment, a man is compelled to despair of himself, to seek the
help which he does not find in himself elsewhere and from someone else, as stated in Hos. [13:9]: "Destruction is your own, O
Israel: your help is only in me." As we fare with respect to one
commandment, so we fare with all, for it is equally impossible for
us to keep any one of them.

Now when a man has learned through the commandments to

recognize his helplessness and is distressed about how he might satisfy the law—since the law must be fulfilled so that not a jot or tittle shall be lost, otherwise man will be condemned without hope—then, being truly humbled and reduced to nothing in his own eyes, he finds in himself nothing whereby he may be justified and saved. Here the second part of Scripture comes to our aid, namely, the promises of God which declare the glory of God, saying, "If you wish to fulfil the law and not covet, as the law demands, come, believe in Christ in whom grace, righteousness, peace, liberty, and all things are promised you. If you believe, you shall have all things; if you do not believe, you shall lack all things." That which is impossible for you to accomplish by trying to fulfil all the works of the law—many and useless as they all are—you will accomplish quickly and easily through faith. God our Father has made all things depend on faith so that whoever has faith will have everything, and whoever does not have faith will have nothing. "For God has consigned all men to disobedience, that He may have mercy upon all," as it is stated in Rom. 11 [:32]. Thus the promises of God give what the commandments of God demand and fulfil what the law prescribes so that all things may be God's alone, both the commandments and the fulfilling of the commandments. He alone commands, He alone fulfils. Therefore the promises of God belong to the New Testament. Indeed, they are the New Testament. . . .

From what has been said it is easy to see from what source faith derives such great power and why a good work or all good works together cannot equal it. No good work can rely upon the word of God or live in the soul, for faith alone and the word of God rule in the soul. Just as the heated iron glows like fire because of the union of fire with it, so the word imparts its qualities to the soul. It is clear, then, that a Christian has all that he needs in faith and needs no works to justify him; and if he has no need of works, he has no need of the law; and if he has no need of the law, surely he is free from the law. It is true that "the law is not laid down for the just" [1 Tim. 1:9]. This is that Christian liberty, our faith, which does not induce us to live in idleness or wickedness but makes the law and works unnecessary for any man's righteousness and salvation.

This is the first power of faith. Let us now examine also the second. It is a further function of faith that it honors him whom it trusts with the most reverent and highest regard since it considers him truthful and trustworthy. There is no other honor equal to the estimate of truthfulness and righteousness with which we honor him whom we trust. Could we ascribe to a man anything greater than truthfulness and righteousness and perfect goodness? On the other hand, there is no way in which we can show greater contempt for a man than to regard him as false and wicked and to be suspicious of him, as we do when we do not trust him. So when the soul firmly trusts God's promises, it regards Him as truthful and righteous. Nothing more excellent than this can be ascribed to God. The very highest worship of God is this that we ascribe to Him truthfulness, righteousness, and whatever else should be ascribed to one who is trusted. When this is done, the soul consents to His will. Then it hallows His name and allows itself to be treated according to God's good pleasure for, clinging to God's promises, it does not doubt that He who is true, just, and wise will do, dispose, and provide all things well.

Is not such a soul most obedient to God in all things by this faith? What commandment is there that such obedience has not completely fulfilled? What more complete fulfilment is there than obedience in all things? This obedience, however, is not rendered by works, but by faith alone. On the other hand, what greater rebellion against God, what greater wickedness, what greater contempt of God is there than not believing His promise? For what is this but to make God a liar or to doubt that He is truthful?—that is, to ascribe truthfulness to one's self but lying and vanity to God? Does not a man who does this deny God and set himself up as an idol in his heart? Then of what good are works done in such wickedness, even if they were the works of angels and apostles? Therefore God has rightly included all things, not under anger or lust, but under unbelief, so that they who imagine that they are fulfilling the law by doing the works of chastity and mercy required by the law (the civil and human virtues) might not be saved. They are included under the sin of unbelief and must either seek mercy or be justly condemned.

When, however, God sees that we consider Him truthful and by the faith of our heart pay Him the great honor which is due Him, He does us that great honor of considering us truthful and righteous for the sake of our faith. Faith works truth and righteousness by giving God what belongs to Him. Therefore God in turn glorifies our righteousness. It is true and just that God is truthful and just, and to consider and confess Him to be so is the same as being truthful and just. Accordingly He says in 1 Sam. 2 [:30], "Those who honor me I will honor, and those who despise me shall be lightly esteemed." So Paul says in Rom. 4 [:3] that Abraham's faith "was reckoned to him as righteousness" because by it he gave glory most perfectly to God, and that for the same reason our faith shall be reckoned to us as righteousness if we believe.

The third incomparable benefit of faith is that it unites the soul with Christ as a bride is united with her bridegroom. By this mystery, as the Apostle teaches, Christ and the soul become one flesh [Eph. 5:31–32]. And if they are one flesh and there is between them a true marriage—indeed the most perfect of all marriages, since human marriages are but poor examples of this one true marriage—it follows that everything they have they hold in common, the good as well as the evil. Accordingly the believing soul can boast of and glory in whatever Christ has as though it were its own, and whatever the soul has Christ claims as His own. Let us compare these and we shall see inestimable benefits. Christ is full of grace, life, and salvation. The soul is full of sins, death, and damnation. Now let faith come between them and sins, death, and damnation will be Christ's, while grace, life, and salvation will be the soul's; for if Christ is a bridegroom, He must take upon Himself the things which are His bride's and bestow upon her the things that are His. If He gives her His body and very self, how shall He not give her all that is His? And if He takes the body of the bride, how shall He not take all that is hers?

Here we have a most pleasing vision not only of communion but of a blessed struggle and victory and salvation and redemption. Christ is God and man in one person. He has neither sinned nor died, and is not condemned, and He cannot sin, die, or be condemned; His righteousness, life, and salvation are unconquerable, eternal, omnipotent. By the wedding ring of faith He shares in the sins, death, and pains of hell which are His bride's. As a matter of fact, He makes them His own and acts as if they were His own and as if He Himself had sinned; He suffered, died, and descended into hell that He might overcome them all. Now since it was such a one who did all this, and death and hell could not swallow Him up, these were necessarily swallowed up by Him in a mighty duel; for His righteousness is greater than the sins of all men, His life stronger than death, His salvation more invincible than hell. Thus the believing soul by means of the pledge of its faith is free in Christ, its bridegroom, free from all sins, secure against death and hell, and is endowed with the eternal righteousness, life, and salvation of Christ its bridegroom. So He takes to Himself a glorious bride, "without spot or wrinkle, cleansing her by the washing of water with the word" [cf. Eph. 5:26–27] of life, that is, by faith in the word of life, righteousness, and salvation. In this way He marries her in faith, steadfast love, and in mercies, righteousness, and justice, as Hos. 2 [:19–20] says. . . .

From this you once more see that much is ascribed to faith, namely, that it alone can fulfil the law and justify without works. You see that the first commandment, which says, "You shall worship one God," is fulfilled by faith alone. Though you were nothing but good works from the soles of your feet to the crown of your head, you would still not be righteous or worship God or fulfil the first commandment, since God cannot be worshipped unless you ascribe to Him the glory of truthfulness and all goodness which is due Him. This cannot be done by works but only by the faith of the heart. Not by the doing of works but by believing do we glorify God and acknowledge that He is truthful. Therefore faith alone is the righteousness of a Christian and the fulfilling of all the commandments, for he who fulfils the first commandment has no difficulty in fulfilling all the rest.

But works, being inanimate things, cannot glorify God, although they can, if faith is present, be done to the glory of God. Here, however, we are not inquiring what works and what kind of works are done, but who it is that does them, who glorifies God and brings forth the works. This is done by faith which dwells in the heart and is the source and substance of all our righteousness. Therefore it is a blind and dangerous doctrine which teaches that the commandments must be fulfilled by works. The commandments must be fulfilled before any works can be done, and the works proceed from the fulfilment of the commandments [Rom. 13:10], as we shall hear. . . .

Hence all of us who believe in Christ are priests and kings in

Christ, as 1 Pet. 2 [:9] says: "You are a chosen race, God's own people, a royal priesthood, a priestly kingdom, that you may declare the wonderful deeds of Him who called you out of darkness into His marvelous light."

The nature of this priesthood and kingship is something like this: First, with respect to the kingship, every Christian is by faith so exalted above all things that, by virtue of a spiritual power, he is lord of all things without exception, so that nothing can do him any harm. As a matter of fact, all things are made subject to him and are compelled to serve him in obtaining salvation. Accordingly Paul says in Rom. 8 [:28], "All things work together for good for the elect," and in 1 Cor. 3 [:21–23], "All things are yours whether . . . life or death or the present or the future, all are yours; and you are Christ's. . . ." This is not to say that every Christian is placed over all things to have and control them by physical power—a madness with which some churchmen are afflicted—for such power belongs to kings, princes, and other men on earth. Our ordinary experience in life shows us that we are subjected to all, suffer many things, and even die. As a matter of fact, the more Christian a man is, the more evils, sufferings, and deaths he must endure, as we see in Christ the first-born prince Himself, and in all His brethren, the saints. The power of which we speak is spiritual. It rules in the midst of enemies and is powerful in the midst of oppression. This means nothing else than that "power is made perfect in weakness" [2 Cor. 12:9] and that in all things I can find profit toward salvation [Rom. 8:28], so that the cross and death itself are compelled to serve me and to work together with me for my salvation. This is a splendid privilege and hard to attain, a truly omnipotent power, a spiritual dominion in which there is nothing so good and nothing so evil but that it shall work together for good to me, if only I believe. Yes, since faith alone suffices for salvation, I need nothing except faith exercising the power and dominion of its own liberty. Lo, this is the inestimable power and liberty of Christians.

Not only are we the freest of kings, we are also priests forever, which is far more excellent than being kings, for as priests we are worthy to appear before God to pray for others and to teach one another divine things. These are the functions of priests, and they cannot be granted to any unbeliever. Thus Christ has made it possible for us, provided we believe in Him, to be not only His brethren, co-heirs, and fellow-kings, but also His fellow-priests. . . .

He, however, who does not believe is not served by anything. On the contrary, nothing works for his good, but he himself is a servant of all, and all things turn out badly for him because he wickedly uses them to his own advantage and not to the glory of God. So he is no priest but a wicked man whose prayer becomes sin and who never comes into the presence of God because God does not hear sinners [John 9:31]. Who then can comprehend the lofty dignity of the Christian? By virtue of his royal power he rules over all things, death, life, and sin, and through his priestly glory is omnipotent with God because he does the things which God asks and desires, as it is written, "He will fulfil the desire of those who fear him; he also will hear their cry and save them" [cf. Phil. 4:13]. To this glory a man attains, certainly not by any works of his, but by faith alone.

From this anyone can clearly see how a Christian is free from all things and over all things so that he needs no works to make him righteous and save him, since faith alone abundantly confers all these things. Should he grow so foolish, however, as to presume to become righteous, free, saved, and a Christian by means of some good work, he would instantly lose faith and all its benefits, a foolishness aptly illustrated in the fable of the dog who runs along a stream with a piece of meat in his mouth and, deceived by the reflection of the meat in the water, opens his mouth to snap at it and so loses both the meat and the reflection.

You will ask, "If all who are in the church are priests, how do these whom we now call priests differ from laymen?" I answer: Injustice is done those words "priest," "cleric," "spiritual," "ecclesiastic," when they are transferred from all Christians to those few who are now by a mischievous usage called "ecclesiastics." Holy Scripture makes no distinction between them, although it gives the name "ministers," "servants," "stewards" to those who are now proudly called popes, bishops, and lords and who should according to the ministry of the word serve others and teach them the faith of Christ and the freedom of believers. Although we are all equally priests, we cannot all publicly minister and teach. We

ought not do so even if we could. Paul writes accordingly in
1 Cor. 4 [:1], "This is how one should regard us, as servants of
Christ and stewards of the mysteries of God.". . .

To return to our purpose, I believe that it has now become
clear that it is not enough or in any sense Christian to preach the
works, life, and words of Christ as historical facts, as if the knowledge of these would suffice for the conduct of life; yet this is the
fashion among those who must today be regarded as our best
preachers. Far less is it sufficient or Christian to say nothing at
all about Christ and to teach instead the laws of men and the decrees of the Fathers. Now there are not a few who preach Christ
and read about Him that they may move men's affections to sym-
pathy with Christ, to anger against the Jews, and such childish
and effeminate nonsense. Rather ought Christ to be preached to
the end that faith in Him may be established that He may not only
be Christ, but be Christ for you and me, and that what is said of
Him and is denoted in His name may be effectual in us. Such faith
is produced and preserved in us by preaching why Christ came,
what He brought and bestowed, what benefit it is to us to accept
Him. This is done when that Christian liberty which He bestows
is rightly taught and we are told in what way we Christians are
all kings and priests and therefore lords of all and may firmly
believe that whatever we have done is pleasing and acceptable in
the sight of God, as I have already said.

What man is there whose heart, upon hearing these things, will
not rejoice to its depth, and when receiving such comfort will not
grow tender so that he will love Christ as he never could by
means of any laws or works? Who would have the power to harm
or frighten such a heart? If the knowledge of sin or the fear of
death should break in upon it, it is ready to hope in the Lord. It
does not grow afraid when it hears tidings of evil. It is not disturbed when it sees its enemies. This is so because it believes that
the righteousness of Christ is its own and that its sin is not its own,
but Christ's, and that all sin is swallowed up by the righteousness
of Christ. This, as has been said above, is a necessary consequence
on account of faith in Christ. So the heart learns to scoff at death
and sin and to say with the Apostle, "O death, where is thy victory? O death, where is thy sting? The sting of death is sin, and

the power of sin is the law. But thanks be to God, who gives us the victory through our Lord Jesus Christ" [1 Cor. 15:55–57]. . . .

Let this suffice concerning the inner man, his liberty, and the source of his liberty, the righteousness of faith. He needs neither laws nor good works but, on the contrary, is injured by them if he believes that he is justified by them.

Now let us turn to the second part, the outer man. Here we shall answer all those who, offended by the word "faith" and by all that has been said, now ask, "If faith does all things and is alone sufficient unto righteousness, why then are good works commanded? We will take our ease and do no works and be content with faith." I answer: not so, you wicked men, not so. That would indeed be proper if we were wholly inner and perfectly spiritual men. But such we shall be only at the last day, the day of the resurrection of the dead. As long as we live in the flesh we only begin to make some progress in that which shall be perfected in the future life. For this reason the Apostle in Rom. 8 [:23] calls all that we attain in this life "the first fruits of the Spirit" because we shall indeed receive the greater portion, even the fulness of the Spirit, in the future. This is the place to assert that which was said above, namely, that a Christian is the servant of all and made subject to all. Insofar as he is free he does no works, but insofar as he is a servant he does all kinds of works. How this is possible we shall see.

Although, as I have said, a man is abundantly and sufficiently justified by faith inwardly, in his spirit, and so has all that he needs, except insofar as this faith and these riches must grow from day to day even to the future life; yet he remains in this mortal life on earth. In this life he must control his own body and have dealings with men. Here the works begin; here a man cannot enjoy leisure; here he must indeed take care to discipline his body by fastings, watchings, labors, and other reasonable discipline and to subject it to the Spirit so that it will obey and conform to the inner man and faith and not revolt against faith and hinder the inner man, as it is the nature of the body to do if it is not held in check. The inner man, who by faith is created in the image of God, is both joyful and happy because of Christ in whom so many benefits are conferred upon him; and therefore it is his one occupation to serve

God joyfully and without thought of gain, in love that is not constrained.

While he is doing this, behold, he meets a contrary will in his own flesh which strives to serve the world and seeks its own advantage. This the spirit of faith cannot tolerate, but with joyful zeal it attempts to put the body under control and hold it in check, as Paul says in Rom. 7 [:22–23], "For I delight in the law of God, in my inmost self, but I see in my members another law at war with the law of my mind and making me captive to the law of sin," and in another place, "But I pommel my body and subdue it, lest after preaching to others I myself should be disqualified" [1 Cor. 9:27], and in Galatians [5:24], "And those who belong to Christ Jesus have crucified the flesh with its passions and desires."

In doing these works, however, we must not think that a man is justified before God by them, for faith, which alone is righteousness before God, cannot endure that erroneous opinion. We must, however, realize that these works reduce the body to subjection and purify it of its evil lusts, and our whole purpose is to be directed only toward the driving out of lusts. Since by faith the soul is cleansed and made to love God, it desires that all things, and especially its own body, shall be purified so that all things may join with it in loving and praising God. Hence a man cannot be idle, for the need of his body drives him and he is compelled to do many good works to reduce it to subjection. Nevertheless the works themselves do not justify him before God, but he does the works out of spontaneous love in obedience to God and considers nothing except the approval of God, whom he would most scrupulously obey in all things. . . .

The following statements are therefore true: "Good works do not make a good man, but a good man does good works; evil works do not make a wicked man, but a wicked man does evil works." Consequently it is always necessary that the substance or person himself be good before there can be any good works, and that good works follow and proceed from the good person, as Christ also says, "A good tree cannot bear evil fruit, nor can a bad tree bear good fruit" [Matt. 7:18]. It is clear that the fruits do not bear the tree and that the tree does not grow on the fruits, also that, on the contrary, the trees bear the fruits and the fruits grow on the trees. As it is necessary, therefore, that the trees exist before their fruits and the fruits do not make trees either good or bad, but rather as the trees are, so are the fruits they bear; so a man must first be good or wicked before he does a good or wicked work, and his works do not make him good or wicked, but he himself makes his works either good or wicked.

Illustrations of the same truth can be seen in all trades. A good or a bad house does not make a good or a bad builder; but a good or a bad builder makes a good or a bad house. And in general, the work never makes the workman like itself, but the workman makes the work like himself. So it is with the works of man. As the man is, whether believer or unbeliever, so also is his work—good if it was done in faith, wicked if it was done in unbelief. But the converse is not true, that the work makes the man either a believer or an unbeliever. As works do not make a man a believer, so also they do not make him righteous. But as faith makes a man a believer and righteous, so faith does good works. Since, then, works justify no one, and a man must be righteous before he does a good work, it is very evident that it is faith alone which, because of the pure mercy of God through Christ and in His word, worthily and sufficiently justifies and saves the person. A Christian has no need of any work or law in order to be saved since through faith he is free from every law and does everything out of pure liberty and freely. He seeks neither benefit nor salvation since he already abounds in all things and is saved through the grace of God because in his faith he now seeks only to please God.

Furthermore, no good work helps justify or save an unbeliever. On the other hand, no evil work makes him wicked or damns him; but the unbelief which makes the person and the tree evil does the evil and damnable works. Hence when a man is good or evil, this is effected not by the works, but by faith or unbelief. . . .

So let him who wishes to do good works begin not with the doing of works, but with believing, which makes the person good, for nothing makes a man good except faith, or evil except unbelief.

It is indeed true that in the sight of men a man is made good or evil by his works; but this being made good or evil only means that the man who is good or evil is pointed out and known as such, as Christ says in Matt. 7 [:20], "Thus you will know them by their fruits." All this remains on the surface, however, and very many have been deceived by this outward appearance and have presumed to write and teach concerning good works by which we may be justified without even mentioning faith. They go their way, always being deceived and deceiving [2 Tim. 3:13], progressing, indeed, but into a worse state, blind leaders of the blind, wearing themselves with many works and still never attaining to true righteousness [Matt. 15:14]. Of such people Paul says in 2 Tim. 3 [:5, 7], "Holding the form of religion but denying the power of it . . . who will listen to anybody and can never arrive at a knowledge of the truth."

Whoever, therefore, does not wish to go astray with those blind men must look beyond works, and beyond laws and doctrines about works. Turning his eyes from works, he must look upon the person and ask how he is justified. For the person is justified and saved, not by works or laws, but by the word of God, that is, by the promise of His grace, and by faith. . . .

From this it is easy to know how far good works are to be rejected or not, and by what standard all the teachings of men concerning works are to be interpreted. If works are sought after as a means to righteousness, are burdened with this perverse leviathan, and are done under the false impression that through them one is justified, they are made necessary and freedom and faith are destroyed; and this addition to them makes them no longer good but truly damnable works. They are not free, and they blaspheme the grace of God since to justify and to save by faith belongs to the grace of God alone. What the works have no power to do they nevertheless—by a godless presumption through this folly of ours—pretend to do and thus violently force themselves into the office and glory of grace. We do not, therefore, reject good works; on the contrary, we cherish and teach them as much as possible. We do not condemn them for their own sake but on account of this godless addition to them and the perverse idea that righteousness is to be sought through them; for that makes them appear good outwardly, when in truth they are not good. They deceive men and lead them to deceive one another like ravening wolves in sheep's clothing [Matt. 7:15].

But this leviathan, or perverse notion concerning works, is unconquerable where sincere faith is wanting. Those work-saints cannot get rid of it unless faith, its destroyer, comes and rules in their hearts. Nature of itself cannot drive it out or even recognize it, but rather regards it as a mark of the most holy will. If the influence of custom is added and confirms this perverseness of nature, as wicked teachers have caused it to do, it becomes an incurable evil and leads astray and destroys countless men beyond all hope of restoration. Therefore, although it is good to preach and write about penitence, confession, and satisfaction, our teaching is unquestionably deceitful and diabolical if we stop with that and do not go on to teach about faith.

Christ, like His forerunner John, not only said, "Repent" [Matt. 3:2; 4:17], but added the word of faith, saying, "The kingdom of heaven is at hand." We are not to preach only one of these words of God, but both; we are to bring forth out of our treasure things new and old, the voice of the law as well as the word of grace [Matt. 13:52]. We must bring forth the voice of the law that men may be made to fear and come to a knowledge of their sins and so be converted to repentance and a better life. But we must not stop with that, for that would only amount to wounding and not binding up, smiting and not healing, killing and not making alive, leading down into hell and not bringing back again, humbling and not exalting. Therefore we must also preach the word of grace and the promise of forgiveness by which faith is taught and aroused. Without this word of grace the works of the law, contrition, penitence, and all the rest are done and taught in vain. . . .

Let this suffice concerning works in general and at the same time concerning the works which a Christian does for himself. Lastly, we shall also speak of the things which he does toward his neighbor. A man does not live for himself alone in this mortal body to work for it alone, but he lives also for all men on earth; rather, he lives only for others and not for himself. To this end he brings his body into subjection that he may the more sincerely and freely serve others, as Paul says in Rom. 14 [:7–8], "None of us lives to himself, and none of us dies to himself. If we live, we live to the Lord, and if we die, we die to the Lord." He cannot ever in this life be idle and without works toward his neighbors, for he will necessarily speak, deal with, and exchange views with men, as Christ also, being made in the likeness of men [Phil. 2:7],

was found in form as a man and conversed with men, as Baruch 3
[:38] says.

Man, however, needs none of these things for his righteousness
and salvation. Therefore he should be guided in all his works by
this thought and contemplate this one thing alone, that he may
serve and benefit others in all that he does, considering nothing
except the need and the advantage of his neighbor. Accordingly
the Apostle commands us to work with our hands so that we may
give to the needy, although he might have said that we should
work to support ourselves. He says, however, "that he may be
able to give to those in need" [Eph. 4:28]. This is what makes
caring for the body a Christian work, that through its health and
comfort we may be able to work, to acquire, and lay by funds
with which to aid those who are in need, that in this way the
strong member may serve the weaker, and we may be sons of God,
each caring for and working for the other, bearing one another's
burdens and so fulfilling the law of Christ [Gal. 6:2]. This is a
truly Christian life. Here faith is truly active through love [Gal.
5:6], that is, it finds expression in works of the freest service,
cheerfully and lovingly done, with which a man willingly serves
another without hope of reward; and for himself he is satisfied
with the fulness and wealth of his faith. . . .

So a Christian, like Christ his head, is filled and made rich by
faith and should be content with this form of God which he has
obtained by faith; only, as I have said, he should increase this
faith until it is made perfect. For this faith is his life, his righteousness, and his salvation: it saves him and makes him acceptable, and
bestows upon him all things that are Christ's, as has been said
above, and as Paul asserts in Gal. 2 [:20] when he says, "And
the life I now live in the flesh I live by faith in the Son of God."
Although the Christian is thus free from all works, he ought in
this liberty to empty himself, take upon himself the form of a
servant, be made in the likeness of men, be found in human form,
and to serve, help, and in every way deal with his neighbor as he
sees that God through Christ has dealt and still deals with him.
This he should do freely, having regard for nothing but divine
approval.

He ought to think: "Although I am an unworthy and condemned man, my God has given me in Christ all the riches of

righteousness and salvation without any merit on my part, out of pure, free mercy, so that from now on I need nothing except faith which believes that this is true. Why should I not therefore freely, joyfully, with all my heart, and with an eager will do all things which I know are pleasing and acceptable to such a Father who has overwhelmed me with his inestimable riches? I will therefore give myself as a Christ to my neighbor, just as Christ offered Himself to me; I will do nothing in this life except what I see is necessary, profitable, and salutary to my neighbor, since through faith I have an abundance of all good things in Christ."

Behold, from faith thus flow forth love and joy in the Lord, and from love a joyful, willing, and free mind that serves one's neighbor willingly and takes no account of gratitude or ingratitude, of praise or blame, of gain or loss. For a man does not serve that he may put men under obligations. He does not distinguish between friends and enemies or anticipate their thankfulness or unthankfulness, but he most freely and most willingly spends himself and all that he has, whether he wastes all on the thankless or whether he gains a reward. As his Father does, distributing all things to all men richly and freely, making "his sun rise on the evil and on the good" [Matt. 5:45], so also the son does all things and suffers all things with that freely bestowing joy which is his delight when through Christ he sees it in God, the dispenser of such great benefits.

Therefore, if we recognize the great and precious things which are given us, as Paul says [Rom. 5:5], our hearts will be filled by the Holy Spirit with the love which makes us free, joyful, almighty workers and conquerors over all tribulations, servants of our neighbors, and yet lords of all. For those who do not recognize the gifts bestowed upon them through Christ, however, Christ has been born in vain; they go their way with their works and shall never come to taste or feel those things. Just as our neighbor is in need and lacks that in which we abound, so we were in need before God and lacked His mercy. Hence, as our heavenly Father has in Christ freely come to our aid, we also ought freely to help our neighbor through our body and its works, and each one should become as it were a Christ to the other that we may be Christs to one another and Christ may be the same in all, that is, that we may be truly Christians.

Who then can comprehend the riches and the glory of the Christian life? It can do all things and has all things and lacks nothing. It is lord over sin, death, and hell, and yet at the same time it serves, ministers to, and benefits all men. But alas in our day this life is unknown throughout the world; it is neither preached about nor sought after; we are altogether ignorant of our own name and do not know why we are Christians or bear the name of Christians. Surely we are named after Christ, not because He is absent from us, but because He dwells in us, that is, • because we believe in Him and are Christs one to another and do to our neighbors as Christ does to us. But in our day we are taught by the doctrine of men to seek nothing but merits, rewards, and the things that are ours; of Christ we have made only a taskmaster far harsher than Moses.

We have a preeminent example of such a faith in the blessed Virgin. As is written in Luke 2 [:22], she was purified according to the law of Moses according to the custom of all women, although she was not bound by that law and did not need to be purified. Out of free and willing love, however, she submitted to the law like other women that she might not offend or despise them. She was not justified by this work, but being righteous she did it freely and willingly. So also our works should be done, not that we may be justified by them, since, being justified beforehand by faith, we ought to do all things freely and joyfully for the sake of others. . . .

Christ also, in Matt. 17 [:24–27], when the tax money was demanded of His disciples, discussed with St. Peter whether the sons of the king were not free from the payment of tribute, and Peter affirmed that they were. Nonetheless, Christ commanded Peter to go to the sea and said, "Not to give offense to them, go to the sea and cast a hook, and take the first fish that comes up, and when you open its mouth you will find a shekel; take that and give it to them for me and for yourself." This incident fits our subject beautifully for Christ here calls Himself and those who are His children sons of the king, who need nothing; and yet He freely submits and pays the tribute. Just as necessary and helpful as this work was to Christ's righteousness or salvation, just so much do all other works of His or His followers avail for righteousness, since they all follow after righteousness and are free and are done

only to serve others and to give them an example of good
works. . . .

Anyone knowing this could easily and without danger find his
way through those numberless mandates and precepts of pope,
bishops, monasteries, churches, princes, and magistrates upon
which some ignorant pastors insist as if they were necessary to
righteousness and salvation, calling them "precepts of the church,"
although they are nothing of the kind. For a Christian, as a free
man, will say, "I will fast, pray, do this and that as men command,
not because it is necessary to my righteousness or salvation; but
that I may show due respect to the pope, the bishop, the community, a magistrate, or my neighbor, and give them an example.
I will do and suffer all things, just as Christ did and suffered far
more for me, although He needed nothing of it all for Himself, and
was made under the law for my sake, although He was not under
the law." Although tyrants do violence or injustice in making their
demands, yet it will do no harm as long as they demand nothing
contrary to God. . . .

This ignorance and suppression of liberty very many blind
pastors take pains to encourage. They stir up and urge on their
people in these practices by praising such works, puffing them up
with their indulgences, and never teaching faith. If, however, you
wish to pray, fast, or establish a foundation in the church, I advise you to be careful not to do it in order to obtain some benefit,
whether temporal or eternal, for you would do injury to your
faith which alone offers you all things. Your one care should be
that faith may grow, whether it is trained by works or sufferings.
Make your gifts freely and for no consideration, so that others
may profit by them and fare well because of you and your goodness. In this way you shall be truly good and Christian. Of what
benefit to you are the good works which you do not need for
keeping your body under control? Your faith is sufficient for you,
through which God has given you all things.

See, according to this rule the good things we have from God
should flow from one to the other and be common to all, so that
everyone should "put on" his neighbor and so conduct himself
toward him as if he himself were in the other's place. From Christ
the good things have flowed and are flowing into us. He has so
"put on" us and acted for us as if He had been what we are. From

us they flow on to those who have need of them so that I should lay before God my faith and my righteousness that they may cover and intercede for the sins of my neighbor which I take upon myself and so labor and serve in them as if they were my very own. That is what Christ did for us. This is true love and the genuine rule of a Christian life. Love is true and genuine where there is true and genuine faith. Hence the Apostle says of love in 1 Cor. 13 [:5] that "it does not seek its own."

We conclude, therefore, that a Christian lives not in himself, but in Christ and in his neighbor. Otherwise he is not a Christian. He lives in Christ through faith, in his neighbor through love. By faith he is caught up beyond himself into God. By love he descends beneath himself into his neighbor. Yet he always remains in God and in His love, as Christ says in John 1 [:51], "Truly, truly, I say to you, you will see heaven opened, and the angels of God ascending and descending upon the Son of man.". . .

Finally, something must be added for the sake of those for whom nothing can be said so well that they will not spoil it by misunderstanding it. It is questionable whether they will understand even what will be said here. There are very many who, when they hear of this freedom of faith, immediately turn it into an occasion for the flesh and think that now all things are allowed them. They want to show that they are free men and Christians only by despising and finding fault with ceremonies, traditions, and human laws; as if they were Christians because on stated days they do not fast or eat meat when others fast, or because they do not use the accustomed prayers, and with upturned nose scoff at the precepts of men, although they utterly disregard all else that pertains to the Christian religion. The extreme opposite of these are those who rely for their salvation solely on their reverent observance of ceremonies, as if they would be saved because on certain days they fast or abstain from meats, or pray certain prayers; these make a boast of the precepts of the church and of the Fathers, and do not care a fig for the things which are of the essence of our faith. Plainly, both are in error because they neglect the weightier things which are necessary to salvation, and quarrel so noisily about trifling and unnecessary matters. . . .

Our faith in Christ does not free us from works but from false opinions concerning works, that is, from the foolish presumption that justification is acquired by works. Faith redeems, corrects, and preserves our consciences so that we know that righteousness does not consist in works, although works neither can nor ought to be wanting; just as we cannot be without food and drink and all the works of this mortal body, yet our righteousness is not in them, but in faith; and yet those works of the body are not to be despised or neglected on that account. In this world we are bound by the needs of our bodily life, but we are not righteous because of them. "My kingship is not of this world" [John 18:36], says Christ. He does not, however, say, "My kingship is not here, that is, in this world." And Paul says, "Though we live in the world we are not carrying on a worldly war" [2 Cor. 10:3], and in Gal. 2 [:20], "The life I now live in the flesh I live by faith in the Son of God." Thus what we do, live, and are in works and ceremonies, we do because of the necessities of this life and of the effort to rule our body. Nevertheless we are righteous, not in these, but in the faith of the Son of God.

Hence the Christian must take a middle course and face those two classes of men. He will meet first the unyielding, stubborn ceremonialists who like deaf adders are not willing to hear the truth of liberty [Ps. 58:4] but, having no faith, boast of, prescribe, and insist upon their ceremonies as means of justification. Such were the Jews of old, who were unwilling to learn how to do good. These he must resist, do the very opposite, and offend them boldly lest by their impious views they drag many with them into error. In the presence of such men it is good to eat meat, break the fasts, and for the sake of the liberty of faith do other things which they regard as the greatest of sins. Of them we must say, "Let them alone; they are blind guides." According to this principle Paul would not circumcise Titus when the Jews insisted that he should [Gal. 2:3], and Christ excused the apostles when they plucked ears of grain on the sabbath [Matt. 12:1–8]. There are many similar instances. The other class of men whom a Christian will meet are the simple-minded, ignorant men, weak in the faith, as the Apostle calls them, who cannot yet grasp the liberty of faith, even if they were willing to do so [Rom. 14:1]. These he must take care not to offend. He must yield to their weakness until they are more fully instructed. Since they do and think as they do, not because they are stubbornly wicked, but only because their faith is weak, the fasts and other things which they consider necessary must be observed to avoid giving them offense. This is the command of love which would harm no one but would serve all men. It is not by their fault that they are weak, but by that of their pastors who have taken them captive with the snares of their traditions and have wickedly used these traditions as rods with which to beat them. They should have been delivered from these pastors by the teachings of faith and freedom. So the Apostle teaches us in Rom. 14: "If food is a cause of my brother's falling, I will never eat meat" [cf. Rom. 14:21 and 1 Cor. 8:13]; and again, "I know and am persuaded in the Lord Jesus that nothing is unclean in itself; but it is unclean for any one who thinks it unclean" [Rom. 14:14].

For this reason, although we should boldly resist those teachers of traditions and sharply censure the laws of the popes by means of which they plunder the people of God, yet we must spare the timid multitude whom those impious tyrants hold captive by means of these laws until they are set free. Therefore fight strenuously against the wolves, but for the sheep and not also against the sheep. This you will do if you inveigh against the laws and the lawgivers and at the same time observe the laws with the weak so that they will not be offended, until they also recognize tyranny and understand their freedom. If you wish to use your freedom, do so in secret, as Paul says, Rom. 14 [:22], "The faith that you have, keep between yourself and God"; but take care not to use your freedom in the sight of the weak. On the other hand, use your freedom constantly and consistently in the sight of and despite the tyrants and the stubborn so that they also may learn that they are impious, that their laws are of no avail for righteousness, and that they had no right to set them up.

Since we cannot live our lives without ceremonies and works, and the perverse and untrained youth need to be restrained and saved from harm by such bonds; and since each one should keep his body under control by means of such works, there is need that the minister of Christ be far-seeing and faithful. He ought so to govern and teach Christians in all these matters that their conscience and faith will not be offended and that there will not spring up in them a suspicion and a root of bitterness and many will thereby be defiled, as Paul admonishes the Hebrews [Heb.

12:15]; that is, that they may not lose faith and become defiled
by the false estimate of the value of works and think that they must
be justified by works. Unless faith is at the same time constantly
taught, this happens easily and defiles a great many, as has been
done until now through the pestilent, impious, soul-destroying
traditions of our popes and the opinions of our theologians. By
these snares numberless souls have been dragged down to hell,
so that you might see in this the work of Antichrist.

In brief, as wealth is the test of poverty, business the test of
faithfulness, honors the test of humility, feasts the test of tem-
perance, pleasures the test of chastity, so ceremonies are the test
of the righteousness of faith. "Can a man," asks Solomon, "carry
fire in his bosom and his clothes and not be burned?" [Prov. 6:27].
Yet as a man must live in the midst of wealth, business, honors,
pleasures, and feasts, so also must he live in the midst of ceremonies,
that is, in the midst of dangers. Indeed, as infant boys need beyond
all else to be cherished in the bosoms and by the hands of maidens
to keep them from perishing, yet when they are grown up their
salvation is endangered if they associate with maidens, so the in-
experienced and perverse youth need to be restrained and trained
by the iron bars of ceremonies lest their unchecked ardor rush
headlong into vice after vice. On the other hand, it would be death
for them always to be held in bondage to ceremonies, thinking
that these justify them. They are rather to be taught that they
have been so imprisoned in ceremonies, not that they should be
made righteous or gain great merit by them, but that they might
thus be kept from doing evil and might more easily be instructed
to the righteousness of faith. Such instruction they would not
endure if the impulsiveness of their youth were not restrained. . . .

We do not despise ceremonies and works, but we set great store
by them; but we despise the false estimate placed upon works in
order that no one may think that they are true righteousness, as
those hypocrites believe who spend and lose their whole lives in
zeal for works and never reach that goal for the sake of which
the works are to be done, who, as the Apostle says, "will listen
to anybody and can never arrive at a knowledge of the truth" [2
Tim. 3:7]. They seem to wish to build, they make their prepara-
tions, and yet they never build. Thus they remain caught in the
form of religion and do not attain unto its power [2 Tim. 3:5].

⎍⎍⎍⎍⎍⎍⎍⎍⎍⎍⎍⎍⎍⎍⎍⎍⎍⎍⎍⎍⎍⎍⎍⎍⎍⎍⎍

3. Martin Luther: *Invocavit* sermons (1522)*

Following his refusal to recant at Worms, Luther disappeared to the Wartburg at the crucial moment when at Wittenberg his reformatory pronouncements had to be translated into ecclesiastical practice. He had called a wide variety of Catholic practices into question: the Mass was declared unscriptural, as were monastic vows and clerical celibacy. Still, the daily religious life continued unchanged in Wittenberg as if nothing had ever been said. Late in 1521 some of Luther's followers sought to solve some of these questions. In December one of them celebrated an "evangelical" communion and early the following year disturbances occurred over the question of additional ecclesiastical change. Luther, informed of this development, returned to Wittenberg early in March and shortly thereafter preached a series of sermons in which he elaborated his own understanding of ecclesiastical reform. Two of these sermons are reprinted here. They illustrate Luther's characteristic concentration on the essential, and show that he found fault with the impatient reformers for having done the right thing at the wrong time: inner change had to precede outer change. Luther charged that the reverse had been advocated in Wittenberg. Moreover, the gospel must not be turned into rigid regimentation; its "may's" can never be translated into "must's." Here spoke a moderate, if not conservative reformer who abhorred external regimentation and felt it wise to make haste slowly.

LITERATURE
E. G. Rupp, "Luther and the Puritans," in *Luther Today* (Decorah, Iowa, 1957).

The First Sermon

THE summons of death comes to us all, and no one can die for another. Every one must fight his own battle with death by him-

* *Luther's Works.* Vol. 51. Sermons I, ed. John W. Doberstein (Philadelphia, 1959), pp. 70–78.

self, alone. We can shout into another's ears, but every one must himself be prepared for the time of death, for I will not be with you then, nor you with me. Therefore every one must himself know and be armed with the chief things which concern a Christian. And these are what you, my beloved, have heard from me many days ago.

In the first place, we must know that we are the children of wrath, and all our works, intentions, and thoughts are nothing at all. Here we need a clear, strong text to bear out this point. Such is the saying of St. Paul in Eph. 2 [:3]. Note this well; and though there are many such in the Bible, I do not wish to overwhelm you with many texts. "We are all the children of wrath." And please do not undertake to say: I have built an altar, given a foundation for Masses, etc.

Secondly, that God has sent us His only-begotten Son that we may believe in Him and that whoever trusts in Him shall be free from sin and a child of God, as John declares in his first chapter, "To all who believed in His name, He gave power to become children of God" [John 1:12]. Here we should all be well versed in the Bible and ready to confront the devil with many passages. With respect to these two points I do not feel that there has been anything wrong or lacking. They have been rightly preached to you, and I should be sorry if it were otherwise. Indeed, I am well aware and I dare say that you are more learned than I, and that there are not only one, two, three, or four, but perhaps ten or more, who have this knowledge and enlightenment.

Thirdly, we must also have love and through love we must do to one another as God has done to us through faith. For without love faith is nothing, as St. Paul says (1 Cor. 2 [13:1]): If I had the tongues of angels and could speak of the highest things in faith, and have not love, I am nothing. And here, dear friends, have you not grievously failed? I see no signs of love among you, and I observe very well that you have not been grateful to God for His rich gifts and treasures.

Here let us beware lest Wittenberg become Capernaum [cf. Matt. 11:23]. I notice that you have a great deal to say of the doctrine of faith and love which is preached to you, and this is no wonder; an ass can almost intone the lessons, and why should you not be able to repeat the doctrines and formulas? Dear friends, the

kingdom of God—and we are that kingdom—does not consist in
talk or words [1 Cor. 4:20], but in activity, in deeds, in works
and exercises. God does not want hearers and repeaters of words
[Jas. 1:22], but followers and doers, and this occurs in faith
through love. For a faith without love is not enough—rather it is
not faith at all, but a counterfeit of faith, just as a face seen in a
mirror is not a real face, but merely the reflection of a face [1 Cor.
13:12].

Fourthly, we also need patience. For whoever has faith, trusts
in God, and shows love to his neighbor, practicing it day by day,
must needs suffer persecution. For the devil never sleeps, but constantly gives him plenty of trouble. But patience works and produces hope [Rom. 5:4], which freely yields itself to God and
vanishes away in Him. Thus faith, by much affliction and persecution, ever increases, and is strengthened day by day. A heart thus
blessed with virtues can never rest or restrain itself, but rather
pours itself out again for the benefit and service of the brethren,
just as God has done to it.

And here, dear friends, one must not insist upon his rights, but
must see what may be useful and helpful to his brother, as Paul
says, *Omnia mihi licent, sed non omnia expediunt,* " 'All things
are lawful for me,' but not all things are helpful" [1 Cor. 6:12].
For we are not all equally strong in faith, some of you have a
stronger faith than I. Therefore we must not look upon ourselves,
or our strength, or our prestige, but upon our neighbor, for God
has said through Moses: I have borne and reared you, as a mother
does her child [Deut. 1:31]. What does a mother do to her child?
First she gives it milk, then gruel, then eggs and soft food, whereas
if she turned about and gave it solid food, the child would never
thrive [cf. 1 Cor. 3:2; Heb. 5:12–13]. So we should also deal with
our brother, have patience with him for a time, have patience with
his weakness and help him bear it; we should also give him milk-
food, too [1 Pet. 2:2; cf. Rom. 14:1–3], as was done with us, until
he, too, grows strong, and thus we do not travel heavenward alone,
but bring our brethren, who are not now our friends, with us. If all
mothers were to abandon their children, where would we have
been? Dear brother, if you have suckled long enough, do not at
once cut off the breast, but let your brother be suckled as you
were suckled. I would not have gone so far as you have done, if

I had been here. The cause is good, but there has been too much haste. For there are still brothers and sisters on the other side who belong to us and must still be won.

Let me illustrate. The sun has two properties, light and heat. No king has power enough to bend or guide the light of the sun; it remains fixed in its place. But the heat may be turned and guided, and yet is ever about the sun. Thus faith must always remain pure and immovable in our hearts, never wavering; but love bends and turns so that our neighbor may grasp and follow it. There are some who can run, others must walk, still others can hardly creep [cf. 1 Cor. 8:7–13]. Therefore we must not look upon our own, but upon our brother's powers, so that he who is weak in faith, and attempts to follow the strong, may not be destroyed of the devil. Therefore, dear brethren, follow me; I have never been a destroyer. And I was also the very first whom God called to this work. I cannot run away, but will remain as long as God allows. I was also the one to whom God first revealed that His word should be preached to you. I am also sure that you have the pure word of God.

Let us, therefore, let us act with fear and humility, cast ourselves at one another's feet, join hands with each other, and help one another. I will do my part, which is no more than my duty, for I love you even as I love my own soul. For here we battle not against pope or bishop, but against the devil [cf. Eph. 6:12], and do you imagine he is asleep? He sleeps not, but sees the true light rising, and to keep it from shining into his eyes he would like to make a flank attack—and he will succeed, if we are not on our guard. I know him well, and I hope, too, that with the help of God, I am his master. But if we yield him but an inch, we must soon look to it how we may be rid of him. Therefore all those have erred who have helped and consented to abolish the Mass; not that it was not a good thing, but that it was not done in an orderly way. You say it was right according to the Scriptures. I agree, but what becomes of order? For it was done in wantonness, with no regard for proper order and with offense to your neighbor. If, beforehand, you had called upon God in earnest prayer, and had obtained the aid of the authorities, one could be certain that it had come from God. I, too, would have taken steps toward the same

end if it had been a good thing to do; and if the Mass were not so
evil a thing, I would introduce it again. For I cannot defend your
action, as I have just said. To the papists and blockheads I could
defend it, for I could say: How do you know whether it was done
with good or bad intention, since the work in itself was really a
good work? But I would not know what to assert before the devil.
For if on their deathbeds the devil reminds those who began this
affair of texts like these, "Every plant which my Father has not
planted will be rooted up" [Matt. 15:13], or "I have not sent them,
yet they ran" [Jer. 23:21], how will they be able to withstand?
He will cast them into hell. But I shall poke the one spear into
his face, so that even the world will become too small for him,
for I know that in spite of my reluctance I was called by the council to preach. Therefore I was willing to accept you as you were
willing to accept me, and, besides, you could have consulted me
about the matter.

I was not so far away that you could not reach me with a letter,
whereas not the slightest communication was sent to me. If you
were going to begin something and make me responsible for it, that
would have been too hard. I will not do it [i.e., assume the respon-
sibility]. Here one can see that you do not have the Spirit, even
though you do have a deep knowledge of the Scriptures. Take note
of these two things, "must" and "free." The "must" is that which
necessity requires, and which must ever be unyielding; as, for instance, the faith, which I shall never permit any one to take away
from me, but must always keep in my heart and freely confess before every one. But "free" is that in which I have choice, and may
use or not, yet in such a way that it profit my brother and not me.
Now do not make a "must" out of what is "free," as you have
done, so that you may not be called to account for those who were
led astray by your loveless exercise of liberty. For if you entice
any one to eat meat on Friday, and he is troubled about it on his
deathbed, and thinks, Woe is me, for I have eaten meat and I am
lost! God will call you to account for that soul. I, too, would like
to begin many things, in which but few would follow me, but
what is the use? For I know that, when it comes to the showdown,
those who have begun this thing cannot maintain themselves, and
will be the first to retreat. How would it be, if I brought the

people to the point of attack, and though I had been the first to exhort others, I would then flee, and not face death with courage? How the poor people would be deceived!

Let us, therefore, feed others also with the milk which we received, until they, too, become strong in faith. For there are many who are otherwise in accord with us and who would also gladly accept this thing, but they do not yet fully understand it—these we drive away. Therefore, let us show love to our neighbors; if we do not do this, our work will not endure. We must have patience with them for a time, and not cast out him who is weak in faith; and do and omit to do many other things, so long as love requires it and it does no harm to our faith. If we do not earnestly pray to God and act rightly in this matter, it looks to me as if all the misery which we have begun to heap upon the papists will fall upon us. Therefore I could no longer remain away, but was compelled to come and say these things to you.

The Second Sermon

Dear friends, you heard yesterday the chief characteristics of a Christian man, that his whole life and being is faith and love. Faith is directed toward God, love toward man and one's neighbor, and consists in such love and service for him as we have received from God without our work and merit. Thus, there are two things: the one, which is the most needful, and which must be done in one way and no other; the other, which is a matter of choice and not of necessity, which may be kept or not, without endangering faith or incurring hell. In both, love must deal with our neighbor in the same manner as God has dealt with us; it must walk the straight road, straying neither to the left nor to the right. In the things which are "musts" and are matters of necessity, such as believing in Christ, love nevertheless never uses force or undue constraint. Thus the Mass is an evil thing, and God is displeased with it, because it is performed as if it were a sacrifice and work of merit. Therefore it must be abolished. Here there can be no question or doubt, any more than you should ask whether you should worship God. Here we are entirely agreed: the private Masses must be abolished. As I have said in my writings, I wish they would be abolished everywhere and only the ordinary evangelical Mass be retained. Yet Christian love should not employ harshness here nor force the matter. However, it should be preached and taught with tongue and pen that to hold Mass in such a manner is sinful, and yet no one should be dragged away from it by the hair; for it should be left to God, and His word should be allowed to work alone, without our work or interference. Why? Because it is not in my power or hand to fashion the hearts of men as the potter molds the clay and fashion them at my pleasure [Eccles. 33:13]. I can get no farther than their ears; their hearts I cannot reach. And since I cannot pour faith into their hearts, I cannot, nor should I, force any one to have faith. That is God's work alone, who causes faith to live in the heart. Therefore we should give free course to the word and not add our works to it. We have the *jus verbi* [right to speak] but not the *executio* [power to accomplish]. We should preach the word, but the results must be left solely to God's good pleasure.

Now if I should rush in and abolish it by force, there are many who would be compelled to consent to it and yet not know where they stand, whether it is right or wrong, and they would say: I do not know if it is right or wrong, I do not know where I stand, I was compelled by force to submit to the majority. And this forcing and commanding results in a mere mockery, an external show, a fool's play, man-made ordinances, sham-saints, and hypocrites. For where the heart is not good, I care nothing at all for the work. We must first win the hearts of the people. But that is done when I teach only the word of God, preach the gospel, and say: Dear lords or pastors, abandon the Mass, it is not right, you are sinning when you do it; I cannot refrain from telling you this. But I would not make it an ordinance for them, nor urge a general law. He who would follow me could do so, and he who refused would remain outside. In the latter case the word would sink into the heart and do its work. Thus he would become convinced and acknowledge his error, and fall away from the Mass; tomorrow another would do the same, and thus God would accomplish more with His word than if you and I were to merge all our power into one heap. So when you have won the heart, you have won the man—and thus the thing must finally fall of its own weight and come to an end. And if the hearts and minds of all are agreed and united, abolish it. But if all are not heart and soul for its abolishment—leave it in God's hands, I beseech you, otherwise the result will not be good. Not that I would again set up the Mass; I let it lie in God's name. Faith must not be chained and imprisoned, nor bound by an ordinance to any work. This is the principle by which you must be governed. For I am sure you will not be able to carry out your plans. And if you should carry them out with such general laws, then I will recant everything that I have written and preached and I will not support you. This I am telling you now. What harm can it do you? You still have your faith in God, pure and strong so that this thing cannot hurt you.

Love, therefore, demands that you have compassion on the weak, as all the apostles had. Once, when Paul came to Athens (Acts 17 [:16–32]), a mighty city, he found in the temple many ancient altars, and he went from one to the other and looked at them all, but he did not kick down a single one of them with his foot. Rather he stood up in the middle of the market place and said they were nothing but idolatrous things and begged the people to forsake them; yet he did not destroy one of them by force. When the word took hold of their hearts, they forsook them of their own accord, and in consequence the thing fell of itself. Likewise, if I had seen them holding Mass, I would have preached to them and admonished them. Had they heeded my admonition, I would have won them; if not, I would nevertheless not have torn them from it by the hair or employed any force, but simply allowed the word to act and prayed for them. For the word created heaven and earth and all things [Ps. 33:6]; the word must do this thing, and not we poor sinners.

In short, I will preach it, teach it, write it, but I will constrain no man by force, for faith must come freely without compulsion. Take myself as an example. I opposed indulgences and all the papists, but never with force. I simply taught, preached, and wrote God's word; otherwise I did nothing. And while I slept [cf. Mark 4:26–29], or drank Wittenberg beer with my friends Philipp [Melanchthon] and Amsdorf, the word so greatly weakened the papacy that no prince or emperor ever inflicted such losses upon it. I did nothing; the word did everything. Had I desired to foment trouble, I could have brought great bloodshed upon Germany; indeed, I could have started such a game that even the emperor would not have been safe. But what would it have been? Mere fool's play. I did nothing; I let the word do its work. What do you suppose is Satan's thought when one tries to do the thing by kicking up a row? He sits back in hell and thinks: Oh, what a fine game the poor fools are up to now! But when we spread the word alone and let it alone do the work, that distresses him. For it is almighty and takes captive the hearts, and when the hearts are captured the work will fall of itself. Let me cite a simple instance. In former times there were sects, too, Jewish and Gentile Christians, differing on the law of Moses with respect to circumcision. The former wanted to keep it, the latter not. Then came Paul and preached that it might be kept or not, for it was of no consequence, and also that they should not make a "must" of it, but leave it to the choice of the individual; to keep it or not was immaterial [1 Cor. 7:18–24; Gal. 5:1]. So it was up to the time of Jerome, who came and wanted to make a "must" out of it, desiring to make it an ordinance and a law that it be prohibited. Then came St. Augustine and he was of the same opinion as St. Paul: it might be kept or not, as one wished. St. Jerome was a hundred miles away from St. Paul's opinion. The two doctors bumped heads rather hard, but when St. Augustine died, St. Jerome was successful in having it prohibited. After that came the popes, who also wanted to add something and they, too, made laws. Thus out of the making of one law grew a thousand laws, until they have completely buried us under laws. And this is what will happen here, too; one law will soon make two, two will increase to three, and so forth.

4. Martin Luther: Preface to the German Translation of the New Testament (1522)*

Luther's insistence that only the Scriptures were to serve as the guide for the Christian faith, together with his conscious effort to challenge the common people with his program of ecclesiastical transformation, made it inevitable that he turn to the task of making the Scriptures

* *Luther's Works*. Vol. 35. Word and Sacrament I, ed. E. T. Bachmann (Philadelphia, 1960), pp. 358–62.

available in German so that people could read them for themselves. His involuntary stay on the Wartburg from May, 1521 to March, 1522 gave him the opportunity to begin the translation of the New Testament, which he completed in a surprisingly short time. Published in September, 1522 it became known as the September Bible. It was a stylistic masterpiece and a superb translation of the words of the gospel writers into the idiom of sixteenth century Saxony.

The September Bible was important in another way. It contained a number of explanatory notes in which Luther formulated his hermeneutical principle for the interpretation of Scripture. The controversy with Catholic theologians had made him aware that his opponents, too, quoted Scripture in support of their position; thus, Catholics were fond of quoting the Epistle of James with its assertion that man is saved by works to counter Luther's stress upon justification by faith. Clearly, it was not sufficient to demand a simple recourse to Scripture. Catholics took this scriptural heterogeneity to underscore the need for an interpreting agent, the church. Luther, on the other hand, argued the need of distinguishing between various levels of Scriptures. This distinction, and the principles underlying it, he set down in the following, which is a slightly condensed version of the preface.

LITERATURE
H. Blum, *Martin Luther. Creative Translator* (St. Louis, 1965).

JUST as the Old Testament is a book in which are written God's laws and commandments, together with the history of those who kept and of those who did not keep them, so the New Testament is a book in which are written the gospel and the promises of God, together with the history of those who believe and of those who do not believe them.

For "gospel" [*Euangelium*] is a Greek word and means in Greek a good message, good tidings, good news, a good report, which one sings and tells with gladness. For example, when David overcame the great Goliath, there came among the Jewish people the good report and encouraging news that their terrible enemy had been struck down and that they had been rescued and given joy and peace; and they sang and danced and were glad for it [1 Sam. 18:6].

Thus this gospel of God or New Testament is a good story and report, sounded forth into all the world by the apostles, telling of a true David who strove with sin, death, and the devil, and overcame them, and thereby rescued all those who were captive in sin, afflicted with death, and overpowered by the devil. Without any merit of their own He made them righteous, gave them life, and saved them, so that they were given peace and brought back to God. For this they sing, and thank and praise God, and are glad forever, if only they believe firmly and remain steadfast in faith.

This report and encouraging tidings, or evangelical and divine news, is also called a New Testament. For it is a testament when a dying man bequeaths his property, after his death, to his legally defined heirs. And Christ, before His death, commanded and ordained that His gospel be preached after His death in all the world [Luke 24:44–47]. Thereby He gave to all who believe, as their possession, everything that He had. This included: His life, in which He swallowed up death; His righteousness, by which He blotted out sin; and His salvation, with which He overcame everlasting damnation. A poor man, dead in sin and consigned to hell, can hear nothing more comforting than this precious and tender message about Christ; from the bottom of his heart he must laugh and be glad over it, if he believes it true.

Now to strengthen this faith, God has promised this gospel and testament in many ways, by the prophets in the Old Testament, as St. Paul says in Rom. 1[:1], "I am set apart to preach the gospel of God which He promised beforehand through His prophets in the holy Scriptures, concerning His Son, who was descended from David," etc.

To mention some of these places: God gave the first promise when He said to the serpent, in Gen. 3[:15], "I will put enmity between you and the woman, and between your seed and her seed; he shall bruise your head, and you shall bruise his heel." Christ is this woman's seed, who has bruised the devil's head, that is, sin, death, hell, and all his power. For without this seed, no man can escape sin, death, or hell.

Again, in Gen. 22[:18], God promised Abraham, "Through your descendant shall all the nations of the earth be blessed." Christ is that descendant of Abraham, says St. Paul in Gal. 3[:16]; He has blessed all the world, through the gospel [Gal. 3:8]. For where Christ is not, there is still the curse that fell upon Adam and his children when he had sinned, so that they all are necessarily guilty and subject to sin, death, and hell. Over against this curse, the gospel now blesses all the world by publicly announcing, "Whoever believes in this descendant of Abraham shall be blessed." That is, he shall be rid of sin, death, and hell, and shall remain righteous, alive, and saved forever, as Christ Himself says in John 11[:26], "Whoever believes in me shall never die."

Again God made this promise to David in 2 Sam. 7[:12–14] when He said, "I will raise up your son after you, who shall build a house for my name, and I will establish the throne of his kingdom forever. I will be his father, and he shall be my son," etc. This is the kingdom of Christ, of which the gospel speaks: an everlasting kingdom, a kingdom of life, salvation, and righteousness, where all those who believe enter in from out of the prison of sin and death.

There are many more such promises of the gospel in the other prophets as well, for example Mic. 5[:2], "But you, O Bethlehem Ephrathah, who are little to be among the clans of Judah, from you shall come forth for me one who is to be ruler in Israel"; and again, Hos. 13[:14], "I shall ransom them from the power of hell and redeem them from death. O death, I will be your plague; O hell, I will be your destruction."

The gospel, then, is nothing but the preaching about Christ, Son of God and of David, true God and man, who by His death and resurrection has overcome for us the sin, death, and hell of all men who believe in Him. Thus the gospel can be either a brief or a lengthy message; one person can write of it briefly, another at length. He writes of it at length, who writes about many words and works of Christ, as do the four evangelists. He writes of it briefly, however, who does not tell of Christ's works, but indicates briefly how by His death and resurrection He has overcome sin, death, and hell for those who believe in Him, as do St. Peter and St. Paul.

See to it, therefore, that you do not make a Moses out of Christ, or a book of laws and doctrines out of the gospel, as has been done heretofore and as certain prefaces put it, even those of St. Jerome. For the gospel does not expressly demand works of our own by which we become righteous and are saved; indeed it condemns such works. Rather the gospel demands faith in Christ: that He has overcome for us sin, death, and hell, and thus gives us righteousness, life, and salvation not through our works, but through His own works, death, and suffering, in order that we may avail ourselves of His death and victory as though we had done it ourselves.

To be sure, Christ in the gospel, and St. Peter and St. Paul besides, do give many commandments and doctrines, and expound the law. But these are to be counted like all Christ's other works and good deeds. To know His works and the things that happened to Him is not yet to know the true gospel, for you do not yet thereby know that He has overcome sin, death, and the devil. So, too, it is not yet knowledge of the gospel when you know these doctrines and commandments, but only when the voice comes that says, "Christ is your own, with His life, teaching, works, death, resurrection, and all that He is, has, does, and can do."

Thus we see also that He does not compel us but invites us kindly and says, "Blessed are the poor," etc. [Matt. 5:3]. And the apostles use the words, "I exhort," "I entreat," "I beg," so that one sees on every hand that the gospel is not a book of law, but really a preaching of the benefits of Christ, shown to us and given to us for our own possession, if we believe. But Moses, in his books, drives, compels, threatens, strikes, and rebukes terribly, for he is a lawgiver and driver.

Hence it comes that to a believer no law is given by which he becomes righteous before God, as St. Paul says in 1 Tim. 1[:9], because he is alive and righteous and saved by faith, and he needs nothing further except to prove his faith by works. Truly, if faith is there, he cannot hold back; he proves himself, breaks out into good works, confesses and teaches this gospel before the people, and stakes his life on it. Everything that he lives and does is directed to his neighbor's profit, in order to help him—not only to the attainment of this grace, but also in body, property, and honor. Seeing that Christ has done this for him, he thus follows Christ's example.

That is what Christ meant when at the last He gave no other commandment than love, by which men were to know who were His disciples [John 13:34-35] and true believers. For where works and love do not break forth, there faith is not right, the gospel does not yet take hold, and Christ is not rightly known. See, then, that you so approach the books of the New Testament as to learn to read them in this way.

Which are the true and noblest books of the New Testament?

From all this you can now judge all the books and decide among them which are the best. John's Gospel and St. Paul's epistles, especially that to the Romans, and St. Peter's first epistle are the true kernel and marrow of all the books. They ought properly to be the foremost books, and it would be advisable for every Christian to read them first and most, and by daily reading to make them as much his own as his daily bread. For in them you do not find many works and miracles of Christ described, but you do find depicted in masterly fashion how faith in Christ overcomes sin, death, and hell, and gives life, righteousness, and salvation. This is the real nature of the gospel, as you have heard.

If I had to do without one or the other—either the works or the preaching of Christ—I would rather do without the works than without His preaching. For the works do not help me, but His words give life, as He Himself says [John 6:63]. Now John writes very little about the works of Christ, but very much about His preaching, while the other evangelists write much about His works and little about His preaching. Therefore John's Gospel is the one, fine, true, and chief gospel, and is far, far to be preferred over the other three and placed high above them. So, too, the epistles of St. Paul and St. Peter far surpass the other three Gospels, Matthew, Mark, and Luke.

In a word St. John's Gospel and his first epistle, St. Paul's epistles, especially Romans, Galatians, and Ephesians, and St. Peter's first epistle are the books that show you Christ and teach you all that is necessary and salvatory for you to know, even if you were never to see or hear any other book or doctrine. Therefore St. James' epistle is really an epistle of straw, compared to these others, for it has nothing of the nature of the gospel about it. But more of this in the other prefaces.

டூட்பட்டையான text...

5. Martin Luther: *On Governmental Authority* (1523)*

The publication of this tract indicated Luther's concern to explore the political consequences of his new understanding of the nature of the church. He set out to describe the proper Christian attitude toward political authority, in light of the medieval background, where church and state had been intimately connected and the church had sought continuously to impose its will upon the political community. Luther was persuaded that the worldly preoccupation of the medieval church had been one of its major shortcomings and he vehemently argued for a clear separation of the two "realms." He stressed that governmental authority was from God, even though its principles are not those of the gospel. In its own way, Luther's treatise is a classical exposition of political theory written from a Christian perspective. It destroyed the medieval understanding of church and state and undoubtedly influenced subsequent development.

Sections from parts I and II of the treatise are reprinted below. (Part III deals with the attributes of a good leader.)

LITERATURE
W. Elert, *The Structure of Lutheranism* (St. Louis, 1962), vol. I.

FIRST, we must provide a sound basis for the civil law and sword so no one will doubt that it is in the world by God's will and ordinance. The passages which do this are the following: Rom. 12, "Let every soul be subject to the governing authority, for there is no authority except from God; the authority which every-

* *Luther's Works*. Vol. 45. The Christian in Society II, ed. Walther I. Bandt (Philadelphia, 1962), pp. 83–117.

where exists has been ordained by God. He then who resists the governing authority resists the ordinance of God, and he who resists God's ordinance will incur judgment." Again, in 1 Pet. 2 [:13–14], "Be subject to every kind of human ordinance, whether it be to the king as supreme, or to governors, as those who have been sent by Him to punish the wicked and to praise the righteous."

The law of this temporal sword has existed from the beginning of the world. For when Cain slew his brother Abel, he was in such great terror of being killed in turn that God even placed a special prohibition on it and suspended the sword for his sake, so that no one was to slay him [Gen. 4:14–15]. He would not have had this fear if he had not seen and heard from Adam that murderers are to be slain. Moreover, after the Flood, God reestablished and confirmed this in unmistakable terms when He said in Gen. 9 [:6], "Whoever sheds the blood of man, by man shall his blood be shed." This cannot be understood as a plague or punishment of God upon murderers, for many murderers who are punished in other ways or pardoned altogether continue to live, and eventually die by means other than the sword. Rather, it is said of the law of the sword, that a murderer is guilty of death and in justice is to be slain by the sword. Now is justice should be hindered or the sword have become negligent so that the murderer dies a natural death, Scripture is not on that account false when it says, "Whoever sheds the blood of man, by man shall his blood be shed." The credit or blame belongs to men if this law instituted by God is not carried out; just as other commandments of God, too, are broken.

Afterward it was also confirmed by the law of Moses, Ex. 21 [:14], "If a man wilfully kills another, you shall take him from my altar, that he may die." And again, in the same chapter, "A life for a life, an eye for an eye, a tooth for a tooth, a foot for a foot, a hand for a hand, a wound for a wound, a stripe for a stripe." In addition, Christ also confirms it when He says to Peter in the garden, "He that takes the sword will perish by the sword" [Matt. 26:52], which is to be interpreted exactly like the Gen. 9 [:6] passage, "Whoever sheds the blood of man," etc. Christ is undoubtedly referring in these words to that very passage which He thereby wishes to cite and to confirm. John the Baptist also teaches the same thing. When the soldiers asked him what they should do, he answered, "Do neither violence nor injustice to any one, and be content with your wages" [Luke 3:14]. If the sword were not a godly estate, he should have directed them to get out of it, since he was supposed to make the people perfect and instruct them in a proper Christian way. Hence, it is certain and clear enough that it is God's will that the temporal sword and law be used for the punishment of the wicked and the protection of the upright.

Second. There appear to be powerful arguments to the contrary. Christ says in Matt. 5 [:38–41], "You have heard that it was said to them of old: An eye for an eye, a tooth for a tooth. But I say to you, Do not resist evil; but if anyone strikes you on the right cheek, turn to him the other also. And if anyone would sue you and take your coat, let him have your cloak as well. And if anyone forces you to go one mile, go with him two miles," etc. Likewise Paul in Rom. 12 [:19], "Beloved, defend not yourselves, but leave it to the wrath of God; for it is written, 'Vengeance is mine; I will repay, says the Lord.'" And in Matt. 5 [:44], "Love your enemies, do good to them that hate you." And again, in 1 Pet. 2 [3:9], "Do not return evil for evil, or reviling for reviling," etc. These and similar passages would certainly make it appear as though in the New Testament Christians were to have no temporal sword.

Hence, the sophists also say that Christ has thereby abolished the law of Moses. Of such commandments they make "counsels" for the perfect. They divide Christian teaching and Christians into two classes. One part they call the perfect, and assign to it such counsels. The other they call the imperfect, and assign to it the commandments. This they do out of sheer wantonness and caprice, without any scriptural basis. They fail to see that in the same passage Christ lays such stress on His teaching that He is unwilling to have the least word of it set aside, and condemns to hell those who do not love their enemies. Therefore, we must interpret these passages differently, so that Christ's words may apply to everyone alike, be he perfect or imperfect. For perfection and imperfection do not consist in works, and do not establish any distinct external order among Christians. They exist in the heart, in faith and love, so that those who believe and love the most are the perfect ones, whether they be outwardly male or female, prince or peasant, monk or layman. For love and faith produce no sects or outward differences.

Third. Here we must divide the children of Adam and all

mankind into two classes, the first belonging to the kingdom of God, the second to the kingdom of the world. Those who belong to the kingdom of God are all the true believers who are in Christ and under Christ, for Christ is King and Lord in the kingdom of God, as Psalm 2 [:6] and all of Scripture says. For this reason He came into the world, that He might begin God's kingdom and establish it in the world. Therefore, He says before Pilate, "My kingdom is not of the world, but every one who is of the truth hears my voice" [John 18:36-37]. In the gospel He continually refers to the kingdom of God, and says, "Amend your ways, the kingdom of God is at hand" [Matt. 4:17, 10:7]; again, "Seek first the kingdom of God and His righteousness" [Matt. 6:33]. He also calls the gospel a gospel of the kingdom of God; because it teaches, governs, and upholds God's kingdom.

Now observe, these people need no temporal law or sword. If all the world were composed of real Christians, that is, true believers, there would be no need for or benefits from prince, king, lord, sword, or law. They would serve no purpose, since Christians have in their heart the Holy Spirit, who both teaches and makes them to do injustice to no one, to love everyone, and to suffer injustice and even death willingly and cheerfully at the hands of anyone. Where there is nothing but the unadulterated doing of right and bearing of wrong, there is no need for any suit, litigation, court, judge, penalty, law, or sword. For this reason it is impossible that the temporal sword and law should find any work to do among Christians, since they do of their own accord much more than all laws and teachings can demand, just as Paul says in 1 Tim. 1 [:9], "The law is not laid down for the just but for the lawless."

Why is this? It is because the righteous man of his own accord does all and more than the law demands. But the unrighteous do nothing that the law demands; therefore, they need the law to instruct, constrain, and compel them to do good. A good tree needs no instruction or law to bear good fruit; its nature causes it to bear according to its kind without any law or instruction. . . .

You ask: Why, then, did God give so many commandments to all mankind, and why does Christ prescribe in the gospel so many things for us to do? Of this I have written at length in the Postils and elsewhere. To put it here as briefly as possible, Paul says that the law has been laid down for the sake of the lawless

[1 Tim. 1:9], that is, so that those who are not Christians may through the law be restrained outwardly from evil deeds, as we shall hear later. Now since no one is by nature Christian or righteous, but altogether sinful and wicked, God through the law puts them all under restraint so they dare not wilfully implement their wickedness in actual deeds. In addition, Paul ascribes to the law another function in Rom. 7 and Gal. 2, that of teaching men to recognize sin in order that it may make them humble unto grace and unto faith in Christ. Christ does the same thing here in Matt. 5 [:39], where He teaches that we should not resist evil; by this He is interpreting the law and teaching what ought to be and must be the state and temper of a true Christian, as we shall hear further later on.

Fourth. All who are not Christians belong to the kingdom of the world and are under the law. There are few true believers, and still fewer who live a Christian life, who do not resist evil and indeed themselves do no evil. For this reason God has provided for them a different government beyond the Christian estate and kingdom of God. He has subjected them to the sword so that, even though they would like to, they are unable to practice their wickedness, and if they do practice it they cannot do so without fear or with success and impunity. In the same way a savage wild beast is bound with chains and ropes so that it cannot bite and tear as it would normally do, even though it would like to; whereas a tame and gentle animal needs no restraint, but is harmless despite the lack of chains and ropes.

If this were not so, men would devour one another, seeing that the whole world is evil and that among thousands there is scarcely a single true Christian. No one could support wife and child, feed himself, and serve God. The world would be reduced to chaos. For this reason God has ordained two governments: the spiritual, by which the Holy Spirit produces Christians and righteous people under Christ; and the temporal, which restrains the un-Christian and wicked so that—no thanks to them—they are obliged to keep still and to maintain an outward peace. Thus does St. Paul interpret the temporal sword in Rom. 13 [:3], when he says it is not a terror to good conduct but to bad. And Peter says it is for the punishment of the wicked [1 Pet. 2:14].

If anyone attempted to rule the world by the gospel and to abolish all temporal law and sword on the plea that all are baptized and Christian, and that, according to the gospel, there shall be among them no law or sword—or need for either—pray tell me, friend, what would he be doing? He would be loosing the ropes and chains of the savage wild beasts and letting them bite and mangle everyone, meanwhile insisting that they were harmless, tame, and gentle creatures; but I would have the proof in my wounds. Just so would the wicked under the name of Christian abuse evangelical freedom, carry on their rascality, and insist that they were Christians subject neither to law nor sword, as some are already raving and ranting.

To such a one we must say: Certainly it is true that Christians, so far as they themselves are concerned, are subject neither to law nor sword, and have need of neither. But take heed and first fill the world with real Christians before you attempt to rule it in a Christian and evangelical manner. This you will never accomplish; for the world and the masses are and always will be un-Christian, even if they are all baptized and Christian in name. Christians are few and far between (as the saying is). Therefore, it is out of the question that there should be a common Christian government over the whole world, or indeed over a single country or any considerable body of people, for the wicked always outnumber the good. Hence, a man who would venture to govern an entire country or the world with the gospel would be like a shepherd who should put together in one fold wolves, lions, eagles, and sheep, and let them mingle freely with one another, saying, "Help yourselves, and be good and peaceful toward one another. The fold is open, there is plenty of food. You need have no fear of dogs and clubs." The sheep would doubtless keep the peace and allow themselves to be fed and governed peacefully, but they would not live long, nor would one beast survive another.

For this reason one must carefully distinguish between these two governments. Both must be permitted to remain; the one to produce righteousness, the other to bring about external peace and prevent evil deeds. Neither one is sufficient in the world without the other. No one can become righteous in the sight of God by means of the temporal government, without Christ's spiritual government. Christ's government does not extend over all men; rather, Christians are always a minority in the midst of non-Christians. Now where temporal government or law alone prevails, there sheer hypocrisy is inevitable, even though the commandments be God's very own. For without the Holy Spirit in the heart no one becomes truly righteous, no matter how fine the works he does. On the other hand, where the spiritual government alone prevails over land and people, there wickedness is given free rein and the door is open for all manner of rascality, for the world as a whole cannot receive or comprehend it.

Now you see the intent of Christ's words which we quoted above from Matt. 5, that Christians should not go to law or use the temporal sword among themselves. Actually, He says this only to His beloved Christians, those who alone accept it and act accordingly, who do not make "counsels" out of it as the sophists do, but in their heart are so disposed and conditioned by the Spirit that they do evil to no one and willingly endure evil at the hands of others. If now the whole world were Christian in this sense, then these words would apply to all, and all would act accordingly. Since the world is un-Christian, however, these words do not apply to all; and all do not act accordingly, but are under another government in which those who are not Christian are kept under external constraint and compelled to keep the peace and do what is good.

This is also why Christ did not wield the sword, or give it a place in His kingdom. For He is a king over Christians and rules by His Holy Spirit alone, without law. Although He sanctions the sword, He did not make use of it, for it serves no purpose in His kingdom, in which there are none but the upright. Hence, David of old was not permitted to build the temple [2 Sam. 7:4–13], because he had wielded the sword and had shed much blood. Not that he had done wrong thereby, but because he could not be a type of Christ, who without the sword was to have a kingdom of peace. It had to be built instead by Solomon, whose name in German means "Friedrich" or "peaceful." . . . Whoever would extend the application of these and similar passages to wherever Christ's name is mentioned, would entirely pervert the Scripture; rather, they are spoken only of true Christians, who really do this among themselves.

Fifth. But you say: if Christians then do not need the temporal sword or law, why does Paul say to all Christians in Rom. 13 [:1], "Let all souls be subject to the governing authority," and St. Peter,

"Be subject to every human ordinance" [1 Pet. 2:13], etc., as quoted above? Answer: I have just said that Christians, among themselves and by and for themselves, need no law or sword, since it is neither necessary nor useful for them. Since a true Christian lives and labors on earth not for himself alone but for his neighbor, he does by the very nature of his spirit even what he himself has no need of, but is needful and useful to his neighbor. Because the sword is most beneficial and necessary for the whole world in order to preserve peace, punish sin, and restrain the wicked, the Christian submits most willingly to the rule of the sword, pays his taxes, honors those in authority, serves, helps, and does all he can to assist the governing authority, that it may continue to function and be held in honor and fear. Although he has no need of these things for himself—to him they are not essential—nevertheless, he concerns himself about what is serviceable and of benefit to others, as Paul teaches in Eph. 5 [:21–6:9].

Just as he performs all other works of love which he himself does not need—he does not visit the sick in order that he himself may be made well, or feed others because he himself needs food—so he serves the governing authority not because he needs it but for the sake of others, that they may be protected and that the wicked may not become worse. He loses nothing by this; such service in no way harms him, yet it is of great benefit to the world. If he did not so serve he would be acting not as a Christian but even contrary to love; he would also be setting a bad example to others who in like manner would not submit to authority, even though they were not Christians. In this way the gospel would be brought into disrepute, as though it taught insurrection and produced self-willed people unwilling to benefit or serve others, when in fact it makes a Christian the servant of all. . . .

Thus you observe in the words of Christ quoted above from Matt. 5 that He clearly teaches that Christians among themselves should have no temporal sword or law. He does not, however, forbid one to serve and be subject to those who do have the secular sword and law. Rather, since you do not need it and should not have it, you are to serve all the more those who have not attained to such heights as you and who therefore do still need it. Although you do not need to have your enemy punished, your afflicted neighbor does. You should help him that he may have peace and that his enemy may be curbed, but this is not possible unless the governing authority is honored and feared. Christ does not say, "You shall not serve the governing authority or be subject to it," but rather, "Do not resist evil" [Matt. 5:39], as much as to say, "Behave in such a way that you bear everything, so that you may not need the governing authority to help you and serve you or be beneficial or essential for you, but that you in turn may help and serve it, being beneficial and essential to it. I would have you be too exalted and far too noble to have any need of it; it should rather have need of you."

Sixth. You ask whether a Christian too may bear the temporal sword and punish the wicked, since Christ's words, "Do not resist evil," are so clear and definite that the sophists have had to make of them a "counsel." Answer: You have now heard two propositions. One is that the sword can have no place among Christians; therefore, you cannot bear it among Christians or hold it over them, for they do not need it. The question, therefore, must be referred to the other group, the non-Christians, whether you may bear it there in a Christian manner. Here the other proposition applies, that you are under obligation to serve and assist the sword by whatever means you can, with body, goods, honor, and soul. For it is something which you do not need, but which is very beneficial and essential for the whole world and for your neighbor. Therefore, if you see that there is a lack of hangmen, constables, judges, lords, or princes, and you find that you are qualified, you should offer your services and seek the position, that the essential governmental authority may not be despised and become enfeebled or perish. The world cannot and dare not dispense with it.

Here is the reason why you should do this: In such a case you would be entering entirely into the service and work of others, which would be of advantage neither to yourself nor your property or honor, but only to your neighbor and to others. You would be doing it not with the purpose of avenging yourself or returning evil for evil, but for the good of your neighbor and for the maintenance of the safety and peace of others. For yourself, you would abide by the gospel and govern yourself according to Christ's word [Matt. 5:39-40], gladly turning the other cheek and letting the cloak go with the coat when the matter concerned you and your cause.

In this way the two propositions are brought into harmony
with one another: at one and the same time you satisfy God's
kingdom inwardly and the kingdom of the world outwardly. You
suffer evil and injustice, and yet at the same time you punish evil
and injustice; you do not resist evil, and yet at the same time,
you do resist it. In the one case, you consider yourself and what
is yours; in the other, you consider your neighbor and what is
his. In what concerns you and yours, you govern yourself by
the gospel and suffer injustice toward yourself as a true Christian;
in what concerns the person or property of others, you govern
yourself according to love and tolerate no injustice toward your
neighbor. The gospel does not forbid this; in fact, in other places
it actually commands it. . . .

Paul says in 1 Cor. 7 [:19] and Gal. 6 [:15] that neither un-
circumcision nor circumcision counts for anything, but only a
new creature in Christ. That is, it is not sin to be uncircumcised,
as the Jews thought, nor is it sin to be circumcised, as the Gentiles
thought. Either is right and permissible for him who does not
think he will thereby become righteous or be saved. The same is
true of all other parts of the Old Testament; it is not wrong to
ignore them and it is not wrong to abide by them, but it is permissible and proper either to follow them or to omit them. Indeed, if
it were necessary or profitable for the salvation of one's neighbor,
it would be necessary to keep all of them. For everyone is under
obligation to do what is for his neighbor's good, be it Old Testament or New, Jewish or Gentile, as Paul teaches in 1 Cor. 12. For
love pervades all and transcends all; it considers only what is necessary and beneficial to others, and does not ask whether it is old or
new. Hence, the precedents for the use of the sword also are matters of freedom, and you may follow them or not. But where you
see that your neighbor needs it, there love constrains you to do as
a matter of necessity that which would otherwise be optional and
not necessary for you either to do or to leave undone. Only do
not suppose that you will thereby become righteous or be saved
—as the Jews presumed to be saved by their works—but leave
this to faith, which without works makes you a new creature.

To prove our position also by the New Testament, the testimony of John the Baptist in Luke 3 [:14] stands unshaken on this
point. There can be no doubt that it was his task to point to

Christ, witness for Him, and teach about Him; that is to say, the teaching of the man who was to lead a truly perfected people to Christ had of necessity to be purely New Testament and evangelical. John confirms the soldiers' calling, saying they should be content with their wages. Now if it had been un-Christian to bear the sword, he ought to have censured them for it and told them to abandon both wages and sword, else he would not have been teaching them Christianity aright. . . .

Moreover, we have the clear and compelling text of St. Paul in Rom. 13 [:1], where he says, "The governing authority has been ordained by God"; and further, "The governing authority does not bear the sword in vain. It is God's servant for your good, an avenger upon him who does evil" [Rom. 13:4]. Be not so wicked, my friend, as to say, "A Christian may not do that which is God's own peculiar work, ordinance, and creation." Else you must also say, "A Christian must not eat, drink, or be married," for these are also God's work and ordinance. If it is God's work and creation, then it is good, so good that everyone can use it in a Christian and salutary way, as Paul says in 2 Tim. 4 [1 Tim. 4:4, 3], "Everything created by God is good, and nothing is to be rejected by those who believe and know the truth." Under "everything created by God" you must include not simply food and drink, clothing and shoes, but also authority and subjection, protection and punishment.

In short, since Paul says here that the governing authority is God's servant, we must allow it to be exercised not only by the heathen but by all men. What can be the meaning of the phrase, "It is God's servant," except that governing authority is by its very nature such that through it one may serve God? Now it would be quite un-Christian to say that there is any service of God in which a Christian should not or must not take part, when service of God is actually more characteristic of Christians than of anyone else. It would even be fine and fitting if all princes were good, true Christians. For the sword and authority, as a particular service of God, belong more appropriately to Christians than to any other men on earth. Therefore, you should esteem the sword or governmental authority as highly as the estate of marriage, or husbandry, or any other calling which God has instituted. Just as one can serve God in the estate of marriage, or

in farming or a trade, for the benefit of others—and must so
serve if his neighbor needs it—so one can serve God in government, and should there serve if the needs of his neighbor demand it.
For those who punish evil and protect the good are God's servants
and workmen. Only, one should also be free not to do it if there
is no need for it, just as we are free not to marry or farm where
there is no need for them. . . .

From all this we gain the true meaning of Christ's words in
Matt. 5 [:39], "Do not resist evil," etc. It is this: A Christian
should be so disposed that he will suffer every evil and injustice
without avenging himself; neither will he seek legal redress in the
courts but have utterly no need of temporal authority and law
for his own sake. On behalf of others, however, he may and
should seek vengeance, justice, protection, and help, and do as
much as he can to achieve it. Likewise, the governing authority
should, on its own initiative or through the instigation of others,
help and protect him too, without any complaint, application, or
instigation on his own part. If it fails to do this, he should permit
himself to be despoiled and slandered; he should not resist evil, as
Christ's words say.

Be certain too that this teaching of Christ is not a counsel
for those who would be perfect, as our sophists blasphemously
and falsely say, but a universally obligatory command for all
Christians. Then you will realize that all those who avenge themselves or go to law and wrangle in the courts over their property
and honor are nothing but heathen masquerading under the name
of Christians. It cannot be otherwise, I tell you. Do not be dis-
suaded by the multitude and common practice; for there are few
Christians on earth—have no doubt about it—and God's word is
something very different from the common practice. . . .

Here you inquire further, whether constables, hangmen, jurists,
lawyers, and others of similar function can also be Christians and
in a state of salvation. Answer: If the governing authority and
its sword are a divine service, as was proved above, then everything that is essential for the authority's bearing of the sword
must also be divine service. There must be those who arrest,
prosecute, execute, and destroy the wicked, and who protect,
acquit, defend, and save the good. Therefore, when they perform
their duties, not with the intention of seeking their own ends but

only of helping the law and the governing authority function to coerce the wicked, there is no peril in that; they may use their office like anybody else would use his trade, as a means of livelihood. For, as has been said, love of neighbor is not concerned about its own; it considers not how great or humble, but how profitable and needful the works are for neighbor or community. . . .

PART TWO. HOW FAR TEMPORAL AUTHORITY EXTENDS

We come now to the main part of this treatise. Having learned that there must be temporal authority on earth, and how it is to be exercised in a Christian and salutary manner, we must now learn how far its arm extends and how widely its hand stretches, lest it extend too far and encroach upon God's kingdom and government. It is essential for us to know this, for where it is given too wide a scope, intolerable and terrible injury follows; on the other hand, injury is also inevitable where it is restricted too narrowly. In the former case, the temporal authority punishes too much; in the latter case, it punishes too little. To err in this direction, however, and punish too little is more tolerable, for it is always better to let a scoundrel live than to put a godly man to death. The world has plenty of scoundrels anyway and must continue to have them, but godly men are scarce.

It is to be noted first that the two classes of Adam's children—the one in God's kingdom under Christ and the other in the kingdom of the world under the governing authority, as was said above—have two kinds of law. For every kingdom must have its own laws and statutes; without law no kingdom or government can survive, as everyday experience amply shows. The temporal government has laws which extend no further than to life and property and external affairs on earth, for God cannot and will not permit anyone but Himself to rule over the soul. Therefore, where the temporal authority presumes to prescribe laws for the soul, it encroaches upon God's government and only misleads souls and destroys them. We want to make this so clear that everyone will grasp it, and that our fine gentlemen, the princes and bishops, will see what fools they are when they seek to coerce the people with their laws and commandments into believing this or that.

When a man-made law is imposed upon the soul to make it

believe this or that as its human author may prescribe, there is certainly no word of God for it. If there is no word of God for it, then we cannot be sure whether God wishes to have it so, for we cannot be certain that something which He does not command is pleasing to Him. Indeed, we are sure that it does not please Him, for He desires that our faith be based simply and entirely on His divine word alone. He says in Matt. 18 [16:18], "On this rock I will build my church"; and in John 10 [:27, 14, 5], "My sheep hear my voice and know me; however, they will not hear the voice of a stranger, but flee from him." From this it follows that with such a wicked command the temporal power is driving souls to eternal death. For it compels them to believe as right and certainly pleasing to God that which is in fact uncertain, indeed, certain to be displeasing to Him since there is no clear word of God for it. Whoever believes something to be right which is wrong or uncertain is denying the truth, which is God Himself. He is believing in lies and errors, and counting as right that which is wrong.

Hence, it is the height of folly when they command that one shall believe the church, the Fathers, and the councils, though there be no word of God for it. It is not the church but the devil's apostles who command such things, for the church commands nothing unless it knows for certain that it is God's word. As St. Peter puts it, "Whoever speaks, let him speak as the word of God" [1 Pet. 4:11]. It will be a long time, however, before they can ever prove that the decrees of the councils are God's word. Still more foolish is it when they assert that kings, princes, and the mass of mankind believe thus and so. My dear man, we are not baptized into kings, or princes, or even into the mass of mankind, but into Christ and God Himself. Neither are we called kings, princes, or common folk, but Christians. No one shall or can command the soul unless he is able to show it the way to heaven; but this no man can do, only God alone. Therefore, in matters which concern the salvation of souls nothing but God's word shall be taught and accepted.

Again, consummate fools though they are, they must confess that they have no power over souls. For no human being can kill a soul or give it life, or conduct it to heaven or hell. If they will not take our word for it, Christ Himself will attend to it strongly enough where He says in the tenth chapter of Matthew, "Do not fear those who kill the body, and after that have nothing that they can do; rather fear him who after he has killed the body, has power to condemn to hell." I think it is clear enough here that the soul is taken out of all human hands and is placed under the authority of God alone.

Now tell me: How much wit must there be in the head of a person who imposes commands in an area where he has no authority whatsoever? Would you not judge the person insane who commanded the moon to shine whenever he wanted it to? How well would it go if the Leipzigers were to impose laws on us Wittenbergers, or if, conversely, we in Wittenberg were to legislate for the people of Leipzig! They would certainly send the lawmakers a thank-offering of hellebore to purge their brains and cure their sniffles. Yet our emperor and clever princes are doing just that today. They are allowing pope, bishop, and sophists to lead them on—one blind man leading the other—to command their subjects to believe, without God's word, whatever they please. And still they would be known as Christian princes, God forbid!

Besides, we cannot conceive how an authority could or should act in a situation except where it can see, know, judge, condemn, change, and modify. What would I think of a judge who should blindly decide cases which he neither hears nor sees? Tell me then: How can a mere man see, know, judge, condemn, and change hearts? That is reserved for God alone, as Psalm 7 [:9] says, "God tries the hearts and reins"; and [v. 8], "The Lord judges the peoples." And Acts 10 says, "God knows the hearts"; and Jer. 1 [17:9-10], "Wicked and unsearchable is the human heart; who can understand it? I the Lord, who search the heart and reins." A court should and must be quite certain and clear about everything if it is to render judgment. But the thoughts and inclinations of the soul can be known to no one but God. Therefore, it is futile and impossible to command or compel anyone by force to believe this or that. The matter must be approached in a different way. Force will not accomplish it. And I am surprised at the big fools, for they themselves all say: *De occultis non iudicat Ecclesia*, the church does not judge secret matters. If the spiritual rule of the church governs only public matters, how dare the mad temporal authority judge and control such a secret, spiritual, hidden matter as faith?

Furthermore, every man runs his own risk in believing as he does, and he must see to it himself that he believes rightly. As nobody else can go to heaven or hell for me, so nobody else can believe or disbelieve for me; as nobody else can open or close heaven or hell to me, so nobody else can drive me to belief or unbelief. How he believes or disbelieves is a matter for the conscience of each individual, and since this takes nothing away from the temporal authority the latter should be content to attend to its own affairs and let men believe this or that as they are able and willing, and constrain no one by force. For faith is a free act, to which no one can be forced. Indeed, it is a work of God in the spirit, not something which outward authority should compel or create. Hence arises the common saying, found also in Augustine, "No one can or ought to be forced to believe."

Moreover, the blind, wretched fellows fail to see how utterly hopeless and impossible a thing they are attempting. For no matter how harshly they lay down the law, or how violently they rage, they can do no more than force an outward compliance of the mouth and the hand; the heart they cannot compel, though they work themselves to a frazzle. For the proverb is true: "Thoughts are tax-free." Why do they persist in trying to force people to believe from the heart when they see that it is impossible? In so doing they only compel weak consciences to lie, to disavow, and to utter what is not in their hearts. They thereby load themselves down with dreadful alien sins, for all the lies and false confessions which such weak consciences utter fall back upon him who compels them. Even if their subjects were in error, it would be much easier simply to let them err than to compel them to lie and to utter what is not in their hearts. In addition, it is not right to prevent evil by something even worse. . . .

Similarly, the temporal lords are supposed to govern lands and people outwardly. This they leave undone. They can do no more than strip and fleece, heap tax upon tax and tribute upon tribute, letting loose here a bear and there a wolf. Besides this, there is no justice, integrity, or truth to be found among them. They behave worse than any thief or scoundrel, and their temporal rule has sunk quite as low as that of the spiritual tyrants. For this reason

God so perverts their minds also, that they rush on into the absurdity of trying to exercise a spiritual rule over souls, just as their counterparts try to establish a temporal rule. They blithely heap alien sins upon themselves and incur the hatred of God and man, until they come to ruin together with bishops, popes, and monks, one scoundrel with the other. Then they lay all the blame on the gospel, and instead of confessing their sin they blaspheme God and say that our preaching has brought about that which their perverse wickedness has deserved—and still unceasingly deserves—just as the Romans did when they were destroyed. Here then you have God's decree concerning the high and mighty. They are not to believe it, however, lest this stern decree of God be hindered by their repentance.

But, you say: Paul said in Rom. 13 [:1] that every soul should be subject to the governing authority; and Peter says that we should be subject to every human ordinance [1 Pet. 2:13]. Answer: Now you are on the right track, for these passages are in my favor. St. Paul is speaking of the governing authority. Now you have just heard that no one but God can have authority over souls. Hence, St. Paul cannot possibly be speaking of any obedience except where there can be corresponding authority. From this it follows that he is not speaking of faith, to the effect that temporal authority should have the right to command faith. He is speaking rather of external things, that should be ordered and governed on earth. His words too make this perfectly clear, where he prescribes limits for both authority and obedience, saying, "Pay all of them their dues, taxes to whom taxes are due, revenue to whom revenue is due, honor to whom honor is due, respect to whom respect is due" [Rom. 13:7]. Temporal obedience and authority, you see, apply only externally to taxes, revenue, honor, and respect. Again, where he says, "The governing authority is not a terror to good conduct, but to bad" [Rom. 13:3], he again so limits the governing authority that it is not to have the mastery over faith or the word of God, but over evil works. . . .

Christ Himself made this distinction, and summed it all up very nicely when He said in Matt. 22 [:21], "Render to Caesar the things that are Caesar's and to God the things that are God's." Now, if the imperial power extended into God's kingdom and authority, and were not something separate, Christ would not have made this distinction. For, as has been said, the soul is not under the authority of Caesar; he can neither teach it nor guide it, neither kill it nor give it life, neither bind it nor loose it, neither judge it nor condemn it, neither hold it fast nor release it. All this he would have to do, had he the authority to command it and to impose laws upon it. But with respect to body, property, and honor he has indeed to do these things, for such matters are under his authority. . . .

If your prince or temporal ruler commands you to side with the pope, to believe thus and so, or to get rid of certain books, you should say, "It is not fitting that Lucifer should sit at the side of God. Gracious sir, I owe you obedience in body and property; command me within the limits of your authority on earth, and I will obey. But if you command me to believe or to get rid of certain books, I will not obey; for then you are a tyrant and overreach yourself, commanding where you have neither the right nor the authority," etc. Should he seize your property on account of this and punish such disobedience, then blessed are you; thank God that you are worthy to suffer for the sake of the divine word. Let him rage, fool that he is; he will meet his judge. For I tell you, if you fail to withstand him, if you give in to him and let him take away your faith and your books, you have truly denied God.

Let me illustrate. In Meissen, Bavaria, the Mark, and other places, the tyrants have issued an order that all copies of the New Testament are everywhere to be turned in to the officials. This should be the response of their subjects: They should not turn in a single page, not even a letter, on pain of losing their salvation. Whoever does so is delivering Christ up into the hands of Herod, for these tyrants act as murderers of Christ just like Herod. If their homes are ordered searched and books or property taken by force, they should suffer it to be done. Outrage is not to be resisted but endured; yet we should not sanction it, or lift a little finger to conform, or obey. For such tyrants are acting as worldly princes are supposed to act, and worldly princes they surely are. But the world is God's enemy; hence, they too have to do what is antagonistic to God and agreeable to the world, that they may not be bereft of honor, but remain worldly princes. Do not won-

der, therefore, that they rage and mock at the gospel; they have
to live up to their name and title.

You must know that since the beginning of the world a wise
prince is a mighty rare bird, and an upright prince even rarer.
They are generally the biggest fools or the worst scoundrels on
earth; therefore, one must constantly expect the worst from them
and look for little good, especially in divine matters which concern the salvation of souls. They are God's executioners and hangmen; His divine wrath uses them to punish the wicked and to
maintain outward peace. Our God is a great lord and ruler; this
is why He must also have such noble, highborn, and rich hangmen and constables. He desires that everyone shall copiously
accord them riches, honor, and fear in abundance. It pleases His
divine will that we call His hangmen gracious lords, fall at their
feet, and be subject to them in all humility, so long as they do
not ply their trade too far and try to become shepherds instead
of hangmen. If a prince should happen to be wise, upright, or
a Christian, that is one of the great miracles, the most precious
token of divine grace upon that land. Ordinarily the course of
events is in accordance with the passage from Is. 3 [:4], "I will
make boys their princes, and gaping fools shall rule over them";
and in Hos. 13 [:11], "I will give you a king in my anger, and
take him away in my wrath." The world is too wicked, and does
not deserve to have many wise and upright princes. Frogs must
have their storks.

Again you say, "The temporal power is not forcing men to
believe; it is simply seeing to it externally that no one deceives
the people by false doctrine; how could heretics otherwise be
restrained?" Answer: This the bishops should do; it is a function
entrusted to them and not to the princes. Heresy can never be
restrained by force. One will have to tackle the problem in some
other way, for heresy must be opposed and dealt with otherwise
than with the sword. Here God's word must do the fighting. If it
does not succeed, certainly the temporal power will not succeed
either, even if it were to drench the world in blood. Heresy is
a spiritual matter which you cannot hack to pieces with iron,
consume with fire, or drown in water. God's word alone avails
here, as Paul says in 2 Cor. 10 [:4–5], "Our weapons are not

carnal, but mighty in God to destroy every argument and proud obstacle that exalts itself against the knowledge of God, and to take every thought captive in the service of Christ."

Moreover, faith and heresy are never so strong as when men oppose them by sheer force, without God's word. For men count it certain that such force is for a wrong cause and is directed against the right, since it proceeds without God's word and knows not how to further its cause except by naked force, as brute beasts do. Even in temporal affairs force can be used only after the wrong has been legally condemned. How much less possible it is to act with force, without justice and God's word, in these lofty spiritual matters! See, therefore, what fine, clever nobles they are! They would drive out heresy, but set about it in such a way that they only strengthen the opposition, rousing suspicion against themselves and justifying the heretics. My friend, if you wish to drive out heresy, you must find some way to tear it first of all from the heart and completely turn men's wills away from it. With force you will not stop it, but only strengthen it. What do you gain by strengthening heresy in the heart, while weakening only its outward expression and forcing the tongue to lie? God's word, however, enlightens the heart, and so all heresies and errors vanish from the heart of their own accord. . . .

Therefore, so long as the devil is not repelled and driven from the heart, it is agreeable to him that I destroy his vessels with fire or sword; it's as if I were to fight lightning with a straw. Job bore abundant witness to this when in his forty-first chapter he said that the devil counts iron as straw, and fears no power on earth. We learn it also from experience, for even if all Jews and heretics were forcibly burned no one ever has been or will be convinced or converted thereby. . . .

But you might say, "Since there is to be no temporal sword among Christians, how then are they to be ruled outwardly? There certainly must be authority even among Christians." Answer: Among Christians there shall and can be no authority; rather all are alike subject to one another, as Paul says in Rom. 12: "Each shall consider the other his superior"; and Peter says in 1 Pet. 5 [:5], "All of you be subject to one another." This is also what Christ means in Luke 14 [:10], "When you are invited to a wedding, go and sit in the lowest place." Among Christians there is no superior but Christ Himself, and Him alone. What kind of authority can there be where all are equal and have the same right, power, possession, and honor, and where no one desires to be the other's superior, but each the other's subordinate? Where there are such people, one could not establish authority even if he wanted to, since in the nature of things it is impossible to have superiors where no one is able or willing to be a superior. Where there are no such people, however, there are no real Christians either.

What, then, are the priests and bishops? Answer: Their government is not a matter of authority or power, but a service and an office, for they are neither higher nor better than other Christians. Therefore, they should impose no law or decree on others without their will and consent. Their ruling is rather nothing more than the inculcating of God's word, by which they guide Christians and overcome heresy. As we have said, Christians can be ruled by nothing except God's word, for Christians must be ruled in faith, not with outward works. Faith, however, can come through no word of man, but only through the word of God, as Paul says in Rom. 10 [:17].

6. The *Twelve Articles* of the peasants (1525)*

The German peasants' uprising of 1524–1525 had only a tenuous relationship with the Protestant Reformation, since the real causes of the peasants' discontent reached back into the preceding century, where they found expression in periodic uprisings and restlessness.

But the Protestant Reformation and its slogans—the freedom of the Christian man, the priesthood of all believers, the repudiation of manmade laws and regulations—seemed to be tailor-made for the peasants, and it was natural that they should embrace the tenets of the Reforma-

* Hans J. Hillerbrand, *The Reformation. A Narrative History* (New York, 1965), pp. 389–91.

tion. When the peasants rose in southwest Germany in the fall of
1524, their pronouncements seemed to express a Lutheran orientation.
The *Twelve Articles*, the most famous of a large number of similar
peasant documents, serves as an excellent illustration; see, for example, the abundant scriptural references, as well as the stipulation that
if any demand was contrary to Scripture it would be withdrawn.

LITERATURE
J. S. Schapiro, *Social Reform and the Reformation* (New York, 1909).

To the Christian Reader Peace and the Grace of God through
Christ.

There are many Antichrists who on account of the assembling
of the peasants, cast scorn upon the gospel, and say: Is this the
fruit of the new teaching, that no one obeys but all everywhere
rise in revolt, and band together to reform, extinguish, indeed kill
the temporal and spiritual authorities. The following articles will
answer these godless and blaspheming fault-finders. They will first
of all remove the reproach from the word of God and secondly
give a Christian excuse for the disobedience or even the revolt of
the entire peasantry. . . . Therefore, Christian reader, read the
following articles with care, and then judge. Here follow the
articles:

The First Article. First, it is our humble petition and desire,
indeed our will and resolution, that in the future we shall have
power and authority so that the entire community should choose
and appoint a minister, and that we should have the right to depose him should he conduct himself improperly. The minister thus
chosen should teach us the holy gospel pure and simple, without
any human addition, doctrine or ordinance. For to teach us continually the true faith will lead us to pray God that through His
grace His faith may increase within us and be confirmed in us.
For if His grace is not within us, we always remain flesh and
blood, which avails nothing; since the Scripture clearly teaches
that only through true faith can we come to God. Only through
His mercy can we become holy. . . .

The Second Article. Since the right tithe is established in the
Old Testament and fulfilled in the New, we are ready and willing

to pay the fair tithe of grain. None the less it should be done properly. The word of God plainly provides that it should be given to God and passed on to His own. If it is to be given to a minister, we will in the future collect the tithe through our church elders, appointed by the congregation and distribute from it, to the sufficient livelihood of the minister and his family elected by the entire congregation, according to the judgment of the whole congregation. The remainder shall be given to the poor of the place, as the circumstances and the general opinion demand. . . .

The Third Article. It has been the custom hitherto for men to hold us as their own property, which is pitiable enough considering that Christ has redeemed and purchased us without exception, by the shedding of His precious blood, the lowly as well as the great. Accordingly, it is consistent with Scripture that we should be free and we wish to be so. Not that we want to be absolutely free and under no authority. God does not teach us that we should lead a disorderly life according to the lusts of the flesh, but that we should live by the commandments, love the Lord our God and our neighbor. . . .

The Fourth Article. In the fourth place it has been the custom heretofore that no poor man was allowed to catch venison or wild fowl, or fish in flowing water, which seems to us quite unseemly and unbrotherly, as well as selfish and not according to the word of God. . . . Accordingly, it is our desire if a man holds possession of waters that he should prove from satisfactory documents that his right has been wittingly acquired by purchase. We do not wish to take it from him by force, but his rights should be exercised in a Christian and brotherly fashion. . . .

The Fifth Article. In the fifth place we are aggrieved in the matter of woodcutting, for our noble folk have appropriated all the woods to themselves alone. . . . It should be free to every member of the community to help himself to such firewood as he needs in his home. Also, if a man requires wood for carpenter's purposes he should have it free, but with the approval of a person appointed by the community for that purpose. . . .

The Sixth Article. Our sixth complaint is in regard to the excessive services demanded of us, which increase from day to day.

We ask that this matter be properly looked into, so that we shall not continue to be oppressed in this way, and that some gracious consideration be given us, since our forefathers served only according to the word of God.

The Seventh Article. Seventh, we will not hereafter allow ourselves to be further oppressed by our lords. What the lords possess is to be held according to the agreement between the lord and the peasant. . . .

The Eighth Article. In the eighth place, we are greatly burdened by holdings which cannot support the rent exacted from them. The peasants suffer loss in this way and are ruined. We ask that the lords may appoint persons of honor to inspect these holdings and fix a rent in accordance with justice, so that the peasant shall not work for nothing, since the laborer is worthy of his hire.

The Ninth Article. In the ninth place, we are burdened with the great evil in the constant making of new laws. We are not judged according to the offense, but sometimes with great ill will, and sometimes much too leniently. In our opinion we should be judged according to the old written law, so that the case shall be decided according to its merits, and not with favors.

The Tenth Article. In the tenth place we are aggrieved that certain individuals have appropriated meadows and fields which at one time belonged to the community. These we will take again into our own hands unless they were rightfully purchased.

The Eleventh Article. In the eleventh place we will entirely abolish the custom called *Todfall* [heriot], and will no longer endure it, nor allow widows and orphans to be thus shamefully robbed against God's will. . . .

Conclusion. In the twelfth place it is our conclusion and final resolution, that if any one or more of these articles should not be in agreement with the word of God, which we do not think, we will willingly recede from such article when it is proved to be against the word of God by a clear explanation of the Scripture. For this we shall pray God, since He can grant all this and He alone. The peace of Christ abide with us all.

ᒥᒪᒥᒪᒥᒪᒥᒪᒥᒪᒥᒪᒥᒪᒥᒪᒥᒪᒥᒪᒥᒪᒥᒪᒥᒪᒥ

7. Martin Luther: *Friendly Admonition to Peace concerning the Twelve Articles of the Swabian Peasants* (1525)*

This tract was Luther's response to the *Twelve Articles*, which had clearly implicated him by the "evangelical" character of their demands. From the insistence that a congregation elect its own minister to the willingness to be corrected by the Scriptures, the *Twelve Articles* seemed to be pages out of Luther's book. Luther responded with this tract, published in April, 1525. Above all, it was meant as an appeal to peace, as a plea that the grievances of the peasants be duly considered and bloodshed avoided. At the same time, Luther left little doubt that he disapproved of the peasants' marshaling of scriptural arguments in support of their economic or social goals and in this tract he expounded his understanding of the relationship of Christianity to social change. No matter how well justified certain social or economic demands may be, the gospel cannot be adduced in their support. Luther rejected the use of the gospel to sustain secular demands, and insisted that the laws of society must provide the answer for social amelioration.

A condensed version of the entire tract is reprinted below.

LITERATURE
H. Mackensen, "Historical Interpretation and Luther's Role in the Peasants' Revolt," *Concordia Theological Monthly*, 35 (1964).

THE peasants who have now banded together in Swabia have put their intolerable grievances against the rulers into twelve

* *Works of Martin Luther*. The Philadelphia Edition. Vol. IV (Philadelphia, 1931), pp. 219–44.

articles, and undertaken to support them with certain passages of Scripture, and have published them in printed form. The thing about them that pleases me best is that, in the twelfth article, they offer to accept instruction gladly and willingly, if there is need or necessity for it, and are willing to be corrected, in so far as that can be done by clear, plain, undeniable passages of Scripture, since it is right and proper that no one's conscience should be instructed or corrected, except by divine Scripture.

Now, if that is their serious and sincere meaning—and it would not be right for me to interpret it otherwise, because in these articles they come out boldly into the open, and show no desire to shun the light—then there is good reason to hope that things will be well. As one who am counted among those who now deal with the divine Scriptures here on earth, and especially as one whom they mention and call upon by name in the second document, it gives me the greater courage and confidence in openly publishing my instruction, which I do in a friendly and Christian spirit, as a duty of brotherly love, in order that, if any misfortune or disaster shall come out of this matter, it may not be attributed to me, or blamed on me, because of my silence. But if this offer of theirs is only pretense and show (and without doubt there are some of that kind of people among them; for it is not possible that so great a crowd should all be true Christians and have good intentions, but a large part of them must be using the good intentions of the rest for their own selfish purposes and seeking their own advantage), then without doubt, it will accomplish very little, or contribute, in fact, to their great injury and eternal ruin.

Because this matter, then, is great and perilous, concerning, as it does, both the kingdom of God and the kingdom of the world (for if this rebellion were to proceed and get the upper hand, both kingdoms would be destroyed and there would be neither worldly government nor word of God, but it would result in the permanent destruction of all Germany), therefore it is necessary to speak boldly and to give advice without regard to anyone. . . .

To the Princes and Lords

We have no one on earth to thank for this mischievous rebellion, except you princes and lords; and especially you blind bishops and mad priests and monks, whose hearts are hardened, even to the present day, and who do not cease to rage and rave against the

holy gospel, although you know that it is true, and that you cannot refute it. Besides, in your temporal government, you do nothing but flay and rob your subjects, in order that you may lead a
life of splendor and pride, until the poor common people can bear
it no longer. The sword is at your throats, but you think yourselves so firm in the saddle that no one can unhorse you. This false
security and stubborn perversity will break your necks, as you
will discover. I have often told you before to beware of the saying, in Psalm 106 [107], *Effundit contemptum super principes*,
"He poureth contempt upon princes." You are striving after it,
and want to be smitten over the head, and no warning or exhorting will help you to avoid it.

Well, then, since you are the cause of this wrath of God, it
will undoubtedly come upon you, if you do not mend your ways
in time. The signs in heaven and the wonders on earth are meant
for you, dear lords; they bode no good for you, and no good
will come to you. A great part of God's wrath has already come,
and God is sending so many false teachers and prophets among
us, so that through error and blasphemy we may richly deserve
hell and everlasting damnation. The rest of it is now here, for the
peasants are mustering, and this must result in the ruin, destruction,
and desolation of Germany by cruel murder and bloodshed, unless
God shall be moved by our repentance to prevent it.

For you ought to know, dear lords, that God is doing this because this raging of yours cannot and will not and ought not be
endured for long. You must become different men and yield to
God's word. If you do not do this amicably and willingly, then
you will be compelled to it by force and destruction. If these
peasants do not do it for you, others will. Even though you were
to beat them all, they would still be unbeaten, for God will raise
up others. It is His will to beat you, and you will be beaten. It is
not the peasants, dear lords, who are resisting you; it is God Himself who is resisting you in order to visit your raging upon you.
There are some of you who have said that they will stake land
and people on the extirpation of Lutheran teaching. What would
you think, if you were to turn out to be your own prophets, and
your land and people were already staked? Do not jest with God,
dear lords! The Jews, too, said, "We have no king," and it became
so serious that they had to be without a king forever.

To make your sin still greater, and ensure your merciless destruction, some of you are beginning to blame this affair on the gospel and say it is the fruit of my teaching. Well, well! Slander away, dear lords. You did not want to know what I taught, and what the gospel is; now there is one at the door who will soon teach you, unless you amend your ways. You, and everyone else, must bear me witness that I have taught with all quietness, have striven earnestly against rebellion, and have diligently held and exhorted subjects to obedience and reverence toward even your tyrannous and ravenous rule. This rebellion cannot be coming from me. But the murder-prophets, who hate me as much as they hate you, have come among these people and have gone about among them for more than three years, and no one has resisted them save me alone. If, therefore, God is minded to punish you, and allows the devil, through his false prophets, to stir up the people against you, and if it is, perhaps, His will that I shall not be able to prevent it any longer; what can I or my gospel do? Not only has it suffered your persecution and murdering and raging; it has also prayed for you and helped protect and maintain your rule over the common people. If I had any desire to be revenged on you, I could laugh in my sleeve, and become a mere onlooker at the doings of the peasants, or even join in with them and help make matters worse; but from this may my God preserve me, as He has done hitherto.

Therefore, my dear lords, enemies or friends, I beg submissively that you will not despise my faithfulness, though I am a poor man. I beg that you will not make light of this rebellion. Not that I believe or fear that they will be too strong for you, or that I would have you be afraid of them on that account. But fear God and have respect for His wrath! If it be His will to punish you as you have deserved (and I am afraid that it is), then He would punish you, even though the peasants were a hundred times fewer than they are. He can make peasants out of stones and slay a hundred of you by one peasant, so that all your armor and your strength will be too little.

If it is still possible to give you advice, my lords, give a little place to the will and wrath of God. . . . Do not begin a struggle with them, for you do not know what the end of it will be. Try kindness first, for you do not know what God wills to do, and do not strike a spark that will kindle all Germany and that no one can quench. Our sins are before God; therefore we have to fear

His wrath when even a leaf rustles, let alone when such multitude sets itself in motion. You lose nothing by kindness; and even though you were to lose something, it can afterwards come back to you ten times over in peace, while in conflict you may, perhaps, lose both life and goods. Why run into danger, when you can get more by another, and a good way?

The peasants have put forth twelve articles, some of which are so fair and just as to take away your reputation in the eyes of God and the world and fulfil the Psalm about pouring contempt upon princes. Nevertheless, almost all of them are framed in their own interest and for their own good, though not for their best good. I should, indeed, have put forth other articles against you that would have dealt with all Germany and its government. . . .

The first article, in which they ask the right to hear the gospel and choose their pastors, you cannot reject with any show of right, though, to be sure, it contains some selfishness, since they allege that these pastors are to be supported by the tithes, and these do not belong to them. Nevertheless, the sense of the article is that permission should be given for the preaching of the gospel, and this no ruler can or ought oppose. Indeed no ruler ought to prevent anyone from teaching or believing what he pleases, whether gospel or lies. It is enough if he prevents the teaching of sedition and rebellion.

The other articles recite physical grievances . . . and they, too, are fair and just. For rulers are not instituted in order that they may seek their own profit and self-will, but in order to provide for the best interests of their subjects. Flaying and extortion are, in the long run, intolerable.

To the Peasants

So far, dear friends, you have learned only that I admit it to be (sad to say!) all too true and certain that the princes and lords, who forbid the preaching of the gospel and oppress the people so unbearably, are worthy, and have well deserved, that God put them down from their seats, as men who have sinned deeply against God and man. And they have no excuse. Nevertheless, you, too, must have a care that you take up your cause with a good conscience and with justice. If you have a good conscience, you have the comforting advantage that God will be with you, and will help you through. Even though you were worsted for a while, and though you suffered death, you would win in the end, and would preserve your soul eternally with all the saints. But if you have not justice and a good conscience, you will be worsted; and even though you were to win for a while, and were to slay all the princes, yet in the end you would be lost eternally, body and soul. This is, therefore, no joking matter for you; it concerns your body and soul eternally. The thing that is most necessary to consider and that must be most seriously regarded, is not how strong you are and how completely wrong they are, but whether you have justice and a good conscience on your side.

Therefore, dear brethren, I beg you, in a kindly and brotherly way, to look diligently to what you do, and not to believe all kinds of spirits and preachers, now that Satan has raised up many evil spirits of disorder and of murder, and filled the world with them. Only listen and give ear, as you offer many times to do. I will not spare you the earnest warning that I owe you, even though some of you, poisoned by the murderous spirits, will hate me for it, and call me a hypocrite. That does not worry me; it is enough for me if I save some of the goodhearted and upright men among you from the danger of God's wrath. The rest I fear as little, as they despise me much; and they shall not harm me. I know one who is greater and mightier than they are, and He teaches me in Psalm 3, "I am not afraid, though many thousands of people set themselves against me." My confidence shall outlast their confidence; that I know for sure.

In the first place, dear brethren, you bear the name of God and call yourselves a "Christian band" or union, and allege that you want to live and act "according to the divine law." Now you know that the name, word, and titles of God are not to be assumed idly or in vain, as He says in the second commandment, "Thou shalt not bear the name of the Lord thy God in vain," and adds "For God will not let him be guiltless who bears His name in vain." Here is a clear, plain text, which applies to you, as to all men. Without regard to your great numbers, your rights, and your terror, it threatens you, as well as us and all others, with God's wrath. He is, as you also know, mighty enough and strong enough to punish you as He here threatens, if His name is borne in vain; and so you have to expect no good fortune, but only misfortune, if you bear His name falsely. Learn from this how to judge yourselves; and accept this kindly warning. For Him who once drowned the whole world in the Flood and sank Sodom with fire, it is a simple thing to slay or to defeat so many thousand peasants. He is an almighty and terrible God.

In the second place, it is easy to prove that you are bearing God's name in vain and putting it to shame; nor is it to be doubted that you will, in the end, encounter all misfortune, unless God is untrue. For here stands God's word, and says through the mouth of Christ, "He who takes the sword shall perish by the sword." That means nothing else than that no one, by his own violence, shall arrogate authority to himself; but as Paul says, "Let every soul be subject to the higher powers with fear and reverence."

How can you get over these sayings and laws of God, when you boast that you are acting according to divine law, and yet take the sword in your own hands, and revolt against the "higher powers" that are ordained of God? Do you not think that Paul's judgment in Rom. 13 will strike you, "He that withstands the ordinance of God shall receive condemnation"? That is "bearing God's name in vain"; alleging God's law and withstanding God's law, under His name. O have a care, dear sirs! It will not turn out that way in the end.

In the third place, you say that the rulers are wicked and intolerable, for they will not allow us the gospel, and they oppress us too hard by the burdens they lay on our temporal goods, and they are ruining us body and soul. I answer: The fact that the rulers are wicked and unjust does not excuse tumult and rebellion, for to punish wickedness does not belong to everybody, but to the worldly rulers who bear the sword. Thus Paul says in Rom. 13, and Peter, in 1 Pet. 3, that they are ordained of God for the punishment of the wicked. Then, too, there is the natural law of all the world, which says that no one may be judge in his own cause or take his own revenge. The proverb is true, "He who resists is wrong," and the other proverb, "He who resists makes strife." The divine law agrees with this, and says, in Deut. 32, "Vengeance is mine, I will repay, saith the Lord." Now you cannot deny that your rebellion proceeds in such a way that you make yourselves your own judges, and avenge yourselves, and are unwilling to suffer any wrong. That is contrary not only to

Christian law and the gospel, but also to natural law and all equity. . . .

On the contrary, because you boast of the divine law and yet act against it, He will let you fall and be punished terribly, as men who dishonor His name; and then He will condemn you eternally, as was said above. For the word of Christ in Matt. 7, applies to you; you see the mote in the eye of the rulers, and see not the beam in your own eye. Also the saying of Paul in Rom. 3, "Let us do evil that good may come; whose damnation is just and right." It is true that the rulers do wrong when they suppress the gospel and oppress you in temporal things; but you do much more wrong when you not only suppress God's word, but tread it underfoot, and invade His authority and His law, and put yourselves above God. Besides, you take from the rulers their authority and right; nay, all that they have. For what have they left, when they have lost their authority? . . .

Can you not imagine it, or figure it out, dear friends? If your enterprise were right, then any man might become judge over another, and there would remain in the world neither authority, nor government, nor order, nor land, but there would be only murder and bloodshed; for as soon as anyone saw that someone was wronging him, he would turn to and judge him and punish him. Now if that is unjust and intolerable when done by an individual, neither can it be endured when done by a band or a crowd. But if it can be endured from a band or a crowd, it cannot be prevented with right and justice when individuals attempt it; for in both cases the cause is the same, namely, a wrong. And what would you do yourselves, if disorder broke out in your band, and one man set himself against another and took his own vengeance on him? Would you put up with that? Would you not say that he must let others, whom you appointed, do the judging and avenging? How, then, do you expect to stand with God and the world, when you do your own judging and avenging upon those who have injured you; nay, upon your rulers, whom God has ordained?

Now, all this has been said concerning the common, divine and natural law which even heathen, Turks, and Jews have to keep, if there is to be any peace or order in the world. Even though you were to keep this whole law, you would do no better and no more than heathen and Turks. For not to be one's own judge and avenger, but to leave this to the authorities and the rulers, makes no man a Christian; it is a thing that must eventually be done whether willingly or not. But because you are acting against this law, you see plainly that you are worse than heathen or Turks, to say nothing of the fact that you are not Christians. But what do you think that Christ will say to this? You bear His name, and call yourselves a "Christian assembly," and yet you are so far from Christian, and your actions and lives are so horribly contrary to His law, that you are not worthy to be called even heathen or Turks, but are much worse than these, because you rage and struggle against the divine and natural law, which all the heathen keep. . . .

If, now, it is really your will to keep the divine law, as you boast, then do it. There it stands! God says, "Vengeance is mine; I will repay"; and again, "Be subject not only to good lords, but also to the wicked." If you do this, well and good; if not, you may, indeed, cause a calamity, but it will finally come upon yourselves. Let no one be in doubt about this! God is just, and will not endure it. Be careful, therefore, with your liberty, that you do not run from the rain and fall in the water, and thinking to gain freedom of body, lose body and goods and soul eternally. God's wrath is there; fear it, I advise you! The devil has sent false prophets among you; beware of them!

And now we would go on, and speak of the law of Christ, and of the gospel, which is not binding on the heathen, as the other law is. For if you boast that you are Christians and are glad when you are called Christians, and want to be known as Christians, then you must allow your law to be held up before you rightly. Listen, then, dear Christians, to your Christian law! Your supreme Lord Christ, whose name you bear, says, in Matt. 6 [5:39] "Ye shall not resist evil, but if any one compels you to go one mile, go with him two miles, and if anyone takes your cloak, let him have your coat, too; and if anyone smites you on one cheek, offer him the other also." Do you hear, "Christian assembly"? How does your undertaking agree with this law? You will not endure it when anyone does you ill or wrong, but will be free, and suffer nothing but good and right; and Christ says that we are not to resist any evil or wrong, but always yield,

suffer it, and let things be taken from us. If you will not bear
this law, then put off the name of Christian, and boast of another name that accords with your actions, or Christ Himself
will tear His name from off you, and that will be too hard for
you.

Thus says Paul, too, in Rom. 12, "Avenge not yourselves,
dearly beloved, but give place to the wrath of God." Again, he
praises the Corinthians, in 2 Cor. 11, because they suffer it gladly
if a man smite or rob them; and in 1 Cor. 6, he rebukes them
because they went to law about property, and did not endure
the wrong. Nay our Leader, Jesus Christ, says, in Matt. 7, that we
are to wish good to those who wrong us, and pray for our persecutors, and do good to those who do evil to us. These are our
Christian laws, dear friends! Now see how far the false prophets
have led you away from them, and yet they call you Christians,
though they have made you worse than heathen. For from these
sayings, a child easily grasps that it is Christian law not to strive
against wrongs, not to grasp after the sword, not to protect oneself, not to avenge oneself, but to give up life and property, and
let who takes it take it; we have enough in our Lord, who will
not leave us, as He has promised. Suffering, suffering; cross, cross!
This and nothing else, is the Christian law! But now you battle
for temporal goods, and will not let the coat go after the cloak,
but want to recover the cloak. How, then, will you die, and give
up your life, or love your enemies, or do good to them? O worthless Christians! Dear friends, Christians are not so common that
so many of them can get together in one crowd. A Christian is
a rare bird! Would to God that the majority of us were good,
pious heathen, who kept the natural law, not to mention the
Christian law!

I will also give you some illustrations of Christian law so that
you may see whither the mad prophets have led you. Look at
St. Peter in the garden. He wanted to defend his Lord Christ with
the sword, and cut off Malchus's ear. Tell me, had not Peter great
right on his side? Was it not an intolerable wrong that they were
going to take from Christ, not only His property, but also His
life? Nay, they not only took from Him life and property, but
in so doing they entirely suppressed the gospel by which they
were to be saved, and thus robbed heaven. Such a wrong you

have not yet suffered, dear friends. But see what Christ does and teaches in this case. However great the wrong was, nevertheless He stopped St. Peter, bade him put up his sword, and would not allow him to avenge or prevent this wrong. In addition He passed a judgment of death upon him, as though upon a murderer, and said, "He that takes the sword shall perish with the sword." From this we must understand that it is not enough that anyone has done us wrong, and that we have a good case, and have right on our side, but we must also have the right and power committed to us by God to use the sword and punish wrong. Moreover, a Christian must also endure it if anyone desires to keep the gospel away from him; if, indeed, it is possible to keep the gospel from anyone, as we shall hear.

A second example is Christ Himself. What did He do when they took His life on the cross and thereby took away from Him the work of preaching for which He had been sent by God Himself for the blessing of the souls of men? He did just what St. Peter says. He committed the whole matter to Him who judgeth righteously, and He endured this intolerable wrong. More than that, He prayed for His persecutors and said, "Father, forgive them, for they know not what they do."

Now, if you are true Christians, you must certainly act in this same way and follow this example. If you do otherwise, then let go the name of Christian and the boast of Christian law; for then you are certainly not Christians but are resisting Christ and His law, His doctrine and His example. . . .

I must also give you an illustration from this present time. Pope and emperor have set themselves against me and have raged. Now how have I brought it about that the more pope and emperor have raged the more my gospel spread? I have never drawn sword nor desired revenge. I have begun no division and no rebellion, but, so far as I was able, I have helped the worldly rulers, even those who persecuted the gospel and me, to maintain their power and honor. But I have stopped with committing the matter to God and relying confidently at all times upon His hand. Therefore, He has not only preserved my life in spite of the pope and all the tyrants (and this many really consider a great miracle; as I myself must also confess that it is), but He has caused my gospel always to increase and spread. Now you interfere with me. You want to help the gospel and do not see that by what you are doing you are hindering it and holding it down in the highest degree.

I say all this, dear friends, as a faithful warning. In this case you should rid yourselves of the name of Christians and cease to boast of Christian law. For no matter how right you are, it is not for a Christian to appeal to law, or to fight, but rather to suffer wrong and endure evil; and there is no other way (1 Cor. 6). You yourselves confess in your Preface, that all who believe in Christ become kindly, peaceful, patient, and united; but in your deeds you are displaying nothing but impatience, turbulence, strife and violence; thus you contradict your own words. You want to be known as patient people, who will endure neither wrong nor evil, but will endure what is right and good. That is fine patience! Any knave can practise it! It does not take a Christian to do that! Therefore I say again, however good and right your cause may be, nevertheless, because you would defend yourselves, and suffer neither violence nor wrong, you may do anything that God does not prevent, but leave the name of Christian out of it; leave out, I say, the name of Christian, and do not make it a cloak for your impatient, disorderly, un-Christian undertaking. I shall not let you have that name, but so long as there is a heartbeat in my body, I shall do all I can to take that name from you. You will not succeed, or will succeed only in ruining your bodies and souls.

In saying this, it is not my intention to justify or defend the rulers in the intolerable wrongs which you suffer from them. They are wrong, and do you cruel wrongs; that I admit. But what I hope is that, if neither party will allow itself to be instructed, and the one party attacks and comes to blows with the other (which God forbid!), neither shall be called Christians, but that, as is usual when one people fights with another, God will punish one knave with another, as the saying goes. If it comes to a conflict (which may God graciously avert!), I hope that you will be counted as people of such a kind and such a name that the rulers may know that they are fighting not against Christians but against heathen; and that you, too, may know that you are fighting the rulers not as Christians but as heathen. For Christians fight for themselves not with sword and gun, but with the cross and with suffering, just as Christ, our leader, does not bear a sword, but hangs on the cross. . . .

If you were Christians, you would stop defying and threatening, and stay inside the Lord's Prayer, and advance your cause with God by praying, and say, "Thy will be done," and "Deliver us from evil. Amen." You see in the Psalter that the true saints take their necessities to God, and lament them, and seek aid from Him, and do not defend themselves or resist evil. Such prayer would have done more to help you, in all your needs, than if the world were full of you, especially if, beside that, you had a good conscience, and a comforting assurance that your prayers were heard, as His promises declare; such as 1 Tim. 4, "He is the helper of all men, especially of the believers," and Psalm 39 [50: 15], "Call upon me in trouble, and I will help thee"; and Psalm 90 [91:15], "He called upon me in trouble, therefore will I deliver him." See! That is the Christian way to get rid of misfortune and evil, namely, endure it and call upon God. But because you do neither—neither call nor endure—but aid yourselves with your own might, and make yourselves your own God and Savior, therefore God cannot and must not be your God or Savior. By God's permission (which, we pray, may not be given!), you might accomplish something as heathen and blasphemers, though only for your eternal and temporal ruin; but as Christians, or evangelicals, you will win nothing; I would wager a thousand necks in it!

On the basis of what has been said, all your articles are easily answered; for even though all of them were right and proper according to the law of nature, nevertheless you have forgotten the Christian law, since you have not put them through by means of patience and prayer to God, as Christian people ought, but have undertaken, with impatience and violence, to wrest them from the rulers, and extort them by force; and this is against the law of the land and against natural justice. The man who framed your articles is no pious and honest man, for he has indicated on the margin many chapters of Scripture, on which the articles are supposed to rest, but keeps the porridge in his mouth, and leaves out the passages by which he would show his own wickedness and that of your enterprise. He has done this to deceive you and urge you on and bring you into danger. For the chapters he ad-

duces, when they are read through, say very little in favor of
your undertaking, but rather the opposite; viz., that men shall
live and act as Christians. He is some prophet of turbulence, who
seeks, through you, to work his will upon the gospel. May God
prevent, and guard you against him!

In the preface you are conciliatory and allege that you would
not be seditious, and make the excuse that you desire to teach
and live according to the gospel. There your own mouth and
your own works rebuke you, for you confess that you are making
disturbances and rising in revolt, and you want to adorn such conduct by means of the gospel. You have heard above that the
gospel teaches that Christians ought to endure and suffer wrong,
and pray to God in all their necessities, yet you are not willing to
suffer, but like heathen, force the rulers to conform to your impatient will. You adduce the children of Israel as an example, saying that God heard their crying and delivered them. Why then do
you not follow the example that you bring forward? Call upon
God and wait until He sends you a Moses, who will prove by
signs and wonders that he is sent from God. The children of
Israel did not riot against Pharaoh, or help themselves as you pro-
pose to do. This illustration, therefore, is dead against you, and
condemns you. You boast of it, and yet you do the opposite.

Again, it is not true when you declare that you teach and
live according to the gospel. There is not one of the articles
which teaches a single point of the gospel, but everything is directed to one purpose; namely, that your bodies and your properties may be free. In a word, they all deal with worldly and
temporal matters. You would have power and wealth, so as not
to suffer wrong; and yet the gospel does not take worldly matters
into account, and makes the external life consist only in suffering,
wrong, cross, patience, and contempt for temporal wealth and
life. How, then, does the gospel agree with you; except that you
are seeking to give your unevangelical and un-Christian enterprise an evangelical appearance, and do not see that you are
thereby bringing shame on the holy gospel of Christ, and making
it a cloak for wickedness? Therefore you must take a different
attitude, and either drop this matter entirely and decide to suffer
these wrongs, if you would be Christians and have the name of

Christian; or else, if you are going on with it, make use of another name and not be called and considered Christians. There is no third course, and no other way.

True enough, you are right in desiring the gospel, if you are really in earnest about it. Indeed, I am willing to make this article even sharper than you do, and say it is intolerable that anyone should be shut out of heaven and driven by force into hell. No one should suffer that; he ought rather lose his neck a hundred times. But he who keeps the gospel from me, shuts heaven against me and drives me by force into hell; for the gospel is the only way and means for the soul's salvation, and on peril of losing my soul, I should not suffer this. Tell me, is that not stated sharply enough? And yet it does not follow that I must set myself with my fist against the rulers who do me this wrong. "But," you say, "how am I at once to suffer it and not suffer it?" The answer is easy. It is impossible that anyone shall have the gospel kept from him. There is no power in heaven or earth that can do this, for it is a public teaching that moves freely about under the heavens and is bound to no one place. In this it is like the star, running through the air, which showed Christ's birth to the wise men from the East.

It is true, indeed, that the rulers may suppress the gospel in cities or places where the gospel is, or where there are preachers; but you can leave these cities or places and follow the gospel to some other place. It is not necessary that, for the gospel's sake, you should capture or hold the city or place; but let the lord have his city, and do you follow the gospel. Thus you suffer men to do you wrong and drive you away; and yet, at the same time you do not suffer men to take the gospel from you or keep it from you. Thus the two things, suffering and not suffering, come to one. If you will hold the city for the sake of the gospel, you rob the lord of the city of what is his, and pretend that you are doing it for the gospel's sake. Dear friend, the gospel does not teach robbing or the taking of things, even though the lord of the property abuses it by using it against God, wrongfully, and to your injury. The gospel needs no bodily place or city to dwell in; it will and must dwell in hearts. This is what Christ taught in Matt. 10, "If they drive you out of one city, flee to another."

He does not say, "If they drive you out of one city, stay there, and capture the city, to the praise of the gospel, and make a riot against the lord of the city," though that is what men now want to do, and what they are teaching. But He says, "Flee, flee straightway into another, until the Son of Man shall come." Thus He says, too, in Matt. 23, that the godless shall drive His evangelists from one city to another; and Paul also says, in 2 Corinthians 4, "We are in no certain place." If it so happen that a Christian must be moving constantly from one place to another, and leaving the place where he is and everything that he has, or if he sit in uncertainty, expecting this to happen any hour, then it is well with him; it is as it should be with a Christian. For because he will not suffer the gospel to be taken from him or kept from him, he has to suffer city, place, property, and everything that he is and has, to be taken and kept from him. Now how does this agree with your undertaking? You capture and hold cities and places that are not yours, and will not suffer them to be taken or kept from you; thought you take and keep them from their natural lords. What kind of Christians are these, who, for the gospel's sake, become robbers, thieves, and scoundrels, and then say they are adherents of the new evangelical faith?

ON THE FIRST ARTICLE

"An entire community shall have the power to choose and depose a pastor." This article is right if only it were understood in a Christian sense, though the chapters indicated on the margin do not help it. If the goods of the parish come from the rulers, and not from the community, then the community cannot apply these goods to the use of him whom they choose, for that would be robbery and theft. If they desire a pastor, let them first humbly ask one from the rulers. If the rulers are unwilling, then let them choose their own pastor, and support him with their own property, and let the rulers have their property, or else secure it from them in a lawful way. But if the rulers will not tolerate the pastor whom they chose and support, then let him flee to another city, and let any flee with him who will, as Christ teaches. That is a Christian and evangelical way to choose and have one's own pastor. Whoever does otherwise, acts in an un-Christian manner, as a robber and brawler.

ON THE SECOND ARTICLE

"The tithes shall be divided out to the pastor and the poor, and the balance kept for needs of the land, etc." This article is nothing but theft and highway robbery. They would appropriate for themselves the tithes, which are not theirs but the rulers', and would do with them what they please. Not so, dear friends! That is the same thing as deposing the rulers altogether, when your preface expressly says that no one is to be deprived of what is his. If you would make gifts and do good, do it out of your own property, as the Wise Man says, for God says by Isaiah, "I hate the sacrifice that is got by robbery." You speak in this article as though you were already lords in the land and had taken all the property of the rulers for your own and would be no one's subjects, and would give nothing. From this one grasps what you have in mind. Stop it, dear sirs, stop it! It will not be you who end it! The chapters of Scripture that your lying preacher and false prophet has smeared on the margin, do not help you at all; they are against you.

ON THE THIRD ARTICLE

"There shall be no serfs, for Christ has made all men free." That is making Christian liberty an utterly carnal thing. Did not Abraham and other patriarchs and prophets have slaves? Read what St. Paul teaches about servants, who, at that time, were all slaves. Therefore this article is dead against the gospel. It is a piece of robbery by which every man takes from his lord the body, which has become his lord's property. For a slave can be a Christian, and have Christian liberty, in the same way that a prisoner or a sick man is a Christian, and yet not free. This article would make all men equal, and turn the spiritual kingdom of Christ into a worldly, external kingdom; and that is impossible. For a worldly kingdom cannot stand unless there is in it an inequality of persons, so that some are free, some imprisoned, some lords, some subjects, etc.; and St. Paul says in Gal. 5, that in Christ master and servant are one thing. . . .

The other articles, about freedom of game, birds, fish, wood, forests; about services, tithe, imposts, excises, *Todfall*, etc.,—these I leave to the lawyers, for it is not fitting that I, an evangelist, should judge or decide them. It is for me to instruct and teach men's consciences in things that concern divine and Christian matters; there are books enough about the other things in the imperial laws. I have said above that these things do not concern a Christian, and that he cares nothing about them. He lets any-one else rob, take, skin, scrape, devour, and rage, for he is a martyr on earth. Therefore the peasants ought rightly let the name of Christian alone, and act in some other name, as men who want human and natural rights, not as those who seek Christian rights. This means that on all these points they should keep still, suffer, and make their complaints to God alone.

See, dear friends, this is the instruction that you asked of me in the second document. I beg that you will remember that you offer willingly to be instructed by the Scriptures. Now when this reaches you, do not cry out at me, "Luther flatters the princes and speaks contrary to the gospel." First read and see my arguments from Scripture; for this is your affair; I am excused in the sight of God and the world. I know well the false prophets that are among you. Do not listen to them. They are surely deceiving you. They do not think of your consciences, but would make Galatians of you, so that by means of you they might come to wealth and honor, and must afterwards, with you, be damned eternally in hell.

Admonition to Both Rulers and Peasants

Therefore, dear sirs, since there is nothing Christian on either side and nothing Christian is at issue between you, but both lords and peasants are dealing with heathenish, or worldly, right and wrong, and with temporal goods; since, moreover, both parties are acting against God and are under His wrath, as you have heard;—therefore, for God's sake, let yourselves be advised, and attack these matters as such matters are to be attacked, that is, with justice and not with force or with strife, and do not start an endless bloodshed in Germany. For because both of you are wrong, and both of you would avenge and defend yourselves, both of you will destroy yourselves and God will use one knave to flog another.

You lords have both Scripture and history against you, for both tell how tyrants are punished. Even the heathen poets say that tyrants seldom die a dry death, but usually have been slain, and have perished in blood. Because, then, it is an assured fact that you rule tyrannically and with rage, prohibit the gospel, and skin and oppress the poor, you have no reason for confidence or hope that you will perish otherwise than your kind have perished.

Look at all the kingdoms that have come to their end by the sword,—Assyria, Persia, Greece, Rome. They have all been destroyed at last in the same way that they destroyed others. Thus God shows that He is judge upon earth and leaves no wrong unpunished. Therefore nothing is more certain than that this same judgment is close to you, whether it come now or later, unless you reform.

You peasants also have Scripture and experience against you. They teach that turbulence has never had a good end, and God has always held strictly to the word, "He that takes the sword shall perish by the sword." Because, then, you are doing wrong by judging yourselves and avenging yourselves, and are bearing the name of Christian unworthily besides, you are certainly under the wrath of God; and even though you win and destroy all the lords, in the end you would have to tear the flesh from one another's bones, like wild beasts. For because not spirit, but flesh and blood, rules among you, God will shortly send an evil spirit among you, as He did to the men of Shechem and to Abimelech. See the end that finally comes to turbulence in the story of Korah, in Numbers 16, and of Absalom, Sheba, Samri and their like. Briefly, God hates both tyrants and rebels; therefore He sets them on each other, so that both parties perish shamefully, and His wrath and judgment upon the godless are fulfilled.

To me the saddest and the really pitiful thing, and that which I would willingly buy off with my own life and death, is that on both sides two inevitable injuries must follow. For because neither party strives with a good conscience, but both fight for the upholding of wrong, it must follow, in the first place, that those who are slain are lost eternally, body and soul, as men who die in their sins, without penitence and without grace, in the wrath of God. There is nothing to be done for them. The lords would be fighting for the strengthening and maintaining of their tyranny, their persecution of the gospel, and their unjust oppression of the poor, or else for the aiding of that kind of rulers. That is a terrible wrong and is against God. He who commits such a sin must be lost eternally. The peasants, on the other hand, would fight to defend their turbulence and their abuse of the name of Christian. Both these things are greatly against God, and he who dies in them or for them must also be lost eternally, and there is no help for it.

The second injury is that Germany will be laid waste, and if this bloodshed once starts, it will scarcely cease until everything is destroyed. It is easy to start a fight, but to stop it when we will is not in our power. What have they ever done to you—all these innocent children, women, and old people, whom you fools are drawing with you into such danger—that you should fill the land with blood and robbery, widows and orphans? Oh. the devil's mind is wicked enough! And God is angry, and threatens to let him loose upon us and cool his rage in our blood and souls. Beware, dear sirs, and be wise! It concerns both of you! What good will it do you to condemn yourselves eternally and wilfully and leave behind you, for your descendants, a desolate and devastated and bloody land besides, when you could arrange things better, while there is still time, by penitence toward God and friendly agreement, or by suffering in the sight of men? With defiance and strife you will do nothing.

It would, therefore, be my faithful counsel to choose from among the nobles certain counts and lords, and from the cities certain councilmen, and have these matters dealt with in a friendly way, and settled; that you lords let down your stubbornness—as you must do in the end, whether you will or will not—and give up a little of your tyranny and oppression, so that poor people get air and room to live; that the peasants for their part, let themselves be instructed, and give over and let go some of the articles that grasp too far and too high, so that the case may be settled by human law and agreement, even though it cannot be dealt with in a Christian way.

If you shall not follow this advice (and God forbid that you do not follow it!), I must let you come to grips, but I am guiltless as regards your souls, your blood, and your property; you will bear the guilt yourselves. I have told you that you are both wrong and that your fighting is wrong. You lords are not fighting against Christians—for Christians do nothing against you, but prefer to suffer all things—but against open robbers and defamers of the Christian name. Those of them who die are already condemned eternally. On the other hand, you peasants are not fighting against Christians, but against tyrants, and persecutors of God and man, and murderers of the holy Christ. Those of them who die are also condemned eternally. There you have God's sure verdict upon both parties; that I know. Do what you please to keep your bodies and souls, if you will not follow this verdict.

ⅬⅬⅬⅬⅬⅬⅬⅬⅬⅬⅬⅬⅬⅬⅬⅬⅬⅬⅬⅬⅬⅬⅬⅬⅬⅬⅼ

8. Martin Luther: *Commentary on St. Paul's Epistle to the Galatians* (1535)*

Above all, Luther was an expositor of Scripture, and his commentaries on biblical books which grew out of his professorial responsibilities at Wittenberg show him at his best. In 1519, and again in 1535, he lectured on the Epistle to the Galatians and published his lectures in the form of a commentary. The commentary of 1535 ranks high as an expression of Luther's theology, for here he expounded in classical form his thoughts about the heart of his religion—justification by faith. Reprinted here are a section from the introduction and also part of the exposition of Galatians 1:16.

Most of Luther's treatises were polemical, written against specific opponents such as Eck, Carlstadt, Zwingli, Erasmus, or dealing with specific issues such as the Lord's Supper or free will. His biblical commentaries, from his first lectures on the Psalms of 1513 to his lectures on the Book of Genesis which occupied him during the last decade of his life, expressed his thought in a different form, neither polemical nor systematic, but in an exegetical exposition whose framework is the argument of the biblical text.

LITERATURE
J. Pelikan, *Luther the Expositor* (St. Louis, 1959).

* *Luther's Works.* Vol. 26. Lectures on Galatians (1535), ed. Jaroslav Pelikan (St. Louis, 1963), pp. 4-12, 122-36.

The Argument of St. Paul's Epistle to the Galatians

Fɪʀsᴛ of all, we must speak of the argument, that is, of the issue
with which Paul deals in this epistle. The argument is this: Paul
wants to establish the doctrine of faith, grace, the forgiveness of
sins or Christian righteousness, so that we may have a perfect
knowledge and know the difference between Christian righteousness and all other kinds of righteousness. For righteousness is of
many kinds. There is a political righteousness, which the emperor,
the princes of the world, philosophers, and lawyers consider.
There is also a ceremonial righteousness, which human traditions
teach, as, for example, the traditions of the pope and other traditions. Parents and teachers may teach this righteousness without
danger, because they do not attribute to it any power to make
satisfaction for sin, to placate God, and to earn grace; but they
teach that these ceremonies are necessary only for moral discipline
and for certain observances. There is, in addition to these, yet another righteousness, the righteousness of the law or of the decalogue which Moses teaches. We, too, teach this, but after the
doctrine of faith.

Over and above all these there is the righteousness of faith or
Christian righteousness, which is to be distinguished most carefully
from all the others. For they are all contrary to this righteousness,
both because they proceed from the laws of emperors, the traditions of the pope, and the commandments of God, and because
they consist in our works and can be achieved by us with "purely
natural endowments," as the scholastics teach, or from a gift of
God. For these kinds of the righteousness of works, too, are gifts
of God, as are all the things we have. But this most excellent
righteousness, the righteousness of faith, which God imputes to us
through Christ without works, is neither political nor ceremonial
nor legal nor work-righteousness but is quite the opposite; it is
a merely passive righteousness, while all the others, listed above,
are active. For here we work nothing, render nothing to God;
we only receive and permit someone else to work in us, namely,
God. Therefore it is appropriate to call the righteousness of faith
or Christian righteousness "passive." This is a righteousness hidden
in a mystery, which the world does not understand. In fact,

Christians themselves do not adequately understand it or grasp it in the midst of their temptations. Therefore it must always be taught and continually exercised. And anyone who does not grasp or take hold of it in afflictions and terrors of conscience cannot stand. For there is no comfort of conscience so solid and certain as is this passive righteousness.

But such is human weakness and misery that in the terrors of conscience and in the danger of death we look at nothing except our own works, our worthiness, and the law. When the law shows us our sin, our past life immediately comes to our mind. Then the sinner, in his great anguish of mind, groans and says to himself: "Oh, how damnably I have lived! If only I could live longer! Then I would amend my life." Thus human reason cannot refrain from looking at active righteousness, that is, its own righteousness; nor can it shift its gaze to passive, that is, Christian righteousness, but it simply rests in the active righteousness. So deeply is this evil rooted in us, and so completely have we acquired this unhappy habit! Taking advantage of the weakness of our nature, Satan increases and aggravates these thoughts in us. Then it is impossible for the conscience to avoid being more seriously troubled, confounded, and frightened. For it is impossible for the human mind to conceive any comfort of itself, or to look only at grace amid its consciousness and terror of sin, or consistently to reject all discussion of works. To do this is beyond human power and thought. Indeed, it is even beyond the law of God. For although the law is the best of all things in the world, it still cannot bring peace to a terrified conscience but makes it even sadder and drives it to despair. For by the law sin becomes exceedingly sinful (Rom. 7:13).

Therefore the afflicted conscience has no remedy against despair and eternal death except to take hold of the promise of grace offered in Christ, that is, this righteousness of faith, this passive or Christian righteousness, which says with confidence: "I do not seek active righteousness. I ought to have and perform it; but I declare that even if I did have it and perform it, I cannot trust in it or stand up before the judgment of God on the basis of it. Thus I put myself beyond all active righteousness, all righteousness of my own or of the divine law, and I embrace only that passive righteousness which is the righteousness of grace, mercy, and the forgiveness of sins." In other words, this is the righteousness of Christ and of the Holy Spirit, which we do not perform but receive, which we do not have but accept, when God the Father grants it to us through Jesus Christ.

As the earth itself does not produce rain and is unable to acquire it by its own strength, worship, and power but receives it only by a heavenly gift from above, so this heavenly righteousness is given to us by God without our work or merit. As much as the dry earth of itself is able to accomplish in obtaining the right and blessed rain, that much can we men accomplish by our own strength and works to obtain that divine, heavenly, and eternal righteousness. Thus we can obtain it only through the free imputation and indescribable gift of God. Therefore the highest art and wisdom of Christians is not to know the law, to ignore works and all active righteousness, just as outside the people of God the highest wisdom is to know and study the law, works, and active righteousness.

It is a marvelous thing and unknown to the world to teach Christians to ignore the law and to live before God as though there were no law whatever. For if you do not ignore the law and thus direct your thoughts to grace as though there were no law but as though there were nothing but grace, you cannot be saved. "For through the law comes knowledge of sin" (Rom. 3:20). On the other hand, works and the performance of the law must be demanded in the world as though there were no promise or grace. This is because of the stubborn, proud, and hardhearted, before whose eyes nothing must be set except the law, in order that they may be terrified and humbled. For the law was given to terrify and kill the stubborn and to exercise the old man. Both words must be correctly divided, according to the Apostle (2 Tim. 2:25 ff.).

This calls for a wise and faithful father who can moderate the law in such a way that it stays within its limits. For if I were to teach men the law in such a way that they suppose themselves to be justified by it before God, I would be going beyond the limit of the law, confusing these two righteousnesses, the active and the passive, and would be a bad dialectician who does not properly distinguish. But when I go beyond the old man, I also go beyond the law. For the flesh or the old man, the law and works, are all joined together. In the same way the spirit or the new man is joined to the promise and to grace. Therefore when I see that a man is sufficiently contrite, oppressed by the law, terrified by sin, and thirsting for comfort, then it is time for me to take the law and active righteousness from his sight and to set forth before him, through the gospel, the passive righteousness which excludes Moses and the law and shows the promise of Christ, who came for the afflicted and for sinners. Here a man is raised up again and gains hope. Nor is he any longer under the law; he is under grace, as the Apostle says (Rom. 6:14): "You are not under law but under grace." How not under law? According to the new man, to whom the law does not apply. For the law had its limits until Christ, as Paul says below (Gal. 3:24): "The Law, until Christ." When He came, Moses and the law stopped. So did circumcision, sacrifices, and the sabbath. So did all the prophets.

This is our theology, by which we teach a precise distinction between these two kinds of righteousness, the active and the passive, so that morality and faith, works and grace, secular society and religion may not be confused. Both are necessary, but both must be kept within their limits. Christian righteousness applies to the new man, and the righteousness of the law applies to the old man, who is born of flesh and blood. Upon this latter, as upon an ass, a burden must be put that will oppress him. He must not enjoy the freedom of the spirit or of grace unless he has first put on the new man by faith in Christ, but this does not happen fully in this life. Then he may enjoy the kingdom and the ineffable gift of grace. I am saying this in order that no one may suppose that we reject or prohibit good works, as the papists falsely accuse us because they understand neither what they themselves are saying nor what we are teaching. They know nothing except the righteousness of the law; and yet they claim the right to judge a doctrine that is far above and beyond the law, a doctrine on which the carnal man is unable to pass judgment. Therefore it is inevitable that they be offended, for they cannot see any higher than the law. Therefore whatever is above the law is the greatest possible offense to them.

We set forth two worlds, as it were, one of them heavenly and the other earthly. Into these we place these two kinds of righteousness, which are distinct and separated from each other. The righteousness of the law is earthly and deals with earthly things; by it we perform good works. But as the earth does not bring forth fruit unless it has first been watered and made fruitful from above —for the earth cannot judge, renew, and rule the heavens, but the heavens judge, renew, rule, and fructify the earth, so that it may do what the Lord has commanded—so also by the righteousness of the law we do nothing even when we do much; we do not fulfil the law even when we fulfil it. Without any merit or work of our own, we must first be justified by Christian righteousness, which has nothing to do with the righteousness of the law or with earthly and active righteousness. But this righteousness is heavenly and passive. We do not have it of ourselves; we receive it from heaven. We do not perform it; we accept it by faith, through which we ascend beyond all laws and works. "As, therefore, we have borne the image of the earthly Adam," as Paul says, "let us bear the image of the heavenly one" (1 Cor. 15:49), who is a new man in a new world, where there is no law, no sin, no conscience, no death, but perfect joy, righteousness, grace, peace, life, salvation, and glory.

Then do we do nothing and work nothing in order to obtain this righteousness? I reply: Nothing at all. For this righteousness means to do nothing, to hear nothing, and to know nothing about the law or about works but to know and believe only this: that Christ has gone to the Father and is now invisible; that He sits in heaven at the right hand of the Father, not as a Judge but as one who has been made for us wisdom, righteousness, sanctification, and redemption from God (1 Cor. 1:30); in short, that He is our High Priest, interceding for us and reigning over us and in us through grace. Here one notices no sin and feels no terror or remorse of conscience. Sin cannot happen in this Christian righteousness; for where there is no law, there cannot be any transgression (Rom. 4:15). If, therefore, sin does not have a place here, there is no conscience, no terror, no sadness. Therefore John says: "No one born of God commits sin" (1 John 3:9). But if there is any conscience or fear present, this is a sign that this righteousness has been withdrawn, that grace has been lost sight of, and that Christ is hidden and out of sight. But where Christ is truly seen, then there must be full and perfect joy in the Lord and peace of heart, where the heart declares: "Although I am a sinner accord-

ing to the law, judged by the righteousness of the law, nevertheless I do not despair. I do not die, because Christ lives who is my
righteousness and my eternal and heavenly life. In that righteousness and life I have no sin, conscience, and death. I am indeed a
sinner according to the present life and its righteousness, as a son
of Adam where the law accuses me, death reigns and devours
me. But above this life I have another righteousness, another life,
which is Christ, the Son of God, who does not know sin and
death but is righteousness and eternal life. For His sake this body
of mine will be raised from the dead and delivered from the
slavery of the law and sin, and will be sanctified together with
the spirit."

Thus as long as we live here, both remain. The flesh is accused,
exercised, saddened, and crushed by the active righteousness of
the law. But the spirit rules, rejoices, and is saved by passive righteousness, because it knows that it has a Lord sitting in heaven at
the right hand of the Father, who has abolished the law, sin, and
death, and has trodden all evils underfoot, has led them captive
and triumphed over them in Himself (Col. 2:15). In this epistle,
therefore, Paul is concerned to instruct, comfort, and sustain us
diligently in a perfect knowledge of this most excellent and
Christian righteousness. For if the doctrine of justification is lost,
the whole of Christian doctrine is lost. And those in the world
who do not teach it are either Jews or Turks or papists or sectarians. For between these two kinds of righteousness, the active
righteousness of the law and the passive righteousness of Christ,
there is no middle ground. Therefore he who has strayed away
from this Christian righteousness will necessarily relapse into the
active righteousness; that is, when he has lost Christ, he must fall
into a trust in his own works.

We see this today in the fanatical spirits and sectarians, who
neither teach nor can teach anything correctly about this righteousness of grace. They have taken the words out of our mouth and
out of our writings, and these only they speak and write. But the
substance itself they cannot discuss, deal with, and urge, because
they neither understand it nor can understand it. They cling only
to the righteousness of the law. Therefore they are and remain
disciplinarians of works; nor can they rise beyond the active righteousness. Thus they remain exactly what they were under the

pope. To be sure, they invent new names and new works; but the content remains the same. So it is that the Turks perform different works from the papists, and the papists perform different works from the Jews, and so forth. But although some do works that are more splendid, great, and difficult than others, the content remains the same, and only the quality is different. That is, the works vary only in appearance and in name. For they are still works. And those who do them are not Christians; they are hirelings, whether they are called Jews, Mohammedans, papists, or sectarians.

Therefore we always repeat, urge, and inculcate this doctrine of faith or Christian righteousness, so that it may be observed by continuous use and may be precisely distinguished from the active righteousness of the law. (For by this doctrine alone and through it alone is the church built, and in this it consists.) Otherwise we shall not be able to observe true theology but shall immediately become lawyers, ceremonialists, legalists, and papists. Christ will be so darkened that no one in the church will be correctly taught or comforted. Therefore if we want to be preachers and teachers of others, we must take great care in these issues and hold to this distinction between the righteousness of the law and that of Christ. This distinction is easy to speak of; but in experience and practice it is the most difficult of all, even if you exercise and practice it diligently. For in the hour of death or in other conflicts of conscience these two kinds of righteousness come together more closely than you would wish or ask. . . .

Therefore let us learn diligently this art of distinguishing between these two kinds of righteousness, in order that we may know how far we should obey the law. We have said above that in a Christian the law must not exceed its limits but should have its dominion only over the flesh, which is subjected to it and remains under it. When this is the case, the law remains within its limits. But if it wants to ascend into the conscience and exert its rule there, see to it that you are a good dialectician and that you make the correct distinction. Give no more to the law than it has coming, and say to it: "Law, you want to ascend into the realm of conscience and rule there. You want to denounce its sin and take away the joy of my heart, which I have through faith in Christ. You want to plunge me into despair, in order that I may perish. You are exceeding your jurisdiction. Stay within your limits, and exercise your dominion over the flesh. You shall not touch my conscience. For I am baptized; and through the gospel I have been called to a fellowship of righteousness and eternal life, to the kingdom of Christ, in which my conscience is at peace, where there is no law but only the forgiveness of sins, peace, quiet, happiness, salvation, and eternal life. Do not disturb me in these matters. In my conscience not the law will reign, that hard tyrant and cruel disciplinarian, but Christ, the Son of God, the King of peace and righteousness, the sweet Savior and Mediator. He will preserve my conscience happy and peaceful in the sound and pure doctrine of the gospel and in the knowledge of this passive righteousness."

When I have this righteousness within me, I descend from heaven like the rain that makes the earth fertile. That is, I come forth into another kingdom, and I perform good works whenever the opportunity arises. If I am a minister of the word, I preach, I comfort the saddened, I administer the sacraments. If I am a father, I rule my household and family, I train my children in piety and honesty. If I am a magistrate, I perform the office which I have received by divine command. If I am a servant, I faithfully tend to my master's affairs. In short, whoever knows for sure that Christ is his righteousness not only cheerfully and gladly works in his calling but also submits himself for the sake of love to magistrates, also to their wicked laws, and to everything else in this present life—even, if need be, to burden and danger. For he knows that God wants this and that this obedience pleases Him. . . .

Chapter 1, verse 16. Yet who know that a man is not justified by works of the law but through faith in Jesus Christ.

These words, "works of the law," are to be taken in the broadest possible sense and are very emphatic. I am saying this because of the smug and idle scholastics and monks, who obscure such words in Paul—in fact, everything in Paul—with their foolish and wicked glosses, which even they themselves do not understand. Therefore take "works of the law" generally, to mean whatever is opposed to grace: Whatever is not grace is law, whether it be the civil law, the ceremonial law, or the decalogue. Therefore even if you were to do the work of the law, according to the commandment, "You shall love the Lord your God with all your heart, etc." (Matt. 22:37), you still would not be justified in the sight of God; for a man is not justified by works of the law. But more detail on this later on.

Thus for Paul "works of the law" means the works of the entire law. Therefore one should not make a distinction between the decalogue and ceremonial laws. Now if the work of the decalogue does not justify, much less will circumcision, which is a work of the ceremonial law. When Paul says, as he often does, that a man is not justified by the law or by the works of the law, which means the same thing in Paul, he is speaking in general about the entire law; he is contrasting the righteousness of faith with the righteousness of the entire law, with everything that can be done on the basis of the law, whether by divine power or by human. For by the righteousness of the law, he says, a man is not pronounced righteous in the sight of God; but God imputes the righteousness of faith freely through His mercy, for the sake of Christ. It is, therefore, with a certain emphasis and vehemence that he said "by works of the law." For there is no doubt that the law is holy, righteous, and good; therefore the works of the law are holy, righteous, and good. Nevertheless, a man is not justified in the sight of God through them.

Hence the opinion of Jerome and others is to be rejected when they imagine that here Paul is speaking about the works of the ceremonial law, not about those of the decalogue. If I concede this, I am forced to concede also that the ceremonial law was good and holy. Surely circumcision and other laws about rites and about the temple were righteous and holy, for they were commanded by God as much as the moral laws were. But then they say: "But after Christ the ceremonial laws were fatal." They invent this out of their own heads, for it does not appear anywhere in Scripture. Besides, Paul is not speaking here about the Gentiles, for whom the ceremonies would be fatal, but about the Jews, for whom they were good; indeed, he himself observed them. Thus even at the time when the ceremonial laws were holy, righteous, and good, they were not able to justify.

Therefore Paul is speaking not only about a part of the law, which is also good and holy, but about the entire law. He means that a work done in accordance with the entire law does not justify. Nor is he speaking about a sin against the law or a deed of the flesh, but about "the work of the law," that is, a work performed in accordance with the law. Therefore refraining from murder or adultery—whether this is done by natural powers or by human strength or by free will or by the gift and power of God—still does not justify.

But the works of the law can be performed either before justification or after justification. Before justification many good men even among the pagans—such as Xenophon, Aristides, Fabius, Cicero, Pomponius Atticus, etc.—performed the works of the law and accomplished great things. Cicero suffered death courageously in a righteous and good cause. Pomponius was a man of integrity and veracity; for he himself never lied, and he could not bear it if others did. Integrity and veracity are, of course, very fine virtues and very beautiful works of the law; but these men were not justified by these works. After justification, moreover, Peter, Paul, and all other Christians have done and still do the works of the law; but they are not justified by them either. "I am not aware of anything against myself," says Paul; that is, "No man can accuse me, but I am not thereby justified" (1 Cor. 4:4). Thus we see that Paul is speaking about the entire law and all its works, not about sins against the law.

Therefore the dangerous and wicked opinion of the papists is to be condemned. They attribute the merit of grace and the forgiveness of sins to the mere performance of the work. For they say that a good work performed before grace can earn a "merit of congruity"; but once grace has been obtained, the work that follows deserves eternal life by the "merit of condignity." If a man outside a state of grace and in mortal sin performs a good work by his own natural inclination—such as reading or hearing Mass, giving alms, etc.—this man deserves grace "by congruity." Once he has obtained grace this way, he goes on to perform a work that merits eternal life "by condignity." Now in the first case God is not indebted to anyone. But because He is good and righteous, it is proper for Him to approve such a good work, even though it is performed in mortal sin, and to grant grace for such a deed. But once grace has been obtained, God has become a debtor and is obliged by right to grant eternal life. For now this is not only a work of the free will, carried out externally; but it is performed in the grace that makes a man pleasing before God, that is, in love.

Such is the theology of the anti-Christian kingdom. I am recounting it here to make Paul's argument more intelligible; for when two opposites are placed side by side, they become more evident. In addition, I want everyone to see how far these "blind guides of the blind" (Matt. 15:14) have strayed. By this wicked and blasphemous teaching they have not only obscured the gospel but have removed it altogether and have buried Christ completely. For if in a state of mortal sin I can do any tiny work that is not only pleasing before God externally and of itself but can even deserve grace "by congruity"; and if, once I have received grace, I am able to perform works according to grace, that is, according to love, and receive eternal life by a right—then what need do I have of the grace of God, the forgiveness of sins, the promise, and the death and victory of Christ? Then Christ has become altogether useless to me; for I have free will and the power to perform good works, and through this I merit grace "by congruity" and eventually eternal life "by condignity."

Such dreadful monstrosities and horrible blasphemies ought to be propounded to Turks and Jews, not to the church of Christ. This whole business clearly shows that the pope with his bishops, theologians, monks, and all the rest has neither knowledge nor concern about sacred things; nor do they care anything about the health of the flock, which is so deserted and so miserably scattered. For if they had seen, though only through a cloud, what Paul calls sin and what he calls grace, they would not have imposed such abominations and wicked lies on Christian people. They take mortal sin to be only the external work committed against the law, such as murder, adultery, theft, etc. They did not see that ignorance, hatred, and contempt of God in the heart, ingratitude, murmuring against God, and resistance to the will of God are also mortal sin, and that the flesh cannot think, say, or do anything except what is diabolical and opposed to God. If they had seen that these huge plagues are rooted in the nature of man, they would not have dreamt so wickedly about the "merit of congruity" and the "merit of condignity."

Therefore there must be a proper and clear definition of what a wicked man or mortal sinner is. He is a holy hypocrite and murderer, as Paul was when he went to Damascus to persecute

Jesus of Nazareth, to abolish the doctrine of Christ, to murder the faithful, and to overthrow the church of Christ altogether. Those were certainly extremely great and horrible sins against God, but Paul was unable to recognize them as such. For he was so completely blinded by a wicked zeal for God that he regarded these unspeakable crimes of his as the height of righteousness and an act of worship and obedience most pleasing to God. Can such saints, who defend such horrible sins as the height of righteousness, be supposed to merit grace? . . .

Now the true meaning of Christianity is this: that a man first acknowledge, through the law, that he is a sinner, for whom it is impossible to perform any good work. For the law says: "You are an evil tree. Therefore everything you think, speak, or do is opposed to God. Hence you cannot deserve grace by your works. But if you try to do so, you make the bad even worse; for since you are an evil tree, you cannot produce anything except evil fruits, that is, sins. 'For whatever does not proceed from faith is sin' (Rom. 14:23)." Trying to merit grace by preceding works, therefore, is trying to placate God with sins, which is nothing but heaping sins upon sins, making fun of God, and provoking His wrath. When a man is taught this way by the law, he is frightened and humbled. Then he really sees the greatness of his sin and finds in himself not one spark of the love of God; thus he justifies God in His word and confesses that he deserves death and eternal damnation. Thus the first step in Christianity is the preaching of repentance and the knowledge of oneself.

The second step is this: If you want to be saved, your salvation does not come by works; but God has sent His only Son into the world that we might live through Him. He was crucified and died for you and bore your sins in His own body (1 Peter 2:24). Here there is no "congruity" or work performed before grace, but only wrath, sin, terror, and death. Therefore the law only shows sin, terrifies, and humbles; thus it prepares us for justification and drives us to Christ. For by His word God has revealed to us that He wants to be a merciful Father to us. Without our merit— since, after all, we cannot merit anything—He wants to give us forgiveness of sins, righteousness, and eternal life for the sake of Christ. For God is He who dispenses His gifts freely to all, and this is the praise of His deity. But He cannot defend this deity of

His against the self-righteous people who are unwilling to accept grace and eternal life from Him freely but want to earn it by their own works. They simply want to rob Him of the glory of His deity. In order to retain it, He is compelled to send forth His law, to terrify and crush those very hard rocks as though it were thunder and lightning.

This, in summary, is our theology about Christian righteousness, in opposition to the abominations and monstrosities of the sophists about "merit of congruity and of condignity" or about works before grace and after grace. Smug people, who have never struggled with any temptations or true terrors of sin and death, were the ones who made up these empty dreams out of their own heads; therefore they do not understand what they are saying or what they are talking about, for they cannot supply any examples of such works done either before grace or after grace. Therefore these are useless fables, with which the papists delude both themselves and others.

The reason is that Paul expressly states here that a man is not justified by the deeds of the law, whether they are those that precede (of which he is speaking here) or those that follow justification. Thus you see that Christian righteousness is not an "inherent form," as they call it. For they say: When a man does a good work, God accepts it; and for this work He infuses charity into him. This infused charity, they say, is a quality that is attached to the heart; they call it "formal righteousness." (It is a good idea for you to know this manner of speaking.) Nothing is more intolerable to them than to be told that this quality, which informs the heart as whiteness does a wall, is not righteousness. They cannot climb any higher than this cogitation of human reason: Man is righteous by means of his formal righteousness, which is grace making him pleasing before God, that is, love. Thus they attribute formal righteousness to an attitude and "form" inherent in the soul, namely, to love, which is a work and gift according to the law; for the law says: "You shall love the Lord" (Matt. 22:37). And they say that this righteousness is worthy of eternal life; that he who has it is "formally righteous"; and, finally, that he is righteous in fact, because he is now performing good works, for which eternal life is due him. This is the opinion of the sophists— and of the best among them at that.

Others are not even that good, such as Scotus and Occam. They said that this love which is given by God is not necessary to obtain the grace of God, but that even by his own natural powers a man is able to produce a love for God above all things. Scotus disputes this way: "If a man can love a creature, a young man love a girl, or a covetous man love money—all of which are a lesser good—he can also love God, who is a greater good. If by his natural powers he has a love for the creature, much more does he have a love for the Creator." This argument left all the sophists confounded, and none of them could refute it. Nevertheless, this is what they said:

"Scripture requires us to say that in addition to our natural love, with which He is not satisfied, God also demands a love that He Himself grants." Thus they accuse God of being a severe tyrant and a cruel taskmaster, who is not content that I observe and fulfil His law but demands also that beyond the law, which I can easily fulfil, I dress up my obedience with additional qualities and adornments. It is as though the lady of the house were not content that her cook had prepared the food very well but scolded her for not wearing precious garments and adorning herself with a golden crown while she prepared the food. What sort of housewife would that be who, after her cook has done everything she is required to do and has done it superbly, would demand that she should also wear a golden crown, which it is impossible for her to have? Likewise, what sort of God would that be who would demand that we fulfil His law, which we otherwise observe by our natural powers, with an ornamentation that we cannot possess?

To avoid the impression of contradicting themselves, they make a distinction at this point and say that the law can be fulfilled in two ways: first, according to the content of the act; secondly, according to the intention of Him who gave the commandment. According to the content of the act, that is, so far as the deed itself is concerned, we can simply fulfil everything that the law commands. But we cannot do so according to the intention of Him who gave the commandment; for this means that God is not content that you have performed and fulfilled everything commanded in the law (although He has no more than this to demand of you), but He requires in addition that you keep the law in love —not the natural love that you have but a supernatural and divine love that He Himself confers. What is this but to make God a tyrant and a tormentor who demands of us what we cannot produce? In a sense it is as though they were saying that if we are damned, the fault is not so much in us as in God, who requires us to keep His law in this fashion.

I am reciting all this to make you see how far they have strayed from the meaning of Scripture with their declaration that by our own natural powers we are able to love God above all things, or at least that by the mere performance of the deed we are able to merit grace and eternal life. And because God is not content if we fulfil the law according to the content of the act but also wants us to fulfil it according to the intention of Him who gave the commandment, therefore sacred Scripture requires us to have a supernatural quality infused into us from heaven, namely, love, which they call the formal righteousness that informs and adorns faith and makes it justify us. Thus faith is the body, the shell, or the color; but love is the life, the kernel, or the form.

Such are the dreams of the scholastics. But where they speak of love, we speak of faith. And while they say that faith is the mere outline but love is its living colors and completion, we say in opposition that faith takes hold of Christ and that He is the form that adorns and informs faith as color does the wall. Therefore Christian faith is not an idle quality or an empty husk in the heart, which may exist in a state of mortal sin until love comes along to make it alive. But if it is true faith, it is a sure trust and firm acceptance in the heart. It takes hold of Christ in such a way that Christ is the object of faith, or rather not the object but, so to speak, the One who is present in the faith itself. Thus faith is a sort of knowledge or darkness that nothing can see. Yet the Christ of whom faith takes hold is sitting in this darkness as God sat in the midst of darkness on Sinai and in the temple. Therefore our "formal righteousness" is not a love that informs faith; but it is faith itself, a cloud in our hearts, that is, trust in a thing we do not see, in Christ, who is present especially when He cannot be seen.

Therefore faith justifies because it takes hold of and possesses this treasure, the present Christ. But how He is present—this is beyond our thought; for there is darkness, as I have said. Where the confidence of the heart is present, therefore, there Christ is present, in that very cloud and faith. This is the formal righteousness on account of which a man is justified; it is not on account of love, as the sophists say. In short, just as the sophists say that love forms and trains faith, so we say that it is Christ who forms and trains faith or who is the form of faith. Therefore the Christ who is grasped by faith and who lives in the heart is the true Christian righteousness, on account of which God counts us righteous and grants us eternal life. Here there is no work of the law, no love; but there is an entirely different kind of righteousness, a new world above and beyond the law. For Christ or faith is neither the law nor the work of the law. But we intend later on to go into more detail on this issue, which the sophists have neither understood nor written about. For the present let it be enough for us to have shown that Paul is speaking here not only about the ceremonial law but about the entire law. . . .

In opposition to these trifles and empty dreams, as we have noted briefly above, we teach faith and the true meaning of Christianity. First, a man must be taught by the law to know himself, so that he may learn to sing: "All have sinned and fall short of the glory of God" (Rom. 3:23); again: "None is righteous, no, not one; no one understands, no one seeks for God. All have turned aside" (Rom. 3:10–12); again: "Against Thee only have I sinned" (Ps. 51:4). By this opposition of ours we drive men away from the merit of congruity and of condignity. Now once a man has thus been humbled by the law and brought to the knowledge of himself, then he becomes truly repentant; for true repentance begins with fear and with the judgment of God. He sees that he is such a great sinner that he cannot find any means to be delivered from his sin by his own strength, effort, or works. Then he understands correctly what Paul means when he says that man is the slave and captive of sin, that God has consigned all men to sin, and that the whole world is guilty in the sight of God. . . .

Now he begins to sigh: "Then who can come to my aid?" Terrified by the law, he despairs of his own strength; he looks about and sighs for the help of the Mediator and Savior. Then there comes, at the appropriate time, the saving word of the gospel, which says: "Take heart, my son; your sins are forgiven (Matt. 9:2). Believe in Jesus Christ, who was crucified for your sins. If you feel your sins, do not consider them in yourself but remember that they have been transferred to Christ, 'with whose stripes you are healed' (Is. 53:3)."

This is the beginning of salvation. By this means we are delivered from sin and justified, and eternal life is granted to us, not for our own merits and works but for our faith, by which we take hold of Christ. Therefore we, too, acknowledge a quality and a formal righteousness in the heart; but we do not mean love, as the sophists do, but faith, because the heart must behold and grasp nothing but Christ the Savior. Here it is necessary to know the true definition of Christ. Ignoring this altogether, the sophists have made Him a judge and a torturer, and have invented this stupid notion about the merit of congruity and of condignity.

But by the true definition Christ is not a lawgiver; He is a Propitiator and a Savior. Faith takes hold of this and believes without doubting that He has performed a superabundance of works and merits of congruity and condignity. He might have made satisfaction for all the sins of the world with only one drop of His blood, but now He has made abundant satisfaction. Heb. 9:12: "With His own blood He entered once for all into the Holy Place." And Rom. 3:24-25: "Justified by His grace as a gift, through the redemption which is in Christ Jesus, whom God put forward as an expiation by His blood." Therefore it is something great to take hold, by faith, of Christ, who bears the sins of the world (John 1:29). And this faith alone is counted for righteousness (Rom. 3-4).

Here it is to be noted that these three things are joined together: faith, Christ, and acceptance or imputation. Faith takes hold of Christ and has Him present, enclosing Him as the ring encloses the gem. And whoever is found having this faith in the Christ who is grasped in the heart, him God accounts as righteous. This is the means and the merit by which we obtain the forgiveness of sins and righteousness. "Because you believe in me," God says, "and your faith takes hold of Christ, whom I have freely given to you as your Justifier and Savior, therefore be righteous." Thus God accepts you or accounts you righteous only on account of Christ, in whom you believe.

Now acceptance or imputation is extremely necessary, first, because we are not yet purely righteous, but sin is still clinging to our flesh during this life. God cleanses this remnant of sin in our flesh. In addition, we are sometimes forsaken by the Holy Spirit, and we fall into sins, as did Peter, David, and other saints. Nevertheless, we always have recourse to this doctrine, that our sins are covered and that God does not want to hold us accountable for them (Rom. 4). This does not mean that there is no sin in us, as the sophists have taught when they said that we must go on doing good until we are no longer conscious of any sin; but sin is always present, and the godly feel it. But it is ignored and hidden in the sight of God, because Christ the Mediator stands between; because we take hold of Him by faith, all our sins are sins no longer. But where Christ and faith are not present, here there is no forgiveness of sins or hiding of sins. On the contrary, here there is the sheer imputation and condemnation of sins. Thus God wants to glorify His Son, and He Himself wants to be glorified in us through Him.

When we have taught faith in Christ this way, then we also teach about good works. Because you have taken hold of Christ by faith, through whom you are righteous, you should now go and love God and your neighbor. Call upon God, give thanks to Him, preach Him, praise Him, confess Him. Do good to your neighbor, and serve him; do your duty. These are truly good works, which flow from this faith and joy conceived in the heart because we have the forgiveness of sins freely through Christ.

Then whatever there is of cross or suffering to be borne later on is easily sustained. For the yoke that Christ lays upon us is sweet, and His burden is light (Matt. 11:30). When sin has been forgiven and the conscience has been liberated from the burden and the sting of sin, then a Christian can bear everything easily. Because everything within is sweet and pleasant, he willingly does and suffers everything. But when a man goes along in his own righteousness, then whatever he does and suffers is painful and tedious for him, because he is doing it unwillingly.

Therefore we define a Christian as follows: A Christian is not someone who has no sin or feels no sin; he is someone to whom, because of his faith in Christ, God does not impute his sin. This doctrine brings firm consolation to troubled consciences amid genuine terrors. It is not in vain, therefore, that so often and so diligently we inculcate the doctrine of the forgiveness of sins and of the imputation of righteousness for the sake of Christ, as well as the doctrine that a Christian does not have anything to do with the law and sin, especially in a time of temptation. For to the extent that he is a Christian, he is above the law and sin, because in his heart he has Christ, the Lord of the law, as a ring has a gem. Therefore when the law accuses and sin troubles, he looks to Christ; and when he has taken hold of Him by faith, he has present with him the Victor over the law, sin, death, and the devil—the Victor whose rule over all these prevents them from harming him.

Therefore a Christian, properly defined, is free of all laws and is subject to nothing, internally or externally. But I purposely said, "to the extent that he is a Christian" (not "to the extent that he is a man or a woman"); that is, to the extent that he has his conscience trained, adorned, and enriched by this faith, this great and inestimable treasure, or, as Paul calls it, "this inexpressible gift" (2 Cor. 9:15), which cannot be exalted and praised enough, since it makes men sons and heirs of God. Thus a Christian is greater than the entire world. For in his heart he has this seemingly small gift; yet the smallness of this gift and treasure, which he holds in faith, is greater than heaven and earth, because Christ, who is this gift, is greater.

When this doctrine, which pacifies consciences, remains pure and intact, Christians are constituted as judges over all kinds of doctrine and become lords over all the laws of the entire world. Then they can freely judge that the Turk with his Koran is damned, because he does not follow the right way; that is, he does not acknowledge that he is a miserable and damned sinner, and he does not take hold of Christ by faith, for whose sake he could believe that his sins are forgiven. With similar confidence they can pronounce sentence against the pope. He is damned with all his kingdom, because he, with all his monks and universities, acts as though we came to grace through the merit of congruity and as though we were then received into heaven by the merit of condignity. Here the Christian says: "That is not the right way to justify. This is not the road to the stars. For through my works preceding grace I cannot merit grace by congruity, nor can I deserve eternal life by condignity through my merits following grace; but sin is forgiven and righteousness is imputed to him who believes in Christ. This confidence makes him a son and heir of God, who in hope possesses the promise of eternal life."

II. *Huldrych Zwingli*

⎍⎍⎍⎍⎍⎍⎍⎍⎍⎍⎍⎍⎍⎍⎍⎍⎍⎍⎍⎍⎍⎍⎍⎍⎍

9. Huldrych Zwingli: *Commentary on True and False Religion* (1525)*

The *Commentary on True and False Religion* is Zwingli's most important theological treatise. Written in an extremely short time at the suggestion of some French Protestants, its principal theme is the contrast between the true religion of the Bible and the false religion of human speculation and striving. Zwingli marshaled his vast competence in the Bible and in philosophy to underscore his contention that false religion was that of the Catholic church and that true religion had been recovered by the reformers. The stress on philosophy is a characteristic feature of his thought. A second distinctive feature appears in the discussion of the Lord's Supper, where Zwingli revealed that he did not share Luther's affirmation of the real presence of Christ in the sacrament. This theological divergence between the two reformers was to lead to the communion controversy which dominated the history of Protestantism for many years.

Reprinted below are the section of the chapter on the Lord's Supper which deals specifically with the interpretation of Jesus' words of institution ("This is my body," "This is my blood") and the conclusion of the entire treatise.

LITERATURE
J. Courvoisier, *Zwingli: A Reformed Theologian* (Richmond, 1963).

I HAVE amplified at somewhat greater length than before the substance of this sixth chapter [of John], as far as it pertains to

*S. M. Jackson, (ed.), *The Latin Works and Correspondence of Huldreich Zwingli* (Philadelphia, 1922), pp. 122 ff.

the Eucharist, but I hope not fruitlessly. . . . Whatever has been plucked from this chapter and distorted into any other meaning than this native one which the Lord has explained through me, whether it be read in decrees of popes or works of theologians, or heralded in churches or pulpits, ought to have so little effect that we should all declare it would have been more pious for those who have done this thing never to have touched the undefiled truth than in their presumption so to have defiled it.

What, therefore, will their authority avail, however great and excellent they are? The truth is more excellent. To the others, who break out with, "You seem to me to hold that the bodily flesh and also the blood of Christ are not present in the Eucharist," I answer: Do you say this of yourself or have others said it to you? If you are a believer, you are aware how salvation comes; and then the word of God has such power with you that you raise no question about bodily flesh. But if others have told you that this is my view, I say to them that in this matter I hold as the church of Christ holds. She will not even brook the question whether the body of Christ is in the sacrament of the Eucharist in actual, physical, or essential form. For when you bring up these elements of the world, she will thrust this buckler in your face: "The flesh profiteth nothing" [John 6:63]; why, then, do you dispute about the flesh? Even if you now cry out, "O heaven! O earth!" nay, even "Stars and seas!" I shall simply say, "The flesh profiteth nothing"; why, then, is it better for you to be curious rather than anxious about it?

Be this, then, a wall of bronze, "The flesh profiteth nothing." Go now, and bring up all your engines of war, catapults, battering-rams, sheds, and every kind of weapon; far from shattering this wall, you will be able not even to shake it. We must, then, hold a different view of the flesh and blood of this sacrament from that which the theologians have thus far laid down, whose opinion is opposed by all sense and reason and understanding and by faith itself. For I do not think we have to listen to those who are so bold as to say, "I have always firmly believed that in this sacrament I eat the essential body, or the bodily and sensible flesh, of Christ." As if in saying this they could persuade any one to believe that his senses perceive what they do not perceive! When, therefore, they say that the whole thing is established by faith and therefore cannot be denied, for we must firmly believe that we have a sense perception of the bodily flesh, I reply: "I know what faith is and I know also what sense is; but you, either not having this knowledge or supposing that I have it not, are trying to cast darkness upon my light. Faith exists in our hearts through the Spirit of God, and we are sensible of it. In fact, that there is an inward change of heart is not an obscure matter, but we do not perceive it by means of the senses." But now these persons come and, because they fancy that faith is a violent and deliberate turning of our hearts toward some even quite incongruous thing, they therefore aver that here the belief that the bodily and sensible flesh is present is held with unwavering faith.

Yet in this they make two mistakes: First, in thinking that faith has its origin in man's decision and election. They make a mistake here because, although faith is hope and trust in things quite remote from sense, nevertheless it does not rest upon our decision or election. The things upon which we set our hopes themselves cause us to put all our hopes upon them; for if we were made believers by our own election or determination, all men could become believers by their own strength, even the impious. Since, therefore, faith has not its origin in sense or reason and looks not to the things of sense, it is easy to discover how they err in the second place. They err in the second place, then, in applying faith to things of sense, and in saying that through these it brings us certainty. But of that there is no need, for what is perceived by sense owes nothing to faith. Why should anyone hope for that which he already sees? For things which are perceived when presented to the senses are things of sense. Let us see now how finely these things fit together: by faith we believe that the bodily and sensible flesh of Christ is here present. By faith things quite remote from sense are believed. But all bodily things are so entirely things of sense that unless they are perceived by sense they are not bodily. Therefore, to believe and to perceive by sense are essentially different. Observe, therefore, what a monstrosity of speech this is: I believe that I eat the sensible and bodily flesh. For if it is bodily, there is no need of faith, for it is perceived by sense; and things perceived by sense have no need of faith, for by sense they are perceived to be perfectly sure. On the other hand, if your eating is a matter of belief, the thing you believe cannot be sensible or bodily. Therefore what you say is simply a monstrosity. Observe, too, that the theologians asserted here another thing, which even the senses knew not, namely, that bread is flesh; for if this had been so, it would have been established by the verdict of sense, not by faith. For faith springs not from things accessible to sense nor are they objects of faith. Nor do I think we have to listen to those who, seeing that the view mentioned is not only crude but even frivolous and impious, make this pronouncement: "We eat, to be sure, the true and bodily flesh of Christ, but spiritually"; for they do not yet see that the two statements cannot stand, "It is body" and "It is eaten spiritually." For body and spirit are such essentially different things that whichever one you take it cannot be the other. If spirit is the one that has come into question, it follows by the law of contraries that body is not; if body is the one, the hearer is sure that spirit is not. Hence, to eat bodily flesh spiritually is simply to assert that to be body which is spirit. I have adduced these things from the philosophers against those men who, in spite of Paul's warning to be on our guard against philosophy, Col. 2:8, have made it the mistress and instructress of the word of God, that they may see clearly how nicely they sometimes weigh their decisions and pronouncements. In short, faith does not compel sense to confess that it perceives what it does not perceive, but it draws us to the invisible and fixes all our hopes on that [cf. Heb. 11:1]. For it dwelleth not amidst the sensible and bodily, and hath nothing in common therewith. . . .

Who, pray, ever made up such nonsense, and that before the eyes of those who clung in their hearts to the true and most high God, and who, as soon as they examined their faith, saw that there was no need of paradoxes of this sort? For what did God ever promise to those who believed that bodily flesh is eaten here? Did not those who were truly faithful know for certain that salvation is found in relying upon the mercy of God, of which we have the sure sign or pledge in Jesus Christ the only begotten Son of God? What, then, do you imagine this invention—subtle forsooth, since it consists of words only (for no mind can take it in, and neither does faith teach it, as we have seen)—effected with the pious? Nothing, by heaven. Hence it undoubtedly came about that those who were truly pious either believed nothing of the kind, or when pressed to believe took to flight in their hearts, even though with their lips they confessed that they believed it was as the impious declared. For who, when confronted with anything so monstrous, did not flee, saying: "Do not examine this thing; believe the Fathers." And whenever the goading voice of the Truth said: "It is a strange thing. How can it be that you should be compelled to believe that which you cannot see to be possible? When the Jews did not comprehend it, Christ showed that it was to be understood spiritually, but now these persons say it is done in a bodily and material sense, which yet you do not perceive nor experience," did not everyone say to himself: "It is not for you to take anxious thought about these things"? . . .

I have now refuted, I hope, this senseless notion about bodily flesh. In doing that my only object was to prove that to teach that the bodily and sensible flesh of Christ is eaten when we give thanks to God is not only impious but also foolish and monstrous, unless perhaps one is living among the Anthropophagi. Meanwhile I leave everyone free to hold what view he will of spiritual manducation, provided he rests on Christ's dicta and not his own, until he has weighed what I am going to bring forward about the words of Christ. Then he may choose what the Lord will give him to choose, for I impose no law upon any man. . . .

The entire difficulty, then, lies not in the pronoun "this," but in a word no larger as far as number of letters is concerned, namely, in the verb "*is*." For this is used in more than one passage in the holy Scriptures for "signifies." I hear (to mention this point first) that Wycliffe earlier held and the Waldensians today hold this view, that "is" was put here for "signifies," but I have not seen their Scripture basis for it. It is possible for persons to hold right views and not rightly support the right views they hold. Perhaps that was the reason why their view was condemned as impious. For I, having through the grace of God often joined battle with many adversaries in regard to the meaning of Scripture passages, have often found that persons, even when they held right views, were sometimes forced to abandon their cause and to surrender it to others because they could not strongly support their right views. Hence I shall without fear of these words, "He is a Wycliffian," "He is a Waldensian," "He is a heretic," bring forward the passages of Scripture in which it cannot be denied that this word "is" certainly is used for "signifies." Afterwards I shall prove clearly that in this passage also "is" must be taken in the sense of "signifies." This will be plain from the testimony following. In Gen. 41:26 Joseph, interpreting Pharaoh's dream, says: "The seven beautiful kine, and the seven full ears, are seven years of plenty: and both contain the same meaning of the dream." What is this, pray? Are the seven fat kine seven years? Certainly not, but the kine he had seen portended seven fruitful years, and nobody but a fool can deny that this is the force of the words. "Are" is used here, therefore, beyond controversy for "signify." A little later there follows [Gen. 41:27], "And the seven lean and thin kine that came up after them, and the seven thin ears that were blasted with the burning wind, are seven years of famine to come, etc." Here again we have "are" used for "signify." Now I come to the New Covenant. In Luke 8:11, when Christ had signified by the parable of the seed falling upon the ground the varied attitudes of people in receiving the word of God, and the disciples failed to understand and asked what He meant by this parable, He discoursed thus: "The seed," of which they had heard so much—"The seed is the word of God." But no seed is the word of God—the word of God was signified by this term. Here, then "is" is again used for "signifies." A little later [Luke 8:14] we have: "And that which fell among the thorns, these are, etc.," that is, "and that which I said fell among the thorns signifies those, etc." And a little later [Luke 8:15]: "But that in the good ground, these are, etc."; that is, "but the seed which I said fell in the good ground signifies those, etc." So in Matt. 13:1–23, in the same parable, "is" is used for "signifies," although the language is a little less direct. In the same passage, when explaining the parable of the tares sown after the wheat, He says [Matt. 13:38]: "The field is the world." But the field is not the world; but it signified the world in this parable. . . . I think testimony enough has now been adduced to prove that "is" and its cognate forms can be used to mean "signify." But since I hear some persons blurt out indignantly, "If we are to force any word we please thus to signify anything we please, nothing in the holy Scriptures will retain its integrity, for license will be given the impious to twist everything into anything you like," it is worth while to give them an answer rather more polite than their objection. Who does not know, then, that there is absolutely no word that is not sometimes taken out of its native soil and planted in a foreign one, where it has a far higher value than if you had left it in the home ground, that is, in its literal meaning? This was specially customary with the Hebrews beyond other peoples, as is most plainly apparent all through Christ's discourse, even when translated into a foreign tongue. Take the despised term "dung." When Christ, in Luke 13:8, makes the husbandman intercede for the barren tree, undertaking to put dung about it, how could He more delightfully have signified a kindly minister of the word, whose duty it certainly is to encourage the backward in every way, and to commend them to the Lord in constant prayers, lest He judge them according to their deserts? Take another term, "stone." Does not this term occupy a more honorable position when it signifies Christ [Matt. 21:42] the stone, than when it means an inert rock projecting in the field, or even one used in the construction of a building? So also with verbs. . . . Yet, according to the intolerance of those who refuse to admit any extension of the meaning of verbs and nouns, He must be a door. Of wood, then, or of stone, or of ivory or horn, as in Pliny and Homer? "I am the way" [John 14:6], "I am the vine" [John 15:5], "I am the light" [John 8:12], etc., force us in spite of ourselves to allow them a signification other than the literal one. Is He a vine? No, but He is like a vine. There is, therefore, no need of this senseless wail: "Look out, fellow citizens, your interests are in jeopardy, you are going to lose your language"; for we cannot conveniently use even everyday speech without metaphors and metalepses. With faith as teacher, then, we shall see in what sense we ought to take each expression; for otherwise we should be doing a thing absolutely unworthy both of Christ and of ourselves in regarding him as actually a lamb or a ram in John [1:36; 21:15–17], and as a fatted calf in Luke [15:23]. When, therefore, He says [John 15:5], "I am the vine," He is saying nothing else than, "I am like a vine to my disciples." Who will make an uproar here? Who complain that an outrage is done? So, also, in our passage we must consult faith, and if she says that in the expression, "This is my body," this verb "is" must not be taken in its literal meaning, we must by all means obey faith and have no fear whatever of those whom we see daring everything in their impiety, for they cannot, however much they rave, wrest the truth out of the hands of the pious. If, however, faith cannot endure this meaning, then the signification of this word in this passage—as was made plain above by many arguments and is made singularly and solidly plain by the expression, "The flesh profiteth nothing"—will be an altogether different one, whatever outcry is made by the ignorant and impious. This verb "is," then, is in my judgment used here for "signifies." . . .

We must, then, now first of all see how everything squares if we use "is" for "signifies" in this fashion. And as everything will square beautifully, it will be proved at the same time that "is" in this passage as well as in others must be taken for "signifies," which was the second thing I undertook to prove. Thus, then, Luke [22:19] has it, and we shall content ourselves with him from among the evangelists: "And he took bread, and when He had given thanks, He brake it, and gave to them, saying, This signifies my body which is given for you: this do in remembrance of me." See, faithful soul but captive of absurd notions, how everything squares here, how nothing is violently taken away or added, but everything squares so perfectly that you wonder you have not always seen this meaning, and wonder all the more that the beautiful harmony of the discourse in question has been so recklessly mangled by certain persons. "He took bread, gave thanks, brake it, and gave to them, saying." Behold how there is no missing link here! "This (that I offer you to eat, namely) is the symbol of my body which is given for you, and this which I now do, ye shall do hereafter in remembrance of me." Does not the saying, "Do this in remembrance of me," plainly indicate that this bread should be eaten in remembrance of Him? The Lord's Supper, then, as Paul calls it [1 Cor. 11:25–26], is a commemoration of Christ's death, not a remitting of sins, for that is the province of Christ's death alone. For He says: "This which I now bid you eat and drink shall be a symbol unto you which ye shall all use in eating and drinking when ye shall make commemoration of me." And that nothing needful for the true understanding of this commemoration may be lacking, Paul, in 1 Cor. 11:26, after having said with regard to the bread as well as with regard to the wine, "This do in remembrance of me," explains as follows: "For as often as ye eat this bread" (symbolical bread, namely, for no one of them all calls it flesh), "and drink this cup, proclaim the Lord's death till he come." But what is it to "proclaim the Lord's death"? To preach, surely, to give thanks and praise, as Peter says, 1 Pet. 2:9: "That ye should show forth the excellencies of him who called you out of darkness into his marvelous light." Paul, therefore, reminds us that even unto the end of the world, when Christ will return and contend in judgment with the human race, this commemoration of Christ's death should be so made that we proclaim the death of the Lord, that is, preach, praise, and give thanks. For this reason the Greeks called it "Eucharist." . . .

EPILOGUE

I want now to gather the substance of all that I have said into a short epilogue, that no one may imagine that the Christian law is so confused and difficult to explain that no one can learn it or explain it in a few words. That I or others have to talk at such length is due to the fault of him who has dared to corrupt everything, to disturb everything, to defile and to pervert everything, in order to satisfy his own greed, so that there is nothing, or at least very little, in the whole true teaching of the true God that this man of sin [cf. 2 Thess. 2:3] has not ventured to destroy. His avarice is so uncontrollable that when he sees himself refused in human things what he needs to satiate himself, he ventures to lay hold of divine things also. When he sees anything holy and undefiled, his first object is to befoul it with his own interpretation; and when he has polluted everything he proceeds to misuse everything in the interest of lust. Hence it has come to pass that we have purchased salvation from the Roman pontiff as from a peddler, and have got the idea that Christianity is an article of merchandise rather than holiness of life. There is no difference between the life of man and that of beasts if you take away the knowledge of God. For what has man that beasts have not also? Men defend themselves and their children, satisfy their desires, flee from want; so do the beasts. Man founds laws and states. The gregarious animals, as cranes, thrushes, starlings, tunnies, deer, cattle, bees, swine, do the same, being governed by fixed laws, dividing the mass now into wedges and now into single lines, now dwelling in one place, now migrating to another, and generally keeping faith better than is done among men. God, therefore, was unwilling to leave man without the knowledge of Himself, and has always taught him in such a way as immediately to call him back when he seemed to have fallen into forgetfulness of God, that he might not in his degeneracy prefer to perish with the beasts rather than to live forever with Him. Hence the anxious inquiry, addressed to fallen man: "Adam, where art thou?" [Gen. 3:9]. Hence the fire and the flood, in order to keep man to his duty by fear also. Again, the splendid promises and benefits. He promised Abraham offspring that should save the world [cf. Gen. 15:6–21, 17:4–9, 22:17 f.]; so to Isaac [Gen. 26:4–5], Israel [Gen. 28:13–15], and Jesse's son David. Unwilling to endure longer the affliction of His people, He brought the whole nation under Moses out of the savage tyranny of Pharaoh, and, after punishing the enemy, supported them in the desert, now with bread from heaven, now with the flesh of quail; and where water was wanting He brought it forth abundantly from the hardest rock, or where it was not good sweetened it so that they could enjoy it in ample measure. He hedged them about with laws as with a guard rail, and thus separated them from the rest of the nations, that they might see that they were the peculiar people of God. In this manner He showed Himself a most loving Father to one race; yet He was nowhere lacking to others, that the whole world might recognize that He is the one and the only one who can do all things, by whom all things exist, by whom all things are governed, that miserable man may not go over to the beasts; for He marked them off from the beasts by bringing their passions into line through laws. Yet who would ever have accepted His laws that had not first dedicated his heart to Him, that had not above all the belief that He was the true and only God? Therefore, it is evident that, whenever God manifested Himself to the world, He also so entered the heart that what was heard or seen was recognized as being divine. For the flesh receiveth not what is opposed to it; and whatever the heavenly Spirit does is opposed to the flesh. Therefore man cannot receive God, cannot listen to the law, unless God Himself draw the heart to Himself [cf. John 6:44], so that it shall recognize that He is its God, and shall receive the law as good. Thus, then, from the foundation of the world God has manifested Himself in various ways to the human race, that we might recognize Him as Father and Dispenser of all things. The first thing, therefore, in piety is that we should firmly believe that He whom we confess as our God is God, the Source and Father of all things; for unless we do so, we shall never obey His laws. The next thing is that we should know ourselves; for when we have not knowledge of ourselves also, we accept no law. For how should one accept a law who thinks nothing lacking to himself? Therefore this Heavenly Householder rises betimes, aye in the night, as the prophet says [cf. Psalms 46:6], to arrange and prescribe everything early, that we may not begin to labor before the allotted task has been assigned. He hedges the human race about with laws, therefore, that it may begin nothing without regard to law; for He not only compassed the people of Israel about with laws, but also inscribed upon the hearts of the Gentiles the so-called laws of nature; for one of their prophets says: "Know thyself came down from heaven." But on knowledge of self rests the law, What you wish done to yourself, do to another [cf. Matt. 7:12], and its counterpart, What you do not wish done to yourself, do not to another [Tobit 4:16]. For our own good, therefore, God manifests Himself to us, for whether He enters into our hearts—which is the greatest miracle—so that we recognize that He is our God and Father, or whether He accomplishes the same thing by miraculous works, He does it solely with a view to benefiting us. And what is this benefit that He provides with such care for us? It is twofold, verily: namely, to live here blamelessly; and, when the course of this life has been finished, to enjoy eternal bliss with Him. For what need would there have been of knowledge of God, and of laws, if the end of the soul were the same as of the body? Would it not have been better to let man remain a brute, if he had been a brute after this fashion, than to raise him to false hope? God willed, therefore, that amid the numerous and varied progeny of created things the human race should so dwell upon earth as to strive toward the inheritance set for it in heaven. So it pleased the Most High. For what other reason should He manifest Himself to man, and kindle him to love of Him? And knowing that man would wonder exceedingly what sort of an inheritance it was that he should hope for in heaven, He gave him a taste, as it were, of that happiness, but through a mist and a lattice, as the saying is. Man sees all things done with reckless greed and turmoil, but when he hears God say, "Thou shalt not covet" [Ex. 20:17; cf. Rom. 7:7], he infers truly that noxious covetousness must be very far from the place where true happiness dwells, and that the author of such happiness must be still farther removed from all greed. He doubts not, therefore, that it would be a very beautiful thing if, also while we are here, we were far removed from all covetousness. Hence the constant struggle and contest. The soul strives to fashion itself upon the pattern of Him toward whom it is hastening, whose face it desires to see, the face, namely, of its righteous and holy Father, aye, of Him who is righteousness itself, holiness, purity, light, rest, refreshment, joy, and all blessedness together. The body resists, because by its nature it scorns whatever the soul greatly values; it yearns for the things of earth and lets those of heaven go, has no hope at all of seeing God any more than the very earth has from which it sprang. Accordingly, it follows its desires, and if it is ever kept by the power of the soul from attaining them, it proceeds to plot and rage against it. Hence that constant battle between the flesh and the spirit, which ceases not until we have reached our goal. Hence would be born desperation of soul, had not a kind God so manifested Himself to it that it can safely trust to His mercy. For the soul, seeing after all its efforts that the flesh throws itself into all sorts of sin (just as the boy possessed of a demon in Mark [9:22] cast himself now into the fire and now into the water), could not help being reduced to the uttermost depths of despair by this ungovernableness of the flesh. But when it does not cast away hope nor give up its efforts for blamelessness, it sees that mercy is better than vengeance. And that man might never lose this hope, when it pleased the divine counsel, the heavenly Father sent His only begotten Son, so to strengthen the hopes of all that they should see clearly that nothing can be refused, now that the Son is given for poor mortals; for "how shall he not with him freely give us all things?" [Rom. 8:32]. He was sent, then, for this purpose, that He might altogether take away this despair of the soul that springs from the ungovernableness of the flesh, as has been said, and that He might also furnish an example of life. For Christ everywhere emphasizes these two things, namely, redemption through Himself, and the obligation of those redeemed through Him to live according to His example. For He says, John 6:57: "So he that eateth me, he shall live because of me"; and John 15:8: "Herein is my Father glorified, that ye bear much fruit; and so shall ye be my disciples." We ought, then, to be as eagerly bent upon a change of life as we trust in redemption through Him. A Christian, therefore, is a man who trusts in the one true and only God; who relies upon His mercy through His Son Christ, God of God; who models himself upon His example; who dies daily [cf. 1 Cor. 15:31]; who daily renounces self; who is intent upon this one thing, not to do anything that can offend his God. Such watchfulness demands so much diligence and zeal that anyone would need many a Theseus to defend his blamelessness, and yet would never come off victorious. The Christian life, then, is a battle, so sharp and full of danger that effort can nowhere be relaxed without loss; again, it is also a lasting victory, for he who fights it wins, if only he remains loyal to Christ the head. Thus has God willed that man be an amphibian among the creatures, dwelling sometimes on earth, sometimes in the heavens; and, again, while on the earth sometimes conquering, sometimes yielding; but we are by no means to ask the reasons for His acts. Since, then, God asks of us these things only, faith and blamelessness, no more baneful plague can be imagined than a varied worship of God, the invention of our own industry. This we (being given to magnifying everything of our own) embrace, instead of that true worship of God which consists of faith and blamelessness; and, according to the words of the prophet Jeremiah, 2:13, "We have committed two evils; we have forsaken God, the fountain of living waters, and hewed us out cisterns, broken cisterns, that can hold no water." We have substituted a vicar for Christ, and in our folly have decreed that he is to be listened to in place of God. When he saw that a way to our purses was open to him through our consciences, what scheme did he not think up? What did he not dare? How many roads to heaven he showed us, but none without a toll! You confessed into the ear of the vicar of Christ; heaven was promised if you counted out so and so much for Masses and mumbling. You joined some order, to which the stupid crowd contributed much, and again you attained the heavens; for the greater the accessions to them, the more power-ful became our vicar. Run thus through everything that reckless greed has prescribed for us, and you will find that it has removed true religion from men, that is, faith and blamelessness, by which singly and alone God is worshiped; nor does He require any other worship of us; nay, He so scorns other inventions as to say that things which seem high to men are an abomination in His sight. God ought to be worshiped with those things alone in which He delights.

III. *The Anabaptists*

10. Conrad Grebel and the Zürich Anabaptists: .Letter to Thomas Müntzer (1524)*

Among the early representatives of radical reform, two stand out: Thomas Müntzer, a former follower of Luther, minister at the Saxon town of Alstadt, author of several vehemently anti-Lutheran tracts published in early 1524, and the Anabaptists, who had their beginning among a group of erstwhile followers of Huldrych Zwingli. Dissatisfied with his slow and seemingly compromising ecclesiastical reform, they set out to delineate the biblical faith as they understood it. Among their tenets was the notion of the believer's church and believer's baptism, both voluntary expressions of authentic biblical faith.

Traditionally scholarship has assumed that the Zürich Anabaptists owe their origin to Thomas Müntzer, though more recently the essential independence of the Zürich group has been persuasively argued. The following letter written in September, 1524 by the Zürich radicals to Müntzer shows both the areas of agreement as well as disagreement. It is thus an important document for understanding the self-consciousness of the emerging Anabaptist movement and the temper of radical dissent at that particular time. Only the main body of the letter is reprinted here, without the lengthy postscript.

LITERATURE
H. S. Bender, *The Life and Letters of Conrad Grebel* (Goshen, 1950).

DEAR Brother Thomas:
For God's sake do not marvel that we address thee without

* George H. Williams (ed.), *Spiritual and Anabaptist Writers* (Philadelphia, 1957), pp. 73–85.

title, and request thee like a brother to communicate with us by writing, and that we have ventured, unasked and unknown to thee, to open communications between us. God's Son, Jesus Christ, who offers Himself as the one master and head of all who would be saved, and bids us be brethren by the one common word given to all brethren and believers, has moved us and compelled us to make friendship and brotherhood and to bring the following points to thy attention. Thy writing of two tracts on fictitious faith has further prompted us. Therefore we ask that thou wilt take it kindly for the sake of Christ our Savior. If God wills, it shall serve and work to our good. Amen.

Just as our forebears fell away from the true God and from the one true, common, divine word, from the divine institutions, from Christian love and life, and lived without God's law and gospel in human, useless, un-Christian customs and ceremonies, and expected to attain salvation therein, yet fell far short of it, as the evangelical preachers have declared, and to some extent are still declaring, so today too every man wants to be saved by superficial faith, without fruits of faith, without baptism of trial and probation, without love and hope, without right Christian practices, and wants to persist in all the old manner of personal vices, and in the common ritualistic and anti-Christian customs of baptism and of the Lord's Supper, in disrespect for the divine word and in respect for the word of the pope and of the anti-papal preachers, which yet is not equal to the divine word nor in harmony with it. In respecting persons and in manifold seduction there is grosser and more pernicious error now than ever has been since the beginning of the world. In the same error we too lingered as long as we heard and read only the evangelical preachers who are to blame for all this, in punishment for our sins. But after we took Scripture in hand too, and consulted it on many points, we have been instructed somewhat and have discovered the great and harmful error of the shepherds, of ours too, namely, that we do not daily beseech God earnestly with constant groaning to be brought out of this destruction of all godly life and out of human abominations, to attain to the true faith and divine practice. The cause of all this is false forbearance, the hiding of the divine word, and the mixing of it with the human. Aye, we say it harms all and frustrates all things divine. There is no need of specifying and reciting.

While we were marking and deploring these facts, thy book against false faith and baptism was brought to us, and we were more fully informed and confirmed, and it rejoiced us wonderfully that we found one who was of the same Christian mind with us and dared to show the evangelical preachers their lack, how that in all the chief points they falsely forbear and act and set their own opinions, and even those of Antichrist, above God and against God, as befits not the ambassadors of God to act and preach. Therefore we beg and admonish thee as a brother by the name, the power, the word, the spirit, and the salvation, which has come to all Christians through Jesus Christ our Master and Savior (*seligmacher*), that thou wilt take earnest heed to preach only the divine word without fear, to set up and guard only divine institutions, to esteem as good and right only what may be found in pure and clear Scripture, to reject, hate, and curse all devices, words, customs, and opinions of men, including thy own.

(1) We understand and have seen that thou hast translated the Mass into German and hast introduced new German hymns. That cannot be for the good, since we find nothing taught in the New Testament about singing, no example of it. Paul scolds the learned among the Corinthians more than he praises them, because they mumbled in meeting as if they sang, just as the Jews and the Italians chant their words song-fashion. (2) Since singing in Latin grew up without divine instruction and apostolic example and custom, without producing good or edifying, it will still less edify in German and will create a faith of outward appearance only. (3) Paul very clearly forbids singing in Eph. 5:19 and Col. 3:16 since he says and teaches that they are to speak to one another and teach one another with psalms and spiritual songs, and if anyone would sing, he should sing and give thanks in his heart. (4) Whatever we are not taught by clear passages or examples must be regarded as forbidden, just as if it were written: "This do not; sing not." (5) Christ in the Old and especially in the New Testament bids his messengers (*botten*) simply proclaim the word. Paul too says that the word of Christ profits us, not the song. Whoever sings poorly gets

vexation by it; whoever can sing well gets conceit. (6) We must not follow our notions; we must add nothing to the word and take nothing from it. (7) If thou wilt abolish the Mass, it cannot be accomplished with German chants, which is thy suggestion perhaps, or comes from Luther. (8) It must be rooted up by the word and command of Christ. (9) For it is not planted by God. (10) The Supper of fellowship Christ did institute and plant. (11) The words found in Matt. 26, Mark 14, Luke 22, and 1 Cor. 11, alone are to be used, no more, no less. (12) The server, a member of the congregation, should pronounce them from one of the evangelists or from Paul. (13) They are the words of the instituted meal of fellowship, not words of consecration. (14) Ordinary bread ought to be used, without idols and additions. (15) For [the latter] creates an external reverence and veneration of the bread, and a turning away from the inward. An ordinary drinking vessel too ought to be used. (16) This would do away with the adoration and bring true understanding and appreciation of the Supper, since the bread is nought but bread. In faith, it is the body of Christ and the incorporation with Christ and the brethren. But one must eat and drink in the Spirit and love, as John shows in chapter 6 and the other passages, Paul in 1 Cor. 10 and 11, and as is clearly learned in Acts 2. (17) Although it is simply bread, yet if faith and brotherly love precede it, it is to be received with joy, since, when it is used in the church, it is to show us that we are truly one bread and one body, and that we are and wish to be true brethren with one another, etc. (18) But if one is found who will not live the brotherly life, he eats unto condemnation, since he eats it without discerning, like any other meal, and dishonors love, which is the inner bond, and the bread, which is the outer bond. (19) For also it does not call to his mind Christ's body and blood, the covenant of the cross, nor that he should be willing to live and suffer for the sake of Christ and the brethren, of the head and the members. (20) Also it ought not to be administered by thee. That was the beginning of the Mass that only a few would partake, for the Supper is an expression of fellowship, not a Mass and sacrament. Therefore none is to receive it alone, neither on his deathbed nor otherwise. Neither is the bread to be locked away, etc., for the use of a single person, since no one should take for himself alone the bread of those in unity, unless he is not one with himself—which no one is, etc. (21) Neither is it to be used in "temples" according to all Scripture and example, since that creates a false reverence. (22) It should be used much and often. (23) It should not be used without the rule of Christ in Matt. 18:15–18, otherwise it is not the Lord's Supper, for without that rule every man will run after the externals. The inner matter, love, is passed by, if brethren and false brethren approach or eat it [together]. (24) If ever thou desirest to serve it, we should wish that it would be done without priestly garment and vestment of the Mass, without singing, without addition. (25) As for the time, we know that Christ gave it to the apostles at supper and that the Corinthians had the same usage. We fix no definite time with us, etc.

Let this suffice, since thou art much better instructed about the Lord's Supper, and we only state things as we understand them. If we are not in the right, teach us better. And do thou drop singing and the Mass, and act in all things only according to the word, and bring forth and establish by the word the usages of the apostles. If that cannot be done, it would be better to leave all things in Latin and unaltered and mediated [by a priest]. If the right cannot be established, do not then administer according to thy *own* or the priestly usage of Antichrist. And at least teach how it ought to be, as Christ does in John 6, and teaches how we must eat and drink His flesh and blood, and takes no heed of backsliding and anti-Christian caution, of which the most learned and foremost evangelical preachers have made a veritable idol and propagated it in all the world. It is much better that a few be rightly taught through the word of God, believing and walking aright in virtues and practices, than that many believe falsely and deceitfully through adulterated doctrine. Though we admonish and beseech thee, we hope that thou wilt do it of thy own accord; and we admonish the more willingly, because thou hast so kindly listened to our brother and confessed that thou too hast yielded too much, and because thou and Carlstadt are esteemed by us the purest proclaimers and preachers of the purest word of God. And if ye two rebuke, and justly, those who mingle the words and customs of men with those of God, ye must by rights cut yourselves loose and be completely purged of popery, benefices, and all new and ancient customs, and of

your own and ancient notions. If your benefices, as with us, are
supported by interest and tithes, which are both true usury, and
it is not the whole congregation which supports you, we beg
that ye free yourselves of your benefices. Ye know well how a
shepherd should be sustained. . . .

Go forward with the word and establish a Christian church
with the help of Christ and His rule, as we find it instituted in
Matt. 18:15–18 and applied in the epistles. Use determination
and common prayer and decision according to faith and love,
without command or compulsion. Then God will help thee and
thy little sheep to all sincerity, and the singing and the tablets
will cease. There is more than enough of wisdom and counsel
in the Scripture, how all classes and all men may be taught, governed, instructed, and turned to piety. Whoever will not amend
and believe, but resists the word and action of God and thus
persists, such a man, after Christ and His word and rule have
been declared to him and he has been admonished in the presence
of the three witnesses and the church, such a man, we say, taught
by God's word, shall not be killed, but regarded as a heathen
and publican and let alone.

Moreover, the gospel and its adherents are not to be protected
by the sword, nor are they thus to protect themselves, which, as
we learn from our brother, is thy opinion and practice. True
Christian believers are sheep among wolves, sheep for the slaughter; they must be baptized in anguish and affliction, tribulation,
persecution, suffering, and death; they must be tried with fire,
and must reach the fatherland of eternal rest, not by killing their
bodily, but by mortifying their spiritual, enemies. Neither do
they use worldly sword or war, since all killing has ceased with
them—unless, indeed, we would still be of the old law. And
even there [in the Old Testament], so far as we recall, war was
a misfortune after they had once conquered the Promised Land.
No more of this.

On the matter of baptism thy book pleases us well, and we
desire to be further instructed by thee. We understand that
even an adult is not to be baptized without Christ's rule of binding and loosing. The Scripture describes baptism for us thus, that
it signifies that, by faith and the blood of Christ, sins have been
washed away for him who is baptized, changes his mind, and

believes before and after; that it signifies that a man is dead and ought to be dead to sin and walks in newness of life and spirit, and that he shall certainly be saved if, according to this meaning, by inner baptism he lives his faith; so that the water does not confirm or increase faith, as the scholars at Wittenberg say, and [does not] give very great comfort [nor] is it the final refuge on the deathbed. Also baptism does not save, as Augustine, Tertullian, Theophylact, and Cyprian have taught, dishonoring faith and the suffering of Christ in the case of the old and adult, and dishonoring the suffering of Christ in the case of the unbaptized infants. We hold (according to the following passages: Gen. 8:21; Deut. 1:39; 30:6; 31:13; and 1 Cor. 14:20; Wisdom of Solomon 12:19; 1 Peter 2:2; Rom. 1; 2; 7; 10 [allusions uncertain]; Matt. 18:1–6; 19:13–15; Mark 9:33–47; 10:13–16; Luke 18:15–17; etc.) that all children who have not yet come to the discernment of the knowledge of good and evil, and have not yet eaten of the tree of knowledge, that they are surely saved by the suffering of Christ, the new Adam, who has restored their vitiated life, because they would have been subject to death and condemnation only if Christ had not suffered; but they're not yet grown up to the infirmity of our broken nature—unless, indeed, it can be proved that Christ did not suffer for children. But as to the objection that faith is demanded of all who are to be saved, we exclude children from this and hold that they are saved without faith, and we do not believe from the above passages [that children must be baptized], and we conclude from the description of baptism and from the accounts of it (according to which no child was baptized), also from the above passages (which alone apply to the question of children, and all other scriptures do not refer to children), that infant baptism is a senseless, blasphemous abomination, contrary to all Scripture, contrary even to the papacy; since we find, from Cyprian and Augustine, that for many years after apostolic times believers and unbelievers were baptized together for six hundred years, etc. Since thou knowest this ten times better and hast published thy protests against infant baptism, we hope that thou art not acting against the eternal word, wisdom, and commandment of God, according to which only believers are to be baptized, and art not baptizing children.

⎾⎿⎾⎿⎾⎿⎾⎿⎾⎿⎾⎿⎾⎿⎾⎿⎾⎿⎾⎿⎾⎿⎾⎿⎾⎿⎾⎿⎾⎿⎿

11. The Schleitheim Confession of Faith (1527)*

The Schleitheim Confession, named after a small town on the Swiss-German border, grew out of a meeting of South German and Swiss Anabaptists in 1527. Its purpose was to clarify the theological heterogeneity of the Anabaptist movement which had expanded too rapidly and become a catch-all for all sorts of radical dissent. While the emphasis upon believer's baptism was shared by Anabaptists everywhere, other tenets were by no means universally accepted. The Schleitheim Confession, acknowledging that not all Anabaptists concurred with its affirmations, expressed a consensus in several other areas and showed that the ramifications of Anabaptist thought were broader than the issue of baptism.

Though Anabaptism was never a heterogeneous movement and soon split into three major groupings—the Swiss and South German Anabaptists, the Mennonites in North Germany and Holland, and the Hutterites in Moravia—the Schleitheim Confession can be taken as a generally normative statement of Anabaptist belief in the sixteenth century. Reprinted here is a condensed version of the entire Confession.

LITERATURE
G. H. Williams, *The Radical Reformation* (Philadelphia, 1962).

MAY joy, peace and mercy from our Father through the atonement of the blood of Christ Jesus, together with the gifts of the Spirit—who is sent from the Father to all believers for their strength and comfort and for their perseverance in all tribulation until the end, Amen—be to all those who love God, who are the children of light, and who are scattered everywhere as it has been ordained of God our Father, where they are with one mind assembled together in one God and Father of us all: Grace and peace of heart be with you all, Amen.

* John C. Wenger, "The Schleitheim Confession of Faith," *Mennonite Quarterly Review*, 19 (1945), 243 ff.

Beloved brethren and sisters in the Lord: First and supremely we are always concerned for your consolation and the assurance of your conscience (which was previously misled) so that you may not always remain foreigners to us and by right almost completely excluded, but that you may turn again to the true implanted members of Christ, who have been armed through patience and knowledge of themselves, and have therefore again been united with us in the strength of a godly Christian spirit and zeal for God.

It is also apparent with what cunning the devil has turned us aside, so that he might destroy and bring to an end the work of God which in mercy and grace has been partly begun in us. But Christ, the true Shepherd of our souls, who has begun this in us, will certainly direct the same and teach us to His honor and our salvation, Amen.

Dear brethren and sisters, we who have been assembled in the Lord at Schleitheim on the Border, make known in points and articles to all who love God that as concerns us we are of one mind to abide in the Lord as God's obedient children, His sons and daughters, we who have been and shall be separated from the world in everything, and completely at peace. To God alone be praise and glory without the contradiction of any brethren. In this we have perceived the oneness of the Spirit of our Father and of our common Christ with us. For the Lord is the Lord of peace and not of quarreling, as Paul points out. That you may understand in what articles this has been formulated you should observe and note the following.

A very great offense has been introduced by certain false brethren among us, so that some have turned aside from the faith, in the way they intend to practice and observe the freedom of the Spirit and of Christ. But such have missed the truth and to their condemnation are given over to the lasciviousness and self-indulgence of the flesh. They think faith and love may do and permit everything, and nothing will harm them nor condemn them, since they are believers.

Observe, you who are God's members in Christ Jesus, that faith in the heavenly Father through Jesus Christ does not take such form. It does not produce and result in such things as these false brethren and sisters do and teach. Guard yourselves and be warned of such people, for they do not serve our Father, but their father, the devil.

But you are not that way. For they that are Christ's have crucified the flesh with its passions and lusts. You understand me well and know the brethren whom we mean. Separate yourselves from them for they are perverted. Petition the Lord that they may have the knowledge which leads to repentance, and pray for us that we may have constancy to persevere in the way which we have espoused, for the honor of God and of Christ, His Son, Amen.

The articles which we discussed and on which we were of one mind are these (1) Baptism; (2) The Ban [Excommunication]; (3) Breaking of Bread; (4) Separation from the Abomination; (5) Pastors in the Church; (6) The Sword; and (7) The Oath.

First. Observe concerning baptism: Baptism shall be given to all those who have learned repentance and amendment of life, and who believe truly that their sins are taken away by Christ, and to all those who walk in the resurrection of Jesus Christ, and wish to be buried with Him in death, so that they may be resurrected with Him, and to all those who with this significance request baptism of us and demand it for themselves. This excludes all infant baptism, the highest and chief abomination of the pope. In this you have the foundation and testimony of the apostles. Matt. 28, Mark 16, Acts 2, 8, 16, 19. This we wish to hold simply, yet firmly and with assurance.

Second. We are agreed as follows on the ban: The ban shall be employed with all those who have given themselves to the Lord, to walk in His commandments, and with all those who are baptized into the one body of Christ and who are called brethren or sisters, and yet who slip sometimes and fall into error and sin, being inadvertently overtaken. The same shall be admonished twice in secret and the third time openly disciplined or banned according to the command of Christ. Matt. 18. But this shall be done according to the regulation of the Spirit (Matt. 5) before the breaking of bread, so that we may break and eat one bread, with one mind and in one love, and may drink of one cup.

Third. In the breaking of bread we are of one mind and are

agreed as follows: All those who wish to break one bread in remembrance of the broken body of Christ, and all who wish to drink of one drink as a remembrance of the shed blood of Christ, shall be united beforehand by baptism in one body of Christ which is the church of God and whose Head is Christ. For as Paul points out we cannot at the same time be partakers of the Lord's table and the table of devils; we cannot at the same time drink the cup of the Lord and the cup of the devil. That is, all those who have fellowship with the dead works of darkness have no part in the light. Therefore all who follow the devil and the world have no part with those who are called unto God out of the world. All who lie in evil have no part in the good.

Therefore it is and must be thus: whoever has not been called by one God to one faith, to one baptism, to one Spirit, to one body, with all the children of God's church, cannot be made [into] one bread with them, as indeed must be done if one is truly to break bread according to the command of Christ.

Fourth. We are agreed as follows on separation: A separation shall be made from the evil and from the wickedness which the devil planted in the world; in this manner, simply that we shall not have fellowship with them, the wicked, and not run with them in the multitude of their abominations. This is the way it is: Since all who do not walk in the obedience of faith, and have not united themselves with God so that they wish to do His will, are a great abomination before God, it is not possible for anything to grow or issue from them except abominable things. For truly all creatures are in but two classes, good and bad, believing and unbelieving, darkness and light, the world and those who have come out of the world, God's temple and idols, Christ and Belial; and none can have part with the other.

To us then the command of the Lord is clear when He calls upon us to be separate from the evil and thus He will be our God and we shall be His sons and daughters.

He further admonishes us to withdraw from Babylon and the earthly Egypt that we may not be partakers of the pain and suffering which the Lord will bring upon them.

From all this we should learn that everything which is not united with our God and Christ cannot be other than an abomination which we should shun and flee from. By this is meant all popish and anti-popish works and church services, meetings and church attendance, drinking houses, civic affairs, the commitments made in unbelief and other things of that kind, which are highly regarded by the world and yet are carried on in flat contradiction to the command of God, in accordance with all the unrighteousness which is in the world. From all these things we shall be separated and have no part with them for they are nothing but an abomination, and they are the cause of our being hated before our Christ Jesus, who has set us free from the slavery of the flesh and fitted us for the service of God through the Spirit whom He has given us.

Therefore there will also unquestionably fall from us the unChristian, devilish weapons of force—such as sword, armor and the like, and all their use either for friends or against one's enemies —by virtue of the word of Christ, Resist not him that is evil.

Fifth. We are agreed as follows on pastors in the church of God: The pastor in the church of God shall, as Paul has prescribed, be one who out-and-out has a good report of those who are outside the faith. This office shall be to read, to admonish and teach, to warn, to discipline, to ban in the church, to lead out in prayer for the advancement of all the brethren and sisters, to lift up the bread when it is to be broken, and in all things to see to the care of the body of Christ, in order that it may be built up and developed, and the mouth of the slanderer be stopped.

This one moreover shall be supported of the church which has chosen him, wherein he may be in need, so that he who serves the gospel may life of the gospel as the Lord has ordained. But if a pastor should do something requiring discipline, he shall not be dealt with except on the testimony of two or three witnesses. And when they sin they shall be disciplined before all in order that the others may fear.

But should it happen that through the cross this pastor should be banished or led to the Lord through martyrdom another shall be ordained in his place in the same hour so that God's little flock and people may not be destroyed.

Sixth. We are agreed as follows concerning the sword: The sword is ordained of God outside the perfection of Christ. It punishes and puts to death the wicked, and guards and protects the good. In the law the sword was ordained for the punishment of the wicked and for their death, and the same sword is now ordained to be used by the worldly magistrates.

In the perfection of Christ, however, only the ban is used for a warning and for the excommunication of the one who has sinned, without putting the flesh to death—simply the warning and the command to sin no more.

Now it will be asked by many who do not recognize this as the will of Christ for us, whether a Christian may or should employ the sword against the wicked for the defence and protection of the good, or for the sake of love.

Our reply is unanimously as follows: Christ teaches and commands us to learn of Him, for He is meek and lowly in heart and so shall we find rest to our souls. Also Christ says to the heathenish woman who was taken in adultery, not that one should stone her according to the law of His Father (and yet He says, As the Father has commanded me, thus I do), but in mercy and forgiveness and warning, to sin no more. Such an attitude we also ought to take completely according to the rule of the ban.

Secondly, it will be asked concerning the sword, whether a Christian shall pass sentence in worldly dispute and strike such as unbelievers have with one another. This is our united answer: Christ did not wish to decide or pass judgment between brother and brother in the case of the inheritance, but refused to do so. Therefore we should do likewise.

Thirdly, it will be asked concerning the sword, Shall one be a magistrate if one should be chosen as such? The answer is as follows: They wished to make Christ king, but He fled and did not view it as the arrangement of His Father. Thus shall we do as He did, and follow Him, and so shall we not walk in darkness. For He Himself says, He who wishes to come after me, let him deny himself and take up his cross and follow me. Also, He Himself forbids the employment of the force of the sword saying, The worldly princes lord it over them, etc., but not so shall it be with you. Further, Paul says, Whom God did foreknow He also did predestinate to be conformed to the image of His Son, etc. Also Peter says, Christ has suffered (not ruled) and left us an example, that ye should follow His steps.

Finally it will be observed that it is not appropriate for a Christian to serve as a magistrate because of these points: The government magistracy is according to the flesh, but the Christians' is according to the Spirit; their houses and dwelling remain in this world, but the Christians' are in heaven; their citizenship is in this world, but the Christians' citizenship is in heaven; the weapons of their conflict and war are carnal and against the flesh only, but the Christians' weapons are spiritual, against the fortification of the devil. The worldlings are armed with steel and iron, but the Christians are armed with the armor of God, with truth, righteousness, peace, faith, salvation and the word of God. In brief, as is the mind of Christ toward us, so shall the mind of the members of the body of Christ be through Him in all things, that there may be no schism in the body through which it would be destroyed. For every kingdom divided against itself will be destroyed. Now since Christ is as it is written of Him, His members must also be the same, that His body may remain complete and united to its own advancement and upbuilding.

Seventh. We are agreed as follows concerning the oath: The oath is a confirmation among those who are quarreling or making promises. In the law it is commanded to be performed in God's name, but only in truth, not falsely. Christ, who teaches the perfection of the law, prohibits all swearing to His followers, whether true or false—neither by heaven, nor by the earth, nor by Jerusalem, nor by our head,—and that for the reason which He shortly thereafter gives, For you are not able to make one hair white or black. So you see it is for this reason that all swearing is forbidden: we cannot fulfil that which we promise when we swear, for we cannot change even the very least thing on us.

Now there are some who do not give credence to the simple command of God, but object with this question: Well now, did not God swear to Abraham by Himself (since He was God) when He promised him that He would be with him and that He would be his God if he would keep His commandments—why then should I not also swear when I promise to someone? Answer: Hear what the Scripture says: God, since He wished more abundantly to show unto the heirs the immutability of His counsel, inserted an oath, that by two immutable things (in which it is impossible for God to lie) we might have a strong consolation. Observe the meaning of this Scripture: What God forbids you to do, He has power to do, for everything is possible for Him. God swore an oath to Abraham, says the Scripture, so that He might show that His counsel is immutable. That is, no one can withstand nor thwart His will; therefore He can keep His oath. But we can do nothing, as is said above by Christ, to keep or perform our oaths: therefore we shall not swear at all.

Then others further say as follows: It is not forbidden of God to swear in the New Testament, when it is actually commanded in the Old, but it is forbidden only to swear by heaven, earth, Jerusalem and our head. Answer: Hear the Scripture, He who swears by heaven swears by God's throne and by Him who sitteth thereon. Observe: it is forbidden to swear by heaven, which is only the throne of God: how much more is it forbidden to swear by God himself! Ye fools and blind, which is greater, the throne or Him that sitteth thereon?

Further some say, Because evil is now in the world, and because man needs God for the establishment of the truth, so did the apostles Peter and Paul also swear. Answer: Peter and Paul only testify of that which God promised to Abraham with the oath. They themselves promise nothing, as the example indicates clearly. Testifying and swearing are two different things. For when a person swears he is in the first place promising future things, as Christ was promised to Abraham whom we a long time afterwards received. But when a person bears testimony he is testifying about the present, whether it is good or evil, as Simeon spoke to Mary about Christ and testified, Behold this (child) is set for the fall and rising of many in Israel, and for a sign which shall be spoken against.

Christ also taught us along the same line when He said, Let your communication be Yea, yea; Nay, nay; for whatsoever is more than these cometh of evil. He says, Your speech or word shall be yea and nay. (However) when one does not wish to understand, he remains closed to the meaning. Christ is simply Yea and Nay, and all those who seek Him simply will understand His word. Amen.

⎍⎍⎍⎍⎍⎍⎍⎍⎍⎍⎍⎍⎍⎍⎍⎍⎍⎍⎍⎍

12. Augustin Würzlburger: Proceedings of his trial (1528)*

The suspicion of the authorities concerning the Anabaptists prompted an extensive system at legal conviction. Of the great number of legal documents dealing with the treatment of the Anabaptists a few excerpts from one case (about half of the extant documents) are printed below. They pertain to Augustin Würzlburger, a simple Anabaptist from near Regensburg in South Germany, and reveal the various facets of the legal suppression of deviate religious sentiment in the sixteenth century. As the excerpts show, the suppression was entirely in the hands of the political authorities.

LITERATURE
H. S. Bender & C. H. Smith (eds.), *The Mennonite Encyclopedia* (4 vols., Scottdale, Pennsylvania, 1955–1959).

HANS Sedlmair, of Oberhaim, confesses and states that one Augustin Würzlburger, of Regensburg, had visited him last Lent; he could not recall the exact date. This Augustin had talked about the gospel and asserted that to eat meat during Lent was not sinful. Also, our first baptism was invalid, for God Himself had said: "He who believes and is baptized, shall be saved; he who does not believe, shall be condemned." . . .

Hans Sedlmair further confesses and states that Augustin visited him again on April 14, [1528], at his house at Oberhaim and from a book proclaimed to him and Hans Weber, who was also arrested, the gospel. Augustin asked him if he believed in our Lord Jesus Christ who suffered death and pain on the cross. He answered affirmatively and Würzlburger inquired of him if he

* *Quellen zur Geschichte der Täufer V*. Bayern, II. Abteilung, von K. Schornbaum (Gütersloh, 1951), pp. 27–49. This translation by Hans J. Hillerbrand.

desired from the bottom of his heart to be baptized? He had answered affirmatively. Afterwards Augustin brought water into the stable in a small pitcher, took some water with his hands and baptized him in the name of the Father, Son, and Holy Spirit. . . . After Würzlburger had baptized him, he prohibited him to attend church, unless the gospel was preached. If he went to church, he should not remove his hat. . . .

May 20, 1528. First interrogation

On May 20, in the year of the Lord 1528, Augustin Würzlburger was interrogated by City Councillor Stuchsen.

Augustin Würzlburger, a schoolteacher, states that he was baptized on November 17 by one Leonhart Freisleben near Prul, south of Regensburg. Two other teachers had gone there with him, but were not baptized. Prior to his baptism he had been preached the gospel of all creatures in the name of the Father, Son, and Holy Spirit and was entreated henceforth to sin no more. He should do all in power to bring others to the right path. . . .

During the week of April 5 a letter from the congregation at Augsburg had been sent to him through someone named Hans, who had been schoolteacher at Weiden and had since then traveled to Austria. He, Augustin, or Hans, who had brought the letter, had been elected by the congregation at Augsburg to be an apostle to preach the gospel. Neither of them had wanted to accept this charge and had agreed to draw a lot to decide. They had made lines with chalk and the lot had fallen on him. He had accepted it and during the Easter holidays he traveled to Sussbach, where he had several friends. There he had baptized one Hans Sedlmair and also a weaver. He had also baptized the two sons of Sedlmair, his wife and a daughter, a shoemaker, and a stranger whose name he did not know. . . .

Sedlmair, the weaver, and he were arrested at Sussbach by a ducal official who examined them and then released them with the charge to move away. He, Würzlburger, had instructed his brother Hans, a butcher from Landshut, to die unto the world and to serve God, but he had not baptized him. He had heard, however, that his brother had been arrested; perhaps he had talked too much about the matter. He had also preached the gospel to several people and challenged them to accept baptism according to the word of God. His wife had been baptized by one Burkhart Praun, of Ofen, in their apartment in the house of Wisen without anyone else present.

He stated furthermore that clear scriptural testimony convinced him that he denied God if he desisted from this position. He would rather let himself be hanged. Luther could write in his Postill what he wanted; he would turn it according to his pleasure. One should not take anything away from Scripture. . . .

There were many apostles among them and wherever one is sent, he has to go and preach, even if it should cause death. They did not mean to offend anyone. There was no special directive concerning food; he had eaten meat during Lent when it was available. . . . He said that all this he clearly found in Scripture. If he were taught better and differently, he would desist.

May 20, 1528. Interrogation of
Würzlburger's wife

Barbara, wife of Augustin Würzlburger, says that she only knows about baptism. A certain Burkhart had baptized her in her house in Regensburg in November in the name of the Father, Son, and Holy Spirit. Only her husband was present. Also, she truly knew no one whom her husband had baptized. She did not know who had baptized him. A priest came to her and told her that her husband had baptized several people at Landshut. Also, her husband said to her that he had baptized several women who thus belonged to him; he had become single again. Her husband had told two men about baptism but they had not received it. She could not desist from this teaching and turn against the Lord, her God. She had trusted God and would remain true to Him, for His will was to be done.

May 22, 1528. Questions for the second
interrogation of Würzlburger

1. How he had accepted this unbelief or error? How, or from whom, he had heard, learned and accepted it?

2. What innovations he had accepted and practiced after he had stained himself with rebaptism?

3. By whom he was baptized and with what words he was entreated to accept it?

4. If he himself had requested baptism?

5. Who had been baptized with him?

6. The other leaders, directors, preachers and helpers: who and where they are?

7. The secret assemblies or services attended by him with his fellows: what sign they used to recognize one another?

8. If he himself had baptized and preached?

9. Their order and regulations concerning common goods?

10. Confession, Mass, reception of the sacrament and church attendance?

11. Why he had accepted this opinion and what he had hoped for?

12. How often and at what places, here at Landshut or elsewhere in Bavaria, he had preached; who was present at this preaching; also from whom he had heard this teaching?

13. The present whereabouts of his associate in his preaching and rebaptizing at Oberhaim. Had this associate also preached in Bavaria and whom had he rebaptized?

14. How often his brother had been present at his preaching? Was he rebaptized by him or others? . . .

16. What were his intentions and why he had accepted this preaching and rebaptism? Had he accepted it for the purpose of insurrection and other evil doings? Whom he had baptized in Bavaria, their names and residence?

17. If he revoked such opinion and repented of it?

May 25, 1528. Second interrogation
of Würzlburger

In response to the first article Augustin said that he had been told the gospel by those who recently had been expelled from Regensburg because of baptism. He had also read for himself and examined the Scriptures and he had found that this alone was the divine truth. Each one must be persecuted and suffer, for the world has no kinship with the Christian. He thinks nothing of his first baptism; one must not baptize unbelievers. Only after one believes and the gospel is preached is one to be baptized, if it is so desired. . . .

Concerning the second question he said that he did not accept anything new except that he would live only for God and not unto himself; for this reason he was baptized. Concerning the third question he said that he was baptized by Leonhart Freisleben, one of those recently expelled because of baptism, at Prul. This had been in November and he was baptized according to God's command in the gospel according to Matthew and Mark, in the name of the Father, Son, and Holy Spirit. There were four of them and one woman who had been expelled from Regensburg on account of baptism.

Fourth: He said yes, since he knew this to be the divine truth he had desired baptism, and nothing else.

Fifth: He said that only he had been baptized at that time.

Sixth: He said that he did not know any, for he had remained here and had only traveled to such places in Bavaria, where there were none of them. He knew only one Burkhart Praun, of Ofen, a tall man, about thirty years of age, whom he had met at Regensburg last winter. He was a leader but had told him nothing but what the one who had baptized him had also told him. Since that time he had heard nothing from him. Also, it was true that the congregation at Augsburg had sent one called Hans to Regensburg with a letter. More than a year ago he had been a choirmaster at Regensburg and before that a schoolteacher at Weiden. The letter had stated that the congregation had named him or Hans to the office of apostle to preach the gospel. They had cast lots as to who should accept the office, and the lot had fallen to him. For this office he had been given the instruction that he should proclaim the divine truth.

Seventh: That he knew of no secret assembly or gathering, nor of a sign by which they might recognize one another.

Eighth: That he had preached and baptized. First, he had baptized a cousin, at Suspach, called Sedlmair. He had preached to him and to his household during the Easter holidays. Present had been Sedlmair, his wife, two sons and a daughter, also a weaver from Suspach, a miller whom he had not known. . . . He had preached to them the gospel of all creatures, that they might recognize God and also how they were to live, and he had also told them that if they follow Christ they would be persecuted. If they wanted to accept this, they should do it. Thereupon they did accept it and

surrendered to the discipline of the Father and the pure word of
God to live henceforth according to the commands of God. . . .

June 2, 1528. Communication of the
Dukes of Bavaria to the Regensburg
City Council

We have received the interrogation records of Augustin Würzlburger together with a letter from our officials who note your
concern and eagerness. . . . Würzlburger has been shown by
his own confession to be a leader and preacher of the heretical
sect of the Anabaptists, against the order of the holy Christian
church and the imperial edict and mandate. He has also caused
several people to be executed despite their revocation. Therefore
it is desired that Würzlburger be on the basis of his own confession and evil heretical misdemeanor sentenced to death according to imperial law. You are not to refuse this or show any mercy.

June 5, 1528. Regensburg City
Council to the Dukes of Bavaria

Your letter concerning Augustin Würzlburger, instructing us to
sentence him to death on the basis of his own confession concerning rebaptism, has caused us great concern. We do not wish
to refuse anything to you either in this case or any other matter
and we are grieved indeed by the Augustin Würzlburger's error,
since he has no other fault than this concerning rebaptism and the
faith. We cannot understand why we are to sentence him to
death. We want to make him desist from his opinion and error.
If this should be unsuccessful, seek the counsel of other Christian
and learned men. . . .

October 10, 1528

On Saturday, October 10, Augustin N., a teacher and Anabaptist,
was led to the city hall, placed on a bench, where he was charged
with having been rebaptized and himself afterwards rebaptizing
others, nine persons all in all. . . . Even though he had deserved,
according to imperial law, death by burning, the Council had
mercifully ruled that he was to be executed by beheading. This
happened . . . the henchman leading him like a butcher leads a
calf. He did not say a word even as no one spoke to him.

⎍⎍⎍⎍⎍⎍⎍⎍⎍⎍⎍⎍⎍⎍⎍⎍⎍⎍⎍⎍

13. Peter Riedemann: *Account of Our Religion* (c. 1545)*

The Hutterite Anabaptists in Moravia developed a unique characteristic of their own. Relatively unmolested by the authorities, they were able to inhabit separate communities and live according to their theological insights. Elsewhere the Anabaptists were like small islands in a huge ocean; in Moravia they had their own corporate and social life. They laid great stress upon communal living, and following what was to them a biblical precedent they practiced complete sharing of goods.

The theological justification for this practice was described in the *Account of Our Religion,* the major confessional document of sixteenth century Hutterite Anabaptism. Its author was Peter Riedemann, who was a leader of the Hutterites from 1542 to his death in 1556 and who composed a number of other theological writings. Reprinted here is the entire section on the Community of Goods.

LITERATURE
R. Friedmann, *Hutterite Studies* (Goshen, 1961).

Concerning community of goods

Now, since all the saints have fellowship in holy things, that is in God, who also hath given to them all things in His Son Christ Jesus—which gift none should have for himself, but each for the other; as Christ also hath nought for Himself, but hath everything for us, even so all the members of His body have nought for themselves, but for the whole body, for all the members. For His gifts are not sanctified and given to one member alone, or for one member's sake, but for the whole body with its members.

Now, since all God's gifts—not only spiritual, but also material

---

* *Account of Our Religion, Doctrine and Faith, Given by Peter Rideman of the Brothers Whom Men Call Hutterians* (London, 1950), pp. 102–21.

things—are given to man, not that he should have them for himself or alone but with all his fellows, therefore the communion of saints itself must show itself not only in spiritual but also in temporal things; that as Paul saith, one might not have abundance and another suffer want, but that there may be equality. This he showeth from the law touching manna, in that he who gathered much had nothing over, whereas he who gathered little had no less, since each was given what he needed according to the measure.

Furthermore, one seeth in all things created, which testify to us still today, that God from the beginning ordained nought private for man, but all things to be common. But through wrong taking, since man took what he should not and forsook what he should take, he drew such things to himself and made them his property, and so grew and became hardened therein. Through such wrong taking and collecting of created things he hath been led so far from God that he hath even forgotten the Creator, and hath even raised up and honored as God the created things which had been put under and made subject to him. And such is still the case if one steppeth out of God's order and forsaketh the same.

Now, however, as hath been said, created things which are too high for man to draw within his grasp and collect, such as the sun with the whole course of the heavens, day, air and such like, show that not they alone, but all other created things are likewise made common to man. That they have thus remained and are not possessed by man is due to their being too high for him to bring under his power, otherwise—so evil had he become through wrong taking—he would have drawn them to himself as well as the rest and made them his property.

That this is so, however, and that the rest is just as little made by God for man's private possession, is shown in that man must forsake all other created things as well as this when he dies, and can carry nothing with him to use as his own. For which reason Christ also called temporal all things foreign to man's essential nature, and saith, "If ye are not faithful in what is not your own, who will entrust to you what is your own?"

Now, because what is temporal doth not belong to us, but is foreign to our true nature, the law commandeth that none covet strange possessions, that is, set his heart upon and cleave to what is temporal and alien. Therefore whosoever will cleave to Christ and follow Him must forsake such taking of created things and property, as He Himself also saith, "Whosoever forsaketh not all that he hath cannot be my disciple." For if a man is to be renewed again into the likeness of God, he must put off all that leadeth him from him—that is the grasping and drawing to himself of created things—for he cannot otherwise attain God's likeness. Therefore Christ saith, "Whosoever shall not receive the kingdom of God as a little child shall not enter therein," or, "Except ye overcome yourselves and become as little children, ye shall not enter into the kingdom of heaven."

Now, he who thus becometh free from created things can then grasp what is true and divine; and when he graspeth it and it becometh his treasure, he turneth his heart toward it, emptieth himself of all else and taketh nought as his, and regardeth it no longer as his but as of all God's children. Therefore we say that as all the saints have community in spiritual gifts, still much more should they show this in material things, and not ascribe the same to and covet them for themselves, for they are not their own; but regard them as of all God's children, that they may thereby show that they are partakers in the community of Christ and are renewed into God's likeness. For the more man yet cleaveth to created things, appropriateth and ascribeth such to himself, the further doth he show himself to be from the likeness of God and the community of Christ.

For this reason the Holy Spirit also at the beginning of the church began such community right gloriously again, so that none said that aught of the things that he possessed was his own, but they had all things in common; and it is his will that this might still be kept, as Paul saith, "Let none seek his own profit but the profit of another," or, "Let none seek what benefiteth himself but what benefiteth many." Where this is not the case it is a blemish upon the church which ought verily to be corrected. If one should say, it was so nowhere except in Jerusalem, therefore it is now not necessary, we say, Even if it were nowhere but in Jerusalem, it followeth not that it ought not to be so now. For neither apostles nor churches were lacking, but rather the opportunity, manner and time.

Therefore this should be no cause for us to hesitate, but rather should it move us to more and better zeal and diligence, for the Lord now giveth us both time and cause so to do. That there was no lack of either apostles or churches is shown by the zeal of both. For the apostles have pointed the people thereto with all diligence and most faithfully prescribed true surrender, as all their epistles still prove today. And the people obeyed with zeal, as Paul beareth witness—especially of those of Macedonia—saying, "I tell you of the grace that is given to the churches in Macedonia. For their joy was the most rapturous since they had been tried by much affliction, and their poverty, though it was indeed deep, overflowed as riches in all simplicity. For I bear witness that with all their power, yea, and beyond their power, they were themselves willing, and besought us earnestly with much admonition to receive the benefit and community of help which is given to the saints; and not as we had hoped, but first gave themselves to the Lord, and then to us also, by the will of God."

Here one can well see with what inclined and willing hearts the churches were ready to keep community not only in spiritual but also in material things, for they desired to follow the master Christ, and become like Him and one with Him, who Himself went before us in such a way, and commanded us to follow Him.

⎍⎍⎍⎍⎍⎍⎍⎍⎍⎍⎍⎍⎍⎍⎍⎍⎍⎍⎍⎍⎍⎍⎍⎍

14. Elizabeth, a Dutch Anabaptist martyr: A letter (1573)*

No matter where it appeared and what form it took, sixteenth century radicalism was severely persecuted by governmental authorities both Catholic and Protestant. In some instances theological deviation provided the rationale for this persecution, in others the fear that the religious radicals intended to overthrow existing law and order. Thus the radicals were rarely free to exercise their faith; usually they were in danger of being arrested and thrown into dungeons; often they were put to the stake. The latter formed the company of the martyrs.

* Thieleman van Braght, *The Bloody Theater or The Martyrs' Mirror* (Scottdale, Pennsylvania, 1951), pp. 984–87.

The documents concerning the Anabaptist martyrs were collected in the seventeenth century by the Dutchman Thieleman van Braght in an impressive volume entitled *The Bloody Theater or The Martyrs' Mirror*. Though generally an accurate historical guide to the suppression and persecution, this martyrology meant to inspire rather than inform the reader. Reprinted below is the letter of a Dutch Anabaptist woman to her infant daughter, written just before her execution.

LITERATURE

Thieleman van Braght, *The Bloody Theater or The Martyrs' Mirror* (Scottdale, Pennsylvania, 1951).

*[Testament] written to Janneken my
own dearest daughter, while I was
(unworthily) confined for the
Lord's sake, in prison, at
Antwerp, A.D. 1573*

THE true love of God and wisdom of the Father strengthen you in virtue, my dearest child; the Lord of heaven and earth, the God of Abraham, the God of Isaac, and the God of Jacob, the Lord in Israel, keep you in His virtue, and strengthen and confirm your understanding in His truth. My dear little child, I commend you to the almighty, great and terrible God, who only is wise, that He will keep you, and let you grow up in His fear, or that He will take you home in your youth, this is my heart's request of the Lord: you who are yet so young, and whom I must leave here in this wicked, evil, perverse world.

Since, then, the Lord has so ordered and foreordained it, that I must leave you here, and you are here deprived of father and mother, I will commend you to the Lord; let Him do with you according to His holy will. He will govern you, and be a Father to you, so that you shall have no lack here, if you only fear God; for He will be the Father of the orphans and the Protector of the widows.

Hence, my dear lamb, I who am imprisoned and bound here for the Lord's sake, can help you in no other way; I had to leave your father for the Lord's sake, and could keep him only a short time.

We were permitted to live together only half a year, after which we were apprehended, because we sought the salvation of our souls. They took him from me, not knowing my condition, and I had to remain in imprisonment, and see him go before me; and it was a great grief to him, that I had to remain here in prison. And now that I have abided the time, and borne you under my heart with great sorrow for nine months, and given birth to you here in prison, in great pain, they have taken you from me. Here I lie, expecting death every morning, and shall now soon follow your dear father. And I, your dear mother, write you, my dearest child, something for a remembrance, that you will thereby remember your dear father and your dear mother.

Since I am now delivered up to death, and must leave you here alone, I must through these lines cause you to remember, that when you have attained your understanding, you endeavor to fear God, and see and examine why and for whose name we both died; and be not ashamed to confess us before the world, for you must know that it is not for the sake of any evil. Hence be not ashamed of us; it is the way which the prophets and the apostles went, and the narrow way which leads into eternal life, for there shall no other way be found by which to be saved.

Hence, my young lamb, for whose sake I still have, and have had, great sorrow, seek, when you have attained your understanding, this narrow way, though there is sometimes much danger in it according to the flesh, as we may see and read, if we diligently examine and read the Scriptures, that much is said concerning the cross of Christ. And there are many in this world who are enemies of the cross, who seek to be free from it among the world, and to escape it. But, my dear child, if we would with Christ seek and inherit salvation, we must also help bear His cross; and this is the cross which He would have us bear: to follow His footsteps, and to help bear His reproach; for Christ Himself says: "Ye shall be persecuted, killed, and dispersed for my name's sake." Yea, He Himself went before us in this way of reproach, and left us an example, that we should follow His steps; for, for His sake all must be forsaken, father, mother, sister, brother, husband, child, yea, one's own life. . . .

Thus, my dear child, it is now fulfilled in your dear father and mother. It was indeed prophesied to us beforehand, that this was awaiting us; but not everyone is chosen hereunto, nor expects it; the Lord has chosen us hereunto. Hence, when you have attained your understanding, follow this example of your father and mother. And, my dear child, this is my request of you, since you are still very little and young; I wrote this when you were but one month old. As I am soon now to offer up my sacrifice, by the help of the Lord, I leave you this: "That you fulfil my request, always uniting with them that fear God; and do not regard the pomp and boasting of the world, nor the great multitude, whose way leads to the abyss of hell, but look at the little flock of Israelites, who have no freedom anywhere, and must always flee from one land to the other, as Abraham did; that you may hereafter obtain your father-land; for if you seek your salvation, it is easy to perceive which is the way that leads to life, or the way that leads into hell. Above all things, seek the kingdom of heaven and His righteousness; and whatever you need besides shall be added unto you. Matt. 6:33."

Further, my dear child, I pray you, that wherever you live when you are grown up, and begin to have understanding, you conduct yourself well and honestly, so that no one need have cause to complain of you. And always be faithful, taking good heed not to wrong any one. Learn to carry your hands always uprightly, and see that you like to work, for Paul says: "If any will not work, neither shall he eat." 2 Thess. 3:10. And Peter says: "He that will love life, and see good days, let him refrain his tongue from evil." 1 Pet. 3:10.

Hence, my dear Janneken, do not accustom your mouth to filthy talk, nor to ugly words that are not proper, nor to lies; for a liar has no part in the kingdom of heaven; for it is written: "The mouth that lieth slayeth the soul." Hence beware of this, and run not in the street as other bad children do; rather take up a book, and learn to seek there that which concerns your salvation.

And where you have your home, obey those whose bread you eat. If they speak evil, do you speak well. And learn always to love to be doing something; and do not think yourself too good for anything, nor exalt yourself, but condescend to the lowly, and always honor the aged wherever you are.

I leave you here; oh, that it had pleased the Lord, that I might have brought you up; I should so gladly have done my best with respect to it; but it seems that it is not the Lord's will. And though it had not come thus, and I had remained with you for a time, the Lord could still take me from you, and then, too, you should have to be without me, even as it has now gone with your father and myself, that we could live together but so short a time, when we were so well joined since the Lord had so well mated us, that we would not have forsaken each other for the whole world, and yet we had to leave each other for the Lord's sake. So I must also leave you here, my dearest lamb; the Lord that created and made you now takes me from you, it is His holy will. I must now pass through this narrow way which the prophets and martyrs of Christ passed through, and many thousands who put off the mortal clothing, who died here for Christ, and now they wait under the altar till their number shall be fulfilled, of which number your dear father is one. And I am now on the point of following him, for I am delivered up to death, as it appears in the eyes of man; but if it were not the will of the Lord (though it seems that I am delivered up to death), He could yet easily deliver me out of their hands and give me back to you, my child. Even as the Lord returned to Abraham his son Isaac, so He could still easily do it; He is still the same God that delivered Daniel out of the lion's den, and the three young men out of the fiery furnace; He could still easily deliver me out of the hands of man. . . .

If they have persecuted the Lord, they will also persecute us; if they have hated Him, they will also hate us; and this they do because they have not known my Father, nor me, says the Almighty Lord. For His kingdom was not of this world; had His kingdom been of this world, the world would have loved Him; but because His kingdom was not of this world; therefore the world hated Him. So it also is now: since our kingdom is not of this world, the world will hate us; but it is better for us to be despised here by the world, than that we should hereafter have to mourn forever. But they that will not taste the bitter here, can hereafter not expect eternal life; for we know that Paul says, that all that will live godly in Christ Jesus shall be persecuted and be a prey to everyone.

Thus, my dear child, this way the prophets and apostles and many thousands of other Godfearing persons went before us, for an example unto us; and Christ Himself did not spare Himself for us, but delivered up Himself unto death for our sakes—how then

should He not give us all things? Hence, my dearest lamb, seek to
follow this way, this I pray you, as much as you value your salvation; for this is the only way which leads to eternal life, yea,
there is no other way by which we can be saved than only through
Jesus Christ, as Paul says: "Other foundation can no man lay than
that is laid, which is Jesus Christ" (1 Cor. 3:11). . . .

My dear lamb, we can merit nothing, but must through grace
inherit salvation; hence always endeavor to fear God, for the fear
of the Lord is the beginning of wisdom, and he that fears the Lord
will do good, and it will be well with him in this world and in
that which is to come. And always join those that seek to fear the
Lord from the heart, and be not conformed to the world, to do
as she does, nor walk in any improper course of life; for the world
shall pass away, and all the nations that serve her shall perish with
her. Nor have fellowship with the unfruitful works of darkness,
but rather reprove them; and be transformed by the renewing of
your life, that you may show forth the virtues in which God has
called you.

O my dearest lamb, that you might know the truth when you
have attained your understanding, and that you might follow
your dear father and mother, who went before you; for your
dear father demonstrated with his blood that it is the genuine
truth, and I also hope to attest the same with my blood, though
flesh and blood must remain on the posts and on the stake, well
knowing that we shall meet hereafter. Do you also follow us my
dear lamb, that you too may come where we shall be, and that we
may find one another there, where the Lord shall say: "Come, ye
blessed of my Father, inherit the kingdom prepared for you from
the beginning." . . .

I leave you here among my friends; I hope that my father, and
my stepmother, and my brothers, and my sisters will do the best
with you as long as they live. Be subject and obedient to them in
everything, so far as it is not contrary to God. I leave you what
comes from my mother's death, namely, thirty guilders and over;
I do not know how much it is, since I have been long imprisoned
here, and do not know what it has all cost. But I hope that Grietge,
my dear sister, who has shown me so much friendship, will do her
best to give you what belongs to you. And as to what may come
to you from your father, I do not know, since I can learn nothing

about his parents, because it is so far from here; if they should inquire after you, my friends may do the best in the matter.

And now, Janneken, my dear lamb, who are yet very little and young, I leave you this letter, together with a gold real, which I had with me in prison, and this I leave you for a perpetual adieu, and for a testament; that you may remember me by it, as also by this letter. Read it, when you have understanding, and keep it as long as you live in remembrance of me and of your father, if peradventure you might be edified by it. And I herewith bid you adieu, my dear Janneken Munstdorp, and kiss you heartily, my dear lamb, with a perpetual kiss of peace. Follow me and your father, and be not ashamed to confess us before the world, for we were not ashamed to confess our faith before the world, and this adulterous generation; hence I pray you, that you be not ashamed to confess our faith, since it is the true evangelical faith, another than which shall never be found.

Let it be your glory, that we did not die for any evil doing, and strive to do likewise, though they should also seek to kill you. And on no account cease to love God above all, for no one can prevent you from fearing God. If you follow that which is good, and seek peace, and ensue it, you shall receive the crown of eternal life; this crown I wish you and the crucified, bleeding, naked, despised, rejected and slain Jesus Christ for your bridegroom.

IV. *John Calvin*

⊔⊔⊔⊓⊔⊓⊔⊓⊔⊓⊔⊓⊔⊓⊔⊓⊔⊓⊔⊓⊔⊓⊔⊓⊔⊓⊔⊓⊔⊓⊔⊓⊔⊓⊔⊓⊔⊓⊔⊓⊓⊓⊐

15. John Calvin: *Reply to Sadoleto* (1540)*

Though overshadowed by the majestic *Institutes of the Christian Religion*, Calvin's *Reply to Sadoleto* is an outstanding expression of his thought, and one of the classic apologies for the Reformation. Cardinal Jacobo Sadoleto, archbishop of Carpentras, was one of the learned and spiritual representatives of the Catholic church of the time. Combining learning and piety with practical churchmanship, he had written an open letter to the Genevan City Council in 1539, skilfully seeking to make the best of the religious uncertainty which had beset Geneva after Calvin's departure one year earlier. Sadoleto bluntly acknowledged the sad state of the Catholic church and agreed that ecclesiastical reform was needed. Still, he argued, it was not necessary to reject the customs of centuries nor to sever the ties with the Roman church. Sadoleto's letter called for a reply, and even though Calvin no longer had any formal ties with Geneva, in September, 1539 he supplied it. In January, 1540 the Genevan Council ordered the reply printed.

Calvin's tract is a dispassionate discussion of the question of whether the ecclesiastical schism was necessary. The resoundingly affirmative answer insisted that the issue was not so much ecclesiastical abuses (which admittedly could be corrected by the church), but the very heart of Catholic thought.

Reprinted below is a slightly condensed version of the entire tract.

LITERATURE
John Calvin & Jacopo Sadoleto, *A Reformation Debate: Sadoleto's Letter to the Genevans and Calvin's Reply*, ed. John C. Olin (New York: Harper Torchbooks, 1966).

* John Calvin & Jacobo Sadoleto, *A Reformation Debate. Sadoleto's Letter to the Genevans and Calvin's Reply*, John C. Olin (ed.), (New York: Harper Torchbooks, 1966), pp. 53–90.

Although your letter has many windings, its whole purport substantially is to recover the Genevese to the power of the Roman pontiff, or to what you call the faith and obedience of the church. But as, from the nature of the case, their feelings required to be softened, you preface with a long oration concerning the incomparable value of eternal life. You afterward come nearer to the point, when you show that there is nothing more pestiferous to souls than a perverse worship of God; and again, that the best rule for the due worship of God is that which is prescribed by the church, and that, therefore, there is no salvation for those who have violated the unity of the church unless they repent. But you next contend that separation from your fellowship is manifest revolt from the church, and then that the gospel which the Genevese received from us is nothing but a large farrago of impious dogmas. From this you infer what kind of divine judgment awaits them if they attend not to your admonitions. But as it was of the greatest importance to your cause to throw complete discredit on our words, you labor to the utmost to fill them with sinister suspicions of the zeal which they saw us manifest for their salvation. Accordingly, you captiously allege that we had no other end in view than to gratify our avarice and ambition. Since, then, your device has been to cast some stain upon us, in order that the minds of your readers, being preoccupied with hatred might give us no credit, I will, before proceeding to other matters, briefly reply to that objection. . . .

Come and consider with me for a little what the honors and powers are which we have gained. All our hearers will bear us witness that we did not covet or aspire to any other riches or dignities than those which fell to our lot. Since in all our words and deeds they not only perceived no trace of the ambition with which you charge us, but, on the contrary, saw clear evidence of our abhorring it with our whole heart, you cannot hope that by one little word their minds are to be so fascinated as to credit a futile slander in opposition to the many certain proofs with which we furnished them. And to appeal to facts rather than words, the power of the sword, and other parts of civil jurisdiction, which bishops and priests under the semblance of immunity had wrested from the magistrate and claimed for themselves, have not we restored to the magistrate? All their usurped instruments of tyranny and ambition have not we detested and struggled to abolish? If there was any hope of rising, why did we not craftily dissemble, so that those powers might have passed to us along with the office of governing the church? And why did we make such exertion to overturn the whole of that dominion, or rather butchery, which they exercised upon souls, without any sanction from the word of God? How did we not consider that it was just so much lost to ourselves? In regard to ecclesiastical revenues, they are still in a great measure swallowed up by these whirlpools. But if there was a hope that they will one day be deprived of them (as at length they certainly must), why did we not devise a way by which they might come to us? But when with clear voice we denounced as a thief any bishop who, out of ecclesiastical revenues, appropriated more to his own use than was necessary for a frugal and sober subsistence; when we protested that the church was exposed to a deadly poison, so long as pastors were loaded with an affluence under which they themselves might ultimately sink; when we declared it inexpedient that these revenues should fall into their possession; finally, when we counseled that as much should be distributed to ministers as might suffice for a frugality befitting their order, not superabound for luxury, and that the rest should be dispensed according to the practice of the ancient church; when we showed that men of weight ought to be elected to manage these revenues, under an obligation to account annually to the church and the magistracy, was this to entrap any of these for ourselves, or was it not rather voluntarily to shake ourselves free of them? All these things, indeed, demonstrate not what we are, but what we wished to be. But if these things are so plainly and generally known that not one iota can be denied, with what face can you proceed to upbraid us with aspiring to extraordinary wealth and power? . . .

I pass in silence many other invectives which you thunder out against us (open-mouthed, as it is said). You call us crafty men, enemies of Christian unity and peace, innovators on things ancient and well-established, seditious, alike pestiferous to souls, and destructive both publicly and privately to society at large. Had you wished to escape rebuke, you either ought not, for the purpose of exciting prejudice, to have attributed to us a magniloquent tongue, or you ought to have kept your own magniloquence considerably more under check. I am unwilling, however, to dwell on each of these points; only I would have you to consider how unbecoming, not to say illiberal, it is thus in many words to accuse the innocent of things which by one word can be instantly refuted; although to inflict injury on man is a small matter when compared with the indignity of that contumely, which, when you come to the question, you offer to Christ and His word. When the Genevese, instructed by our preaching, escaped from the gulf of error in which they were immersed, and betook themselves to a purer teaching of the gospel, you call it defection from the truth of God; when they threw off the tyranny of the Roman pontiff, in order that they might establish among themselves a better form of church, you call it a desertion from the church. Come, then, and let us discuss both points in their order.

I have also no difficulty in conceding to you that there is nothing more perilous to our salvation than a preposterous and perverse worship of God. The primary rudiments by which we are wont to train to piety those whom we wish to gain as disciples to Christ are these; viz., not to frame any new worship of God for themselves at random, and after their own pleasure, but to know that the only legitimate worship is that which He Himself approved from the beginning. For we maintain what the sacred oracle declared, that obedience is more excellent than any sacrifice (1 Sam. 15:22). In short, we train them by every means to be contented with the one rule of worship which they have received from His mouth, and bid adieu to all fictitious worship.

Therefore, Sadoleto, when you uttered this voluntary confession, you laid the foundation of my defense. For if you admit it to be a fearful destruction to the soul when, by false opinions, divine truth is turned into a lie, it now only remains for us to inquire which of the two parties retains that worship of God which is alone legitimate. In order that you may claim it for your party, you assume that the most certain rule of worship is that which is prescribed by the church, although, as if we here opposed you, you bring the matter under consideration in the manner which is usually observed in regard to doubtful questions. But, Sadoleto, as I see you toiling in vain, I will relieve you from all trouble on this head. You are mistaken in supposing that we desire to lead away the people from that method of worshiping God which the Catholic church always observed. You either labor under a delusion as to the term *church*, or, at least, knowingly and willingly give it a gloss. I will immediately show the latter to be the case, though it may also be that you are somewhat in error. First, in defining the term, you omit what would have helped you in no small degree to the right understanding of it. When you describe it as that which in all parts, as well as at the present time in every region of the earth, being united and consenting in Christ, has been always and everywhere directed by the one Spirit of Christ, what comes of the word of the Lord, that clearest of all marks, and which the Lord himself, in pointing out the church, so often recommends to us? For seeing how dangerous it would be to boast of the Spirit without the word, He declared that the church is indeed governed by the Holy Spirit, but in order that that government might not be vague and unstable, He annexed it to the word. For this reason Christ exclaims that those who are of God hear the word of God—that His sheep are those which recognize His voice as that of their Shepherd, and any other voice as that of a stranger (John 10:27). For this reason the Spirit, by the mouth of Paul, declares (Eph. 2:20) that the church is built upon the foundation of the apostles and prophets. Also, that the church is made holy to the Lord, by the washing of water in the word of life. The same thing is declared still more clearly by the mouth of Peter, when he teaches that people are regenerated to God by that incorruptible seed (1 Pet. 1:23). In short, why is the preaching of the gospel so often styled the kingdom of God, but because it is the scepter by which the heavenly king rules His people?

Nor will you find this in the apostolical writings only, but whenever the prophets foretell the renewal of the church, or its extension over the whole globe, they always assign the first place to the word. For they tell that from Jerusalem will issue forth living water which, being divided into four rivers, will inundate the whole earth (Zech. 14:8). And what these living waters are they themselves explain when they say, "The law will come forth from Zion, and the word of the Lord from Jerusalem" (Is. 2:3). Well, then, does Chrysostom admonish us to reject all who, under the pretense of the Spirit, lead us away from the simple doctrine of the gospel? . . . As if those who seek the way of God were standing where two ways meet and destitute of any certain sign, you are forced to introduce them as hesitating whether it be more expedient to follow the authority of the church, or to listen to those whom you call the inventors of new dogmas. Had you known, or been unwilling to disguise the fact, that the Spirit goes before the church, to enlighten her in understanding the word, while the word itself is like the Lydian stone, by which she tests all doctrines, would you have taken refuge in that most perplexing and thorny question? Learn, then, by your own experience, that it is no less unreasonable to boast of the Spirit without the word than it would be absurd to bring forward the word itself without the Spirit. Now, if you can bear to receive a truer definition of the church than your own, say, in future, that it is the society of all the saints, a society which, spread over the whole world, and existing in all ages, yet bound together by the one doctrine and the one Spirit of Christ, cultivates and observes unity of faith and brotherly concord. With this church we deny that we have any disagreement. Nay, rather, as we revere her as our mother, so we desire to remain in her bosom.

But here you bring a charge against us. For you teach that all which has been approved for fifteen hundred years or more, by the uniform consent of the faithful, is, by our headstrong rashness, torn up and destroyed. Here I will not require you to deal truly and candidly by us (though this should be spontaneously offered by a philosopher, not to say a Christian). I will only ask you not to stoop to an illiberal indulgence in calumny, which, even though we be silent, must be extremely injurious to your reputation with grave and honest men. You know, Sadoleto, and if you venture to deny, I will make it palpable to all that you knew, yet cunningly and craftily disguised the fact, not only that our agreement with antiquity is far closer than yours, but that all we have attempted has been to renew that ancient form of the church, which, at first sullied and distorted by illiterate men of indifferent character, was afterward flagitiously mangled and almost destroyed by the Roman pontiff and his faction.

I will not press you so closely as to call you back to that form which the apostles instituted (though in it we have the only model of a true church, and whosoever deviates from it in the smallest degree is in error), but to indulge you so far, place, I pray, before your eyes, that ancient form of the church, such as their writings prove it to have been in the age of Chrysostom and Basil, among the Greeks, and of Cyprian, Ambrose, and Augustine, among the Latins; after so doing, contemplate the ruins of that church, as now surviving among yourselves. Assuredly, the difference will appear as great as that which the prophets describe between the famous church which flourished under David and Solomon, and that which under Zedekiah and Jehoiakim had lapsed into every kind of superstition, and utterly vitiated the purity of divine worship. Will you here give the name of an enemy of antiquity to him who, zealous for ancient piety and holiness, and dissatisfied with the state of matters as existing in a dissolute and depraved church, attempts to ameliorate its condition, and restore it to pristine splendor?

Since there are three things on which the safety of the church is founded, viz., doctrine, discipline, and the sacraments, and to these a fourth is added, viz., ceremonies, by which to exercise the people in offices of piety, in order that we may be most sparing of the honor of your church, by which of these things would you have us to judge her? The truth of prophetical and evangelical doctrine, on which the church ought to be founded, has not only in a great measure perished in your church, but is violently driven away by fire and sword. Will you obtrude upon me, for the church, a body which furiously persecutes everything sanctioned by our religion, both as delivered by the oracles of God, and embodied in the writings of holy Fathers, and approved by ancient councils? Where, pray, exist among you any vestiges of that true and holy discipline which the ancient bishops exercised in the church? Have you not scorned all their institutions? Have you not trampled all the canons under foot? Then, your nefarious profanation of the sacraments I cannot think of without the utmost horror.

Of ceremonies, indeed, you have more than enough, but for the most part so childish in their import, and vitiated by innumerable forms of superstition, as to be utterly unavailing for the preservation of the church. None of these things, you must be aware, is exaggerated by me in a captious spirit. They all appear so openly that they may be pointed out with the finger wherever there are eyes to behold them. Now, if you please, test us in the same way. You will, assuredly, fall far short of making good the charges which you have brought against us.

In the sacraments, all we have attempted is to restore the native purity from which they had degenerated, and so enable them to resume their dignity. Ceremonies we have in a great measure abolished, but we were compelled to do so; partly because by their multitude they had degenerated into a kind of Judaism, partly because they had filled the minds of the people with superstition, and could not possibly remain without doing the greatest injury to the piety which it was their office to promote. Still we have retained those which seemed sufficient for the circumstances of the times.

That our discipline is not such as the ancient church professed we do not deny. But with what fairness is a charge of subverting discipline brought against us by those who themselves have utterly abolished it, and in our attempts to reinstate it in its rights have hitherto opposed us? As to our doctrine, we hesitate not to appeal to the ancient church. And since, for the sake of example, you have touched on certain heads, as to which you thought had some ground for accusing us, I will briefly show how unfairly and falsely you allege that these are things which have been devised by us against the opinion of the church.

Before descending to particulars, however, I have already cautioned you, and would have you again and again consider with what reason you can charge it upon our people, as a fault, that they have studied to explain the Scriptures. For you are aware that by this study they have thrown such light on the word of God, that, in this respect, even Envy herself is ashamed to defraud them of all praise. You are just as uncandid when you aver that we have seduced the people by thorny and subtle questions, and so enticed them by that philosophy of which Paul bids Christians beware. What? Do you remember what kind of time it was when our [reformers] appeared, and what kind of doctrine candidates for the ministry learned in the schools? You yourself know that it was mere sophistry, and sophistry so twisted, involved, tortuous, and puzzling, that scholastic theology might well be described as a species of secret magic. . . .

Not to go over every point, what sermons in Europe then exhibited that simplicity with which Paul wishes a Christian people to be always occupied? Nay, what one sermon was there from which old wives might not carry off more whimsies than they could devise at their own fireside in a month? For as sermons were then usually divided, the first half was devoted to those misty questions of the schools which might astonish the rude populace, while the second contained sweet stories, or not unamusing speculations, by which the hearers might be kept on the alert. Only a few expressions were thrown in from the word of God, that by their majesty they might procure credit for these frivolities. But as soon as our [reformers] raised the standard, all these absurdities, in one moment, disappeared from amongst us. Your preachers, again, partly profited by our books, and partly compelled by shame and the general murmur, conformed to our example, though they still, with open throat, exhale the old absurdity. Hence, any one who compares our method of procedure with the old method, or with that which is still in repute among you, will perceive that you have done us no small injustice. . . .

Even you yourself afterwards acquit us by your own testimony; for among those of our doctrines which you have thought proper to assail, you do not adduce one, the knowledge of which is not essentially necessary for the edification of the church.

You, in the first place, touch upon justification by faith, the first and keenest subject of controversy between us. Is this a knotty and useless question? Wherever the knowledge of it is taken away, the glory of Christ is extinguished, religion abolished, the church destroyed, and the hope of salvation utterly overthrown. That doctrine, then, though of the highest moment, we maintain that you have nefariously effaced from the memory of men. Our books are filled with convincing proofs of this fact, and the gross ignorance of this doctrine, which even still continues in all your churches, declares that our complaint is by no means illfounded. But you very maliciously stir up prejudice against us, alleging that by attributing everything to faith, we leave no room for works. . . .

First, we bid a man begin by examining himself, and this not in a superficial and perfunctory manner, but to cite his conscience before the tribunal of God, and when sufficiently convinced of his iniquity, to reflect on the strictness of the sentence pronounced upon all sinners. Thus confounded and amazed at his misery, he is prostrated and humbled before God; and, casting away all self-confidence, groans as if given up to final perdition. Then we show that the only haven of safety is in the mercy of God, as manifested in Christ, in whom every part of our salvation is complete. As all mankind are, in the sight of God, lost sinners, we hold that Christ is their only righteousness, since, by His obedience, He has wiped off our transgressions; by His sacrifice, appeased the divine anger; by His blood, washed away our sins; by His cross, borne our curse; and by His death, made satisfaction for us. We maintain that in this way man is reconciled in Christ to God the Father, by no merit of his own, by no value of works, but by gratuitous mercy. When we embrace Christ by faith, and come, as it were, into communion with Him, this we term, after the manner of Scripture, *the righteousness of faith.*

What have you here, Sadoleto, to bite or carp at? Is it that we leave no room for works? Assuredly we do deny that in justifying a man they are worth one single straw. For Scripture everywhere cries aloud, that all are lost; and every man's own conscience bitterly accuses him. The same Scripture teaches that no hope is left but in the mere goodness of God, by which sin is pardoned, and righteousness imputed to us. It declares both to be gratuitous, and finally concludes that a man is justified without works (Rom. 4:7). But what notion, you ask, does the very term *righteousness* suggest to us if respect is not paid to good works? I answer, if you would attend to the true meaning of the term *justifying* in Scripture, you would have no difficulty. For it does not refer to a man's own righteousness, but to the mercy of God, which contrary to the sinner's deserts, accepts of a righteousness for him, and that by not imputing his unrighteousness. Our righteousness, I say, is that which is described by Paul (2 Cor. 5:19) that God hath reconciled us to Himself in Jesus Christ. The mode is afterwards subjoined—by not imputing sin. He demonstrates that it is by faith only we become partakers of that blessing, when he says that the ministry of reconciliation is contained in the gospel. But faith, you say, is a general term, and has a larger signification. I answer that Paul, whenever he attributes to it the power of justifying, at the same time restricts it to a gratuitous promise of the divine favor, and keeps it far removed from all respect to works. Hence his familiar inference—if by faith, then not by works. On the other hand—if by works, then not by faith.

But, it seems, injury is done to Christ, if, under the pretense of His grace, good works are repudiated, He having come to prepare a people acceptable to God, zealous of good works, while to the same effect, are many similar passages which prove that Christ came in order that we, doing good works, might, through Him, be accepted by God. This calumny, which our opponents have ever in their mouths, viz., that we take away the desire of well-doing from the Christian life by recommending gratuitous righteousness, is too frivolous to give us much concern. We deny that good works have any share in justification, but we claim full authority for them in the lives of the righteous. For if he who has obtained justification possesses Christ, and at the same time, Christ never is where His Spirit is not, it is obvious that gratuitous righteousness is necessarily connected with regeneration. Therefore, if you would duly understand how inseparable faith and works are, look to Christ, who, as the Apostle teaches (1 Cor. 1:30) has been given to us for justification and for sanctification. Wherever, therefore, that righteousness of faith, which we maintain to be gratuitous, is, there too Christ is, and where Christ is, there too is the Spirit of holiness, who regenerates the soul to newness of life. On the contrary, where zeal for integrity and holiness is not in vigor, there neither is the Spirit of Christ nor Christ Himself; and wherever Christ is not, there is no righteousness, nay, there is no faith; for faith cannot apprehend Christ for righteousness without the Spirit of sanctification.

Since, therefore, according to us, Christ regenerates to a blessed life those whom He justifies, and after rescuing them from the dominion of sin, hands them over to the dominion of righteousness, transforms them into the image of God, and so trains them by His Spirit into obedience to His will, there is no ground to complain that, by our doctrine, lust is left with loosened reins. The passages which you adduce have not a meaning at variance with our doctrine. But if you will pervert them in assailing gratuitous justification, see how unskilfully you argue. Paul elsewhere says (Eph. 1:4) that we were chosen in Christ, before the creation of the world, to be holy and unblameable in the sight of God through love. Who will venture thence to infer either that election is not gratuitous, or that our love is its cause? Nay, rather, as the end of gratuitous election, so also that of gratuitous justification is, that we may lead pure and unpolluted lives before God. For the saying of Paul is true (1 Thess. 4:7) we have not been called to impurity, but to holiness. This, meanwhile, we constantly maintain, that man is not only justified freely once for all, without any merit of works, but that on this gratuitous justification the salvation of man perpetually depends. Nor is it possible that any work of man can be accepted by God unless it be gratuitously approved. Wherefore, I was amazed when I read your assertion, that love is the first and chief cause of our salvation. O, Sadoleto, who could ever have expected such a saying from you? Undoubtedly the very blind, while in darkness, feel the mercy of God too surely to dare to claim for their love the first cause of their salvation, while those who have merely one spark of divine light feel that their salvation consists in nothing else than their being adopted by God. For eternal salvation is the inheritance of the heavenly Father, and has been prepared solely for His children. Moreover, who can assign any other cause of our adoption than that which is uniformly announced in Scripture, viz., that we did not first love Him, but were spontaneously received by Him into favor and affection? . . .

In the case of the Eucharist, you blame us for attempting to confine the Lord of the universe, and His divine and spiritual power (which is perfectly free and infinite) within the corners of a corporeal nature with its circumscribed boundaries. What end, pray, will there be to calumny? We have always distinctly testified, that not only the divine power of Christ, but His essence also, is diffused over all, and defined by no limits, and yet you hesitate not to upbraid us with confining it within the corners of corporeal nature! How so? Because we are unwilling with you to chain down His body to earthly elements. But had you any regard for sincerity, assuredly you are not ignorant how great a difference there is between the two things—between removing the local presence of Christ's body from bread, and circumscribing His spiritual power within bodily limits. Nor ought you to charge our doctrine with novelty, since it was always held by the Church as an acknowledged point. But as this subject alone would extend to a volume, in order that both of us may escape so toilsome a discussion, the better course will be for you to read Augustine's Epistle to Dardanus, where you will find how one and the same Christ more than fills heaven and earth with the vastness of His divinity, and yet is not everywhere diffused in respect of His humanity.

We loudly proclaim the communion of flesh and blood, which is exhibited to believers in the Supper; and we distinctly show that that flesh is truly meat, and that blood truly drink—that the soul, not contented with an imaginary conception, enjoys them in very truth. That presence of Christ, by which we are ingrafted in Him, we by no means exclude from the Supper, nor shroud in darkness, though we hold that there must be no local limitation, that the glorious body of Christ must not be degraded to earthly elements; that there must be no fiction of transubstantiating the bread into Christ, and afterward worshiping it as Christ. We explain the dignity and end of this solemn rite in the loftiest terms which we can employ, and then declare how great the advantages which we derive from it. Almost all these things are neglected by you. For overlooking the divine beneficence which is here bestowed upon us, overlooking the legitimate use of so great a benefit (the topics on which it were becoming most especially to dwell), you count it enough that the people gaze stupidly at the visible sign, without any understanding of the spiritual mystery. In condemning your gross dogma of transubstantiation, and declaring that stupid adoration which detains the minds of men among the elements, and permits them not to rise to Christ, to be perverse and impious, we have not acted without the concurrence of the ancient church, under whose shadow you endeavor in vain to hide the very vile superstitions to which you are here addicted.

In auricular confession we have disapproved of that law of Innocent, which enjoins every man once a year to pass all his sins in review before his priest. It would be tedious to enumerate all the reasons which induced us to abrogate it. But that the thing was nefarious is apparent even from this, that pious consciences, which formerly boiled with perpetual anxiety, have at length begun, after being freed from that dire torment, to rest with confidence in the divine favor; to say nothing, meanwhile, of the many disasters which it brought upon the church, and which justly entitle us to hold it in execration. For the present, take this for our answer, that it was neither commanded by Christ, nor practiced by the ancient church. We have forcibly wrested from the hands of the sophists all the passages of Scripture which they had contrived to distort in support of it, while the common books on ecclesiastical history show that it had no existence in an earlier age. The testimonies of the Fathers are to the same effect. It is, therefore, mere deception when you say that the humility therein manifested was enjoined and instituted by Christ and the church. For though there appears in it a certain show of humility, it is very far from being true that every kind of abasement, which assumes the name of humility, is commended by God. . . .

That I may altogether disarm you of the authority of the church, which, as your shield of Ajax, you ever and anon oppose to us, I will show, by some additional examples, how widely you differ from that holy antiquity.

We accuse you of overthrowing the ministry, of which the empty name remains with you without the reality. As far as the office of feeding the people is concerned, the very children perceive that bishops and priests are dumb statues, while men of all ranks know by experience that they are active only in robbing and devouring. We are indignant that in the room of the sacred Supper has been substituted a sacrifice, by which the death of Christ is emptied of its virtues. We exclaim against the execrable traffic in Masses, and we complain that the Supper of the Lord, as to one of its halves, has been stolen from the Christian people. We inveigh against the accursed worship of images. We show that the sacraments are vitiated by many profane notions. We tell how indulgences crept in with fearful dishonor to the cross of Christ. We lament that, by means of human traditions, Christian liberty has been crushed and destroyed. Of these and similar pests, we have been careful to purge the churches which the Lord has committed to us. Expostulate with us, if you can, for the injury which we inflicted on the Catholic church, by daring to violate its sacred sanctions. The fact is now too notorious for you to gain anything by denying it, viz., that in all these points, the ancient church is clearly on our side, and opposes you, not less than we ourselves do.

But here we are met by what you say, when, in order to palliate matters, you allege that though your manners should be irregular, that is no reason why we should make a schism in the holy church. It is scarcely possible that the minds of the common people should not be greatly alienated from you by the many examples of cruelty, avarice, intemperance, arrogance, insolence, lust, and all sorts of wickedness, which are openly manifested by men of your order, but none of those things would have driven us to the attempt which we made under a much stronger necessity. That necessity was that the light of divine truth had been extinguished, the word of God buried, the virtue of Christ left in profound oblivion, and the pastoral office subverted. Meanwhile, impiety so stalked abroad that almost no doctrine of religion was pure from admixture, no ceremony free from error, no part, however minute, of divine worship untarnished by superstition. Do those who contend against such evils declare war against the church, and not rather assist her in her extreme distress? And yet you would take credit for your obedience and humility in refraining, through veneration for the church, from applying your hand to the removal of these abominations. What has a Christian man to do with that prevaricating obedience, which, while the word of God is licentiously condemned, yields its homage to human vanity? What has he to do with that contumacious and rude humility, which despising the majesty of God only looks up with reverence to men? Have done with empty names of virtue, employed merely as cloaks for vice, and let us exhibit the thing itself in its true colors. Ours be the humility which, beginning with the lowest, and paying respect to each in his degree, yields the highest honor and respect to the church, in subordination, however, to Christ the church's head; ours the obedience which, while it disposes us to listen to our elders and superiors, tests all obedience by the word of God; in fine, ours the church whose supreme care it is humbly and religiously to venerate the word of God, and submit to its authority.

But what arrogance, you will say, to boast that the church is with you alone, and to deny it to all the world besides! We indeed, Sadoleto, deny not that those over which you preside are churches of Christ, but we maintain that the Roman pontiff, with his whole herd of pseudo-bishops, who have seized upon the pastor's office, are ravening wolves, whose only study has hitherto been to scatter and trample upon the kingdom of Christ, filling it with ruin and devastation. Nor are we the first to make the complaint. With what vehemence does Bernard thunder against Eugenius and all the bishops of his own age? Yet how much more tolerable was its condition then than now? For iniquity has reached its height, and now those shadowy prelates, by whom you think the church stands or perishes, and by whom we say that she has been cruelly torn and mutilated, and brought to the very brink of destruction, can bear neither their vices nor the cure of them. Destroyed the church would have been, had not God, with singular goodness, prevented. For in all places where the tyranny of the Roman pontiff prevails, you scarcely see as many stray and tattered vestiges as will enable you to perceive that there churches lie half buried. Nor should you think this absurd, since Paul tells you (2 Thess. 2:4) that Antichrist would have his seat in no other place than in the midst of God's sanctuary. Ought not this single warning to put us on our guard against tricks and devices which may be practised in the name of the church?

But whatever the character of the men, still you say it is written, "What they tell you, do." No doubt, if they sit in the chair of Moses. But when from the chair of verity, they intoxicate the people with folly, it is written, "Beware of the leaven of the Pharisees", (Matt. 16:6). It is not ours, Sadoleto, to rob the church of any right which the goodness of God not only has conceded to her, but strictly guarded for her by numerous prohibitions. For as pastors are not sent forth by Him to rule the church with a licentious and lawless authority, but are astricted to a certain rule of duty which they must not exceed, so the church is ordered (1 Thess. 5:21; 1 John 4:1) to see that those who are appointed over her on these terms faithfully accord with their vocation. But we must either hold the testimony of Christ of little moment, or must hold it impious to infringe in the least degree on the authority of those whom He has invested with such splendid titles! Nay, it is you who are mistaken in supposing that the Lord set tyrants over his people to rule them at pleasure, when He bestowed so much authority on those whom He sent to promulgate the gospel. Your error lies here, viz., in not reflecting that their power, before they were furnished with it, was circumscribed within certain limits. We admit, therefore, that ecclesiastical pastors are to be heard just like Christ Himself, but they must be pastors who execute the office entrusted to them. And this office, we maintain, is not presumptuously to introduce whatever their own pleasure has rashly devised, but religiously and in good faith to deliver the oracles which they have received at the mouth of the Lord. For within these boundaries Christ confined the reverence which He required to be paid to the apostles; nor does Peter (1 Pet. 4:11) either claim for himself or allow to others anything more than that, as often as they speak among the faithful, they speak as from the mouth of the Lord. Paul, indeed, justly extols (2 Cor. 13:10) the spiritual power with which he was invested, but with this proviso, that it was to avail only for edification, was to wear no semblance of domination, was not to be employed in subjugating faith. . . .

As to your assertion that our only aim in shaking off this tyrannical yoke was to set ourselves free for unbridled licentiousness after (so help us!) casting away all thoughts of future life, let judgment be given after comparing our conduct with yours. We abound, indeed, in numerous faults; too often do we sin and fall; still, though truth would, modesty will not, permit me to boast how far we excel you in every respect, unless, perchance, you are to except Rome, that famous abode of sanctity, which having burst asunder the cords of pure discipline, and trodden all honor under foot, has so overflowed with all kinds of iniquity, that scarcely anything so abominable has ever been before. We behooved, forsooth, to expose our heads to so many perils and dangers that we might not, after her example, be placed under too severe constraint! But we have not the least objection that the discipline which was sanctioned by ancient canons should be in force in the present day, and be carefully and faithfully observed; nay, we have always protested that the miserable condition into which the church had fallen was owing to nothing more than to its enervation by luxury and indulgence. For the body of the church, to cohere well, must be bound together by discipline as with sinews. But how, on your part, is discipline either observed or desired? Where are those ancient canons with which, like a bridle, bishops and priests were kept to their duty? How are your bishops elected? after what trial? what examination? what care? what caution? How are they inducted to their office? with what order? what solemnity? They merely take an official oath that they will perform the pastoral office, and this apparently for no other end than that they may add perjury to their other iniquities. Since, then, in seizing upon ecclesiastical offices they seem to enter upon an authority astricted by no law, they think themselves free to do as they please, and hence it is that among pirates and robbers there is apparently more justice and regular government, more effect given to law, than by all your order. . . .

Nor will those who, instructed by our preaching, have adhered to our cause, be at a loss what to say for themselves, since each will be ready with this defence:

"I, O Lord, as I had been educated from a boy, always professed the Christian faith. But at first I had no other reason for my faith than that which then everywhere prevailed. Thy word, which ought to have shone on all thy people like a lamp, was taken away, or at least suppressed as to us. And lest anyone should long for greater light, an idea had been instilled into the minds of all, that the investigation of that hidden celestial philosophy was better delegated to a few, whom the others might consult as oracles—that the highest knowledge befitting plebeian minds was to subdue themselves into obedience to the church. Then, the rudiments in which I had been instructed were of a kind which could neither properly train me to the legitimate worship of thy Deity, nor pave the way for me to a sure hope of salvation, nor train me aright for the duties of the Christian life. I had learned, indeed, to worship thee only as my God, but as the true method of worshiping was altogether unknown to me, I stumbled at the very threshold. I believed, as I had been taught, that I was redeemed by the death of thy Son from liability to eternal death, but the redemption I thought of was one whose virtue could never reach me. I anticipated a future resurrection, but hated to think of it, as being an event most dreadful. And this feeling not only had dominion over me in private, but was derived from the doctrine which was then uniformly delivered to the people by their Christian teachers. They, indeed, preached of thy clemency towards men, but confined it to those who should show themselves deserving of it. They, moreover, placed this desert in the righteousness of works, so that he only was received into thy favor who reconciled himself to thee by works. Nor, meanwhile, did they disguise the fact, that we are miserable sinners, that we often fall through infirmity of the flesh, and that to all, therefore, thy mercy behooved to be the common haven of salvation; but the method of obtaining it, which they pointed out, was by making satisfaction to thee for offenses. Then, the satisfaction enjoined was, first, after confessing all our sins to a priest, suppliantly to ask pardon and absolution; and, secondly, by good to efface from thy remembrance our bad actions. Lastly, in order to supply what was still wanting, we were to add sacrifices and solemn expiations. Then, because thou wert a stern judge and strict avenger of iniquity, they showed how dreadful thy presence must be. Hence they bade us flee first to the saints, that by their intercession thou mightest be rendered exorable and propitious to us.

"When, however, I had performed all these things, though I had some intervals of quiet, I was still far off from true peace of conscience; for, whenever I descended into myself, or raised my mind to thee, extreme terror seized me—terror which no expiations nor satisfactions could cure. And the more closely I examined myself, the sharper the stings with which my conscience was pricked, so that the only solace which remained to me was to delude myself by obliviousness. Still, as nothing better offered, I continued the course which I had begun, when, lo, a very different form of doctrine started up, not one which led us away from the Christian profession, but one which brought it back to its fountainhead, and, as it were, clearing away the dross, restored it to its original purity. Offended by the novelty, I lent an unwilling ear, and at first, I confess, strenuously and passionately resisted; for (such is the firmness or effrontery with which it is natural to men to persist in the course which they have once undertaken) it was with the greatest difficulty I was induced to confess that I had all my life long been in ignorance and error. One thing in particular made me averse to those new teachers, viz., reverence for the church. But when once I opened my ears, and allowed myself to be taught, I perceived that this fear of derogating from the majesty of the church was groundless. For they reminded me how great the difference is between schism from the church, and studying to correct the faults by which the church herself was contaminated. They spoke nobly of the church, and showed the greatest desire to cultivate unity. And lest it should seem they quibbled on the term *church,* they showed it was no new thing for Antichrists to preside there in place of pastors. Of this they produced not a few examples, from which it appeared that they aimed at nothing but the edification of the church, and in that respect were similarly circumstanced with many of Christ's servants whom we ourselves included in the catalogue of saints. For inveighing more freely against the Roman pontiff, who was reverenced as the viceregent of Christ, the successor of Peter, and the head of the church, they excused themselves thus: such titles as those are empty bugbears, by which the eyes of the pious ought not to be so blinded as not to venture to look at them, and sift the reality. It was when the world was plunged in ignorance and sloth, as in a deep sleep, that the pope had risen to such an eminence; certainly neither appointed head of the church by the Word of God, nor ordained by a legitimate act of the church, but of his own accord, self elected. Moreover, the tyranny which he let loose against the people of God was not to be endured, if we wished to have the kingdom of Christ among us in safety."

16. Ecclesiastical Ordinances. Geneva (1541)*

The adoption of a church order for Geneva was the price for Calvin's return to the city in 1541. Drafted by Calvin himself, and subsequently slightly modified, this order was to fashion a church according to the biblical paradigm and was moreover to allow Calvin to put his understanding of the life of the church into practice. The so-called *Ecclesiastical Ordinances,* approved by the Genevan citizens in November, 1541, sought to provide for a wide variety of ecclesiastical functions. Four church offices were established—pastor, teacher, elder, and

* Reprinted with the help of Corpus Reformatorum 38, 21 ff. from Hans J. Hillerbrand, *The Reformation. A Narrative History* (New York, 1965), pp. 191-94.

deacon—in accord with the New Testament, each with its particular responsibilities and functions. Other provisions of the *Ordinances* stipulated the election of the ministers, the frequency of preaching, etc.

One of the most distinctive features of the *Ordinances*, and of those church orders in the Calvinist tradition modeled after it, was the provision for church discipline, the supervision of the lives of the people. This discipline was to be exercised by the consistory, consisting of the ministers and the twelve elders, which sought to suppress both moral and theological deviation.

Reprinted here is the middle section of the *Ordinances*.

LITERATURE
F. Wendel, *The Origin and Development of Calvin's Thought* (New York, 1963).

Of the Frequency, Place and Time of Preaching

EACH Sunday, at daybreak, there shall be a sermon in St. Peter's and St. Gervaise's, also at the customary hour at St. Peter, Magdalene and St. Gervaise. At three o'clock, as well, in all three parishes, the second sermon.

For purposes of catechetical instruction and the administration of the sacraments, the boundaries of the parishes are to be observed as possible. St. Gervaise is to be used by those who have done so in the past; likewise with Magdalene. Those who formerly attended St. Germain, Holy Cross, the new church of Our Lady and St. Legier are to attend St. Peter's.

On work days, besides the two sermons mentioned, there shall be preaching three times each week, on Monday, Wednesday, and Friday. These sermons shall be announced for an early hour so that they may be finished before the day's work begins. On special days of prayer the Sunday order is to be observed.

To carry out these provisions and the other responsibilities pertaining to the ministry, five ministers and three coadjutors will be needed. The latter will also be ministers and help and reinforce the others as the occasion arises.

Concerning the Second Order, Called Teachers

The proper duty of teachers is to instruct the faithful in sound doctrine so that the purity of the gospel is not corrupted by ignorance or evil opinions. We include here the aids and instructions necessary to preserve the doctrines and to keep the church from becoming desolate for lack of pastors and ministers. To use a more familiar expression, we shall call it the order of the schools.

The order nearest to the ministry and most closely associated with the government of the church is that of lecturer in theology who teaches the Old and the New Testament.

Since it is impossible to profit by such instruction without first knowing languages and the humanities, and also since it is necessary to prepare for the future in order that the church may not be neglected by the young, it will be necessary to establish a school to instruct the youth, to prepare them not only for the ministry but for government.

First of all, a proper place for teaching purposes must be designated, fit to accommodate children and others who wish to profit by such instruction; to secure someone who is both learned in subject matter and capable of looking after the building, who can also read. This person is to be employed and placed under contract on condition that he provide under his charge readers in the languages and in dialectics, if it be possible. Also to secure men with bachelor degrees to teach the children. This we hope to do to further the work of God.

These teachers shall be subject to the same ecclesiastical discipline as the ministers. There shall be no other school in the city for small children; the girls shall have their school apart, as before.

No one shall be appointed unless he is approved by the ministers, who will make their selection known to the authorities, after which he shall be presented to the council with their recommendation. In any case, when he is examined, two members of the Little Council shall be present.

The Third Order Is That of Elders, Those Commissioned or Appointed to the Consistory by the Authorities

Their office is to keep watch over the lives of everyone, to admonish in love those whom they see in error and leading disorderly lives. Whenever necessary they shall make a report concerning these to the ministers who will be designated to make brotherly corrections and join with the others in making such corrections.

If the church deems it wise, it will be well to choose two from the Little Council, four from the Council of Two Hundred, honest men of good demeanor, without reproach and free from all suspicion, above all fearing God and possessed of good and spiritual judgment. It will be well to elect them from every part of the city so as to be able to maintain supervision over all. This we desire to be instituted.

This shall be the manner of their selection, inasmuch as the Little Council advises that the best men be nominated, and to call the minister so as to confer with them, after which those whom they suggest may be presented to the Council of Two Hundred for their approval. If they are found worthy, after being approved, they shall take an oath similar to that required of the ministers. At the end of the year, after the election of the council, they shall present themselves to the authorities in order that it may be decided if they are to remain in office or be replaced. It will not be expedient to replace them often without cause, or so long as they faithfully perform their duties.

The Fourth Order or the Deacons

There were two orders of deacons in the ancient church, the one concerned with receiving, distributing and guarding the goods of the poor, their possessions, income and pensions as well as the quarterly offerings; the other, to take heed to and care for the sick and administer the pittance for the poor. This custom we have preserved to the present. In order to avoid confusion, for we have both stewards and managers, one of the four stewards of the hospital is to act as receiver of all its goods and is to receive adequate remuneration in order that he may better exercise his office.

The number of four stewards shall remain as it is, of which number one shall be charged with the common funds, as directed, not only that there may be greater efficiency, but also that those who wish to make special gifts may be better assured that these will be distributed only as they desire. If the income which the officials assign is not sufficient, or if some emergency should arise, the authorities shall instruct him to make adjustments according to the need.

The election of the managers, as well as of the stewards, is to be conducted as that of the elders; in their election the rule is to be followed which was delivered by St. Paul respecting deacons.

Concerning the office and authority of stewards, we confirm the articles which have already been proposed, on condition that, in urgent matters, especially when the issue is no great matter and the expenditure involved is small, they not be required to assemble for every action taken, but that one or two of them may be permitted to act in the absence of the others, in a reasonable way.

It will be his task to take diligent care that the public hospital is well administered and that it is open not only to the sick but also to aged persons who are unable to work, to widows, orphans and other needy persons. Those who are sick are to be kept in a separate lodging, away from those who cannot work, old persons, widows, orphans and other needy persons.

Also the care of the poor who are scattered throughout the city is to be conducted as the stewards may order.

Also, that another hospital is established for the transients who should be helped. Separate provision is to be made for any who are worthy of special charity. To accomplish this, a room is to be set aside for those who shall be recommended by the stewards, and it is to be used for no other purpose.

Above all, the families of the managers are to be well managed in an efficient and godly fashion, since they are to manage the houses dedicated to God.

The ministers and the commissioners or elders, with one of the syndics, for their part, are carefully to watch for any fault or negligence of any sort, in order to beg and admonish the authorities to set it in order. Every three months they are to cause certain of their company, with the stewards, to visit the hospital to ascertain if everything is in order.

It will be necessary, also, for the benefit of the poor in the hospital and for the poor of the city who cannot help themselves, that a doctor and a competent surgeon be secured from among those who practice in the city to have the care of the hospital and to visit the poor.

The hospital, for the pestilence in any case, is to be set apart; especially should it happen that the city is visited by this rod from God.

Moreover, to prevent begging, which is contrary to good order, it will be necessary that the authorities delegate certain officers. They are to be stationed at the doors of the churches to drive away any who try to resist and, if they act impudently or answer insolently, to take them to one of the syndics. In like manner, the heads of the precincts should always watch that the law against begging is well observed.

The Persons Whom the Elders Should Admonish, and Proper Procedure in This Regard

If there shall be anyone who lays down opinions contrary to received doctrine, he is to be summoned. If he recants, he is to be dismissed without prejudice. If he is stubborn, he is to be admonished from time to time until it shall be evident that he deserves greater severity. Then, he is to be excommunicated and this action reported to the magistrate.

If anyone is negligent in attending worship so that a noticeable offense is evident for the communion of the faithful, or if anyone shows himself contemptuous of ecclesiastical discipline, he is to be admonished. If he becomes obedient, he is to be dismissed in love. If he persists, passing from bad to worse, after having been admonished three times, he is to be excommunicated and the matter reported to the authorities.

For the correction of faults, it is necessary to proceed after the ordinance of our Lord. That is, vices are to be dealt with secretly and no one is to be brought before the church for accusation if the fault is neither public nor scandalous, unless he has been found rebellious in the matter.

For the rest, those who scorn private admonitions are to be admonished again by the church. If they will not come to reason nor recognize their error, they are to be ordered to abstain from communion until they improve.

As for obvious and public evil, which the church cannot overlook: if the faults merit nothing more than admonition, the duty of the elders shall be to summon those concerned, deal with them in love in order that they may be reformed and, if they correct the fault, to dismiss the matter. If they persevere, they are to be admonished again. If, in the end, such procedure proves unsuccessful, they are to be denounced as contemptuous of God, and ordered to abstain from communion until it is evident that they have changed their way of life.

As for crimes that merit not only admonition but punitive correction: if any fall into such error, according to the requirements of the case, it will be necessary to command them to abstain from communion so that they humble themselves before God and repent of their error.

If anyone by being contumacious or rebellious attempts that which is forbidden, the duty of the ministers shall be to reject him, since it is not proper that he receive the sacrament.

Nevertheless, let all these measures be moderate; let there not be such a degree of rigor that anyone should be cast down, for all corrections are but medicinal, to bring back sinners to the Lord.

And let all be done in such a manner as to keep from the ministers any civil jurisdiction whatever, so that they use only the spiritual sword of the word of God as St. Paul ordered them. Thus the consistory may in no wise take from the authority of the officers or of civil justice. On the contrary, the civil power is to be kept intact. Likewise, when it shall be necessary to exercise punishment or restraint against any party, the ministers and the consistory are to hear the party concerned, deal with them and admonish them as it may seem good, reporting all to the council which, for its part, shall deliberate and then pass judgment according to the merits of the case.

17. John Calvin: *The Institutes of the Christian Religion* (1559)*

John Calvin was the great theological systematician of the Reformation and his *Institutes of the Christian Religion*, first published in 1536

* John Calvin, *The Institutes of the Christian Religion*, ed. John T. McNeill (Philadelphia, 1960), pp. 920–61; 1229–39.

and afterwards substantially enlarged, remain one of the classical statements of Protestant thought. Written at the early age of twenty-six, the *Institutes* in their initial form showed Calvin's dependence upon Luther. Subsequent editions, however, increasingly expressed the author's own theological genius. All of Calvin's religion is found within the covers of this book.

Scholars still disagree about the heart of Calvin's religion. Predestination is often cited, and even though other doctrines might be mentioned with equal validity there can be little doubt that predestination formed an important aspect of Calvin's thought; a lengthy section in the *Institutes* is devoted to it. Calvin believed that it was a biblical doctrine and he went to considerable lengths to underscore its biblical basis. Equally noteworthy is the systematic exposition of this doctrine, where all possible objections are considered and discussed. The setting of Calvin's exposition is also worth noting; predestination is not discussed in conjunction with the nature of God, as might be expected, but in the context of a description of God's redemptive work in Christ.

The sections reprinted here are from Book III, "The way in which we receive the grace of Christ. What benefits come to us from it, and what effects follow" and from Book IV, "The external means or aids by which God invites us into the society of Christ and holds us therein." (Books I and II deal with the knowledge of God the creator and God the redeemer in Christ.)

LITERATURE
F. Wendel, *The Origin and Development of Calvin's Thought* (New York, 1963).

Chapter XXI
Eternal Election, by Which God Has Predestined Some to Salvation, Others to Destruction

(Importance of the doctrine of predestination excludes both presumption and reticence in speaking of it, 1–4)
1. *Necessity and beneficial effect of the doctrine of election; danger of curiosity*

In actual fact, the covenant of life is not preached equally among all men, and among those to whom it is preached, it does not gain the same acceptance either constantly or in equal degree. In this diversity the wonderful depth of God's judgment is made known. For there is no doubt that this variety also serves the decision of God's eternal election. If it is plain that it comes to pass by God's bidding that salvation is freely offered to some while others are barred from access to it, at once great and difficult questions spring up, explicable only when reverent minds regard as settled what they may suitably hold concerning election and predestination. A baffling question this seems to many. For they think nothing more inconsistent than that out of the common multitude of men some should be predestined to salvation, others to destruction. . . .

How much the ignorance of this principle detracts from God's glory, how much it takes away from true humility, is well known. Yet Paul denies that this which needs so much to be known can be known unless God, utterly disregarding works, chooses those whom He has decreed within Himself. "At the present time," he says, "a remnant has been saved according to the election of grace. But if it is by grace, it is no more of works; otherwise grace would no more be grace. But if it is of works, it is no more of grace; otherwise work would not be work" [Rom. 11:5–6]. If—to make it clear that our salvation comes about solely from God's mere generosity—we must be called back to the course of election, those who wish to get rid of all this are obscuring as maliciously as they can what ought to have been gloriously and vociferously proclaimed, and they tear humility up by the very roots. Paul clearly testifies that, when the salvation of a remnant of the people is ascribed to the election of grace, then only is it acknowledged that God of His mere good pleasure preserves whom He will, and moreover that He pays no reward, since He can owe none.

They who shut the gates that no one may dare seek a taste of this doctrine wrong men no less than God. For neither will anything else suffice to make us humble as we ought to be nor shall we otherwise sincerely feel how much we are obliged to God. And as Christ teaches, here is our only ground for firmness and confidence: in order to free us of all fear and render us victorious amid so many dangers, snares, and mortal struggles, He promises that whatever the Father has entrusted into His keeping will be safe [John 10:28–29]. From this we infer that all those who do not know that they are God's own will be miserable through constant fear. Hence, those who by being blind to the three benefits we have noted would wish the foundation of our salva-

tion to be removed from our midst, very badly serve the interests
of themselves and of all other believers. . . .

But before I enter into the matter itself, I need to mention by
way of preface two kinds of men.

Human curiosity renders the discussion of predestination, already somewhat difficult of itself, very confusing and even dangerous. No restraints can hold it back from wandering in forbidden bypaths and thrusting upward to the heights. If allowed, it
will leave no secret to God that it will not search out and unravel.
Since we see so many on all sides rushing into this audacity and
impudence, among them certain men not otherwise bad, they
should in due season be reminded of the measure of their duty
in this regard.

First, then, let them remember that when they inquire into
predestination they are penetrating the sacred precincts of divine
wisdom. If anyone with carefree assurance breaks into this place,
he will not succeed in satisfying his curiosity and he will enter a
labyrinth from which he can find no exit. For it is not right for
man unrestrainedly to search out things that the Lord has willed
to be hid in Himself, and to unfold from eternity itself the sub-
limest wisdom, which He would have us revere but not understand that through this also He should fill us with wonder. He
has set forth by His word the secrets of His will that He has decided to reveal to us. These He decided to reveal in so far as He
foresaw that they would concern us and benefit us.

2. *Doctrine of predestination to be sought in Scripture only*

"We have entered the pathway of faith," says Augustine, "let
us hold steadfastly to it. It leads us to the King's chamber, in
which are hid all treasures of knowledge and wisdom. For the
Lord Christ Himself did not bear a grudge against His great and
most select disciples when He said: 'I have . . . many things to
say to you, but you cannot bear them now' [John 16:12]. We
must walk, we must advance, we must grow, that our hearts may
be capable of those things which we cannot yet grasp. But if the
Last Day finds us advancing, there we shall learn what we could
not learn here." If this thought prevails with us, that the word
of the Lord is the sole way that can lead us in our search for
all that it is lawful to hold concerning Him, and is the sole light
to illumine our vision of all that we should see of Him, it will

readily keep and restrain us from all rashness. For we shall know that the moment we exceed the bounds of the word, our course is outside the pathway and in darkness, and that there we must repeatedly wander, slip, and stumble. Let this, therefore, first of all be before our eyes: to seek any other knowledge of predestination than what the word of God discloses is not less insane than if one should purpose to walk in a pathless waste [cf. Job 12:24], or to see in darkness. And let us not be ashamed to be ignorant of something in this matter, wherein there is a certain learned ignorance. Rather, let us willingly refrain from inquiring into a kind of knowledge, the ardent desire for which is both foolish and dangerous, nay, even deadly. But if a wanton curiosity agitates us, we shall always do well to oppose to it this restraining thought: just as too much honey is not good, so for the curious the investigation of glory is not turned into glory [Prov. 25:27]. For there is good reason for us to be deterred from this insolence which can only plunge us into ruin.

3. *The second danger: anxious silence about the doctrine of election*

There are others who, wishing to cure this evil, all but require that every mention of predestination be buried; indeed, they teach us to avoid any question of it, as we would a reef. Even though their moderation in this matter is rightly to be praised, because they feel that these mysteries ought to be discussed with great soberness, yet because they descend to too low a level, they make little progress with the human understanding, which does not allow itself to be easily restrained. Therefore, to hold to a proper limit in this regard also, we shall have to turn back to the word of the Lord, in which we have a sure rule for the understanding. For Scripture is the school of the Holy Spirit, in which, as nothing is omitted that is both necessary and useful to know, so nothing is taught but what is expedient to know. Therefore we must guard against depriving believers of anything disclosed about predestination in Scripture, lest we seem either wickedly to defraud them of the blessing of their God or to accuse and scoff at the Holy Spirit for having published what it is in any way profitable to suppress.

Let us, I say, permit the Christian man to open his mind and ears to every utterance of God directed to him, provided it be with such restraint that when the Lord closes His holy lips, he also shall at once close the way to inquiry. The best limit of sobriety for us will be not only to follow God's lead always in learning but, when He sets an end to teaching, to stop trying to be wise. The fact that they fear danger is not sufficiently important that we should on that account turn away our minds from the oracles of God. . . . Moses clearly expresses this in a few words: "The secret things," he says, "belong to . . . our God, but He has manifested them to us and to our children" [Deut. 29:29]. We see how he urges the people to study the teaching of the law only on the ground of a heavenly decree, because it pleased God to publish it; and how he held the same people within these bounds for this reason alone: that it is not lawful for mortal men to intrude upon the secrets of God.

4. *The alleged peril in the doctrine dismissed*

Profane men, I admit, in the matter of predestination abruptly seize upon something to carp, rail, bark, or scoff at. But if their shamelessness deters us, we shall have to keep secret the chief doctrines of the faith, almost none of which they or their like leave untouched by blasphemy. An obstinate person would be no less insolently puffed up on hearing that within the essence of God there are three Persons than if he were told that God foresaw what would happen to man when He created him. And they will not refrain from guffaws when they are informed that but little more than five thousand years have passed since the creation of the universe, for they ask why God's power was idle and asleep for so long. Nothing, in short, can be brought forth that they do not assail with their mockery. Should we, to silence these blasphemies, forbear to speak of the deity of Son and Spirit? Must we pass over in silence the creation of the universe? No! God's truth is so powerful, both in this respect and in every other, that it has nothing to fear from the evilspeaking of wicked men.

So Augustine stoutly maintains in his little treatise *The Gift of Perseverance*. For we see that the false apostles could not make Paul ashamed by defaming and accusing his true doctrine. They say that this whole discussion is dangerous for godly minds— because it hinders exhortations, because it shakes faith, because it disturbs and terrifies the heart itself—but this is nonsense! . . . I desire only to have them generally admit that we should not investigate what the Lord has left hidden in secret, that we should not neglect what He has brought into the open, so that we may not be convicted of excessive curiosity on the one hand, or of excessive ingratitude on the other. For Augustine also skilfully expressed this idea: we can safely follow Scripture, which proceeds at the pace of a mother stooping to her child, so to speak, so as not to leave us behind in our weakness. But for those who are so cautious or fearful that they desire to bury predestination in order not to disturb weak souls—with what color will they cloak their arrogance when they accuse God indirectly of stupid thoughtlessness, as if He had not foreseen the peril that they feel they have wisely met? Whoever, then, heaps odium upon the doctrine of predestination openly reproaches God, as if He had unadvisedly let slip something hurtful to the church.

(Predestination defined and explained in relation to the Israelitish nation, and to individuals, 5–7)

5. Predestination and foreknowledge of God; the election of Israel

No one who wishes to be thought religious dares simply deny predestination, by which God adopts some to hope of life, and sentences others to eternal death. But our opponents, especially those who make foreknowledge its cause, envelop it in numerous petty objections. We, indeed, place both doctrines in God, but we say that subjecting one to the other is absurd.

When we attribute foreknowledge to God, we mean that all things always were, and perpetually remain, under His eyes, so that to His knowledge there is nothing future or past, but all things are present. And they are present in such a way that He not only conceives them through ideas, as we have before us those things which our minds remember, but He truly looks upon them and discerns them as things placed before Him. And this foreknowledge is extended throughout the universe to every creature. We call predestination God's eternal decree, by which He determined with Himself what He willed to become of each man. For all are not created in equal condition; rather, eternal life is foreordained for some, eternal damnation for others. Therefore, as any man has been created to one or the other of these ends, we speak of him as predestined to life or to death.

God has attested this not only in individual persons but has given us an example of it in the whole offspring of Abraham, to make it clear that in His choice rests the future condition of each nation. "When the Most High divided the nations, and separated the sons of Adam . . . the people of Israel were His portion, . . . the cord of His inheritance" [Deut. 32:8–9]. The separation is apparent to all men: in the person of Abraham, as in a dry tree trunk, one people is peculiarly chosen, while the others are rejected; but the cause does not appear except that Moses, to cut off from posterity any occasion to boast, teaches that they excel solely by God's freely given love. For he declares this the cause of their deliverance: that God loved the patriarchs, "and chose their seed after them" [Deut. 4:37].

More explicitly, in another chapter: "Not because you surpassed all other peoples in number did He take pleasure in you to choose you, . . . but because He loved you" [Deut. 7:7–8]. . . . Believers also proclaim this with one voice: "He chooses our heritage for us, the glory of Jacob, whom He has loved" [Psalms 47:4]. For all who have been adorned with gifts by God credit them to His freely given love because they knew not only that they had not merited them but that even the holy patriarch himself was not endowed with such virtue as to acquire such a high honor for himself and his descendants. And in order more effectively to crush all pride, he reproaches them as deserving no such thing, since they were a stubborn and stiff-necked people [Ex. 32:9; cf. Deut. 9:6]. Also, the prophets often confront the Jews with this election, to the latters' displeasure and by way of reproach, since they had samefully fallen away from it [cf. Amos 3:2].

Be this as it may, let those now come forward who would bind God's election either to the worthiness of men or to the merit of works. Since they see one nation preferred above all others, and hear that God was not for any reason moved to be more favorably inclined to a few, ignoble—indeed, even wicked and stubborn—men, will they quarrel with Him because He chose to give such evidence of His mercy? But they shall neither hinder His work with their clamorous voices nor strike and hurt His righteousness by hurling the stones of their insults toward heaven. Rather, these will fall back on their own heads! Also, the Israelites are recalled to this principle of a freely given covenant when thanks are to be given to God, or when hope is to be aroused for the age to come. "He has made us and not we ourselves," says the prophet, "we are His people and the sheep of His pastures." [Psalms 100:3; Psalms 99:3.] The negative, which is added to exclude "ourselves," is not superfluous, since by it they may know that God is not only the Author of all good things in which they abound but has derived the cause from Himself, because nothing in them was worthy of so great honor. . . .

In this way, David also arms himself for battle when his faith is assailed: "The blessed one whom thou hast elected . . . will dwell in thy courts" [Psalms 65:4]. Moreover, because the election, being hidden in God, was confirmed by the first liberation, as well as by the second and other intermediate benefits, the word "to elect" is applied to this effect in Isaiah: "God will have mercy on Jacob and will yet elect out of Israel" [Is. 14:1]. In describing the time to come, the prophet says that the gathering together of the remnant of the people, whom He had seemed to forsake, will be a sign of the stability and firmness of His election, which at that very moment had seemingly failed. When He also says in another place, "I have elected you and not cast you off" [Is. 41:9], He emphasizes the ceaseless course of the remarkable generosity of His fatherly benevolence. The angel in Zechariah expresses this more clearly: "God . . . will yet elect Jerusalem" [Zech. 2:12]. It is as though He, by more harshly chastening, had rejected her, or as though the exile had been an interruption of election. Yet election remains inviolable, although its signs do not always appear.

6. *The second stage: election and reprobation of individual Israelites*

We must now add a second, more limited degree of election, or one in which God's more special grace was evident, that is, when from the same race of Abraham God rejected some but showed that He kept others among His sons by cherishing them in the church. Ishmael had at first obtained equal rank with his brother, Isaac, for in him the spiritual covenant had been equally sealed by the sign of circumcision. Ishmael is cut off; then Esau; afterward, a countless multitude, and well-nigh all Israel. In Isaac the seed was called; the same calling continued in Jacob. God showed a similar example in rejecting Saul. This is also wonderfully proclaimed in the psalm: "He rejected the tribe of Joseph, and chose not the tribe of Ephraim but chose the tribe of Judah" [Psalms 78:67-68; cf. Psalms 77:67-68]. This is several times repeated in the sacred history, the better to reveal in this change the marvelous secret of God's grace. By their own defect and guilt, I admit, Ishmael, Esau, and the like were cut off from adoption. For the condition had been laid down that they should faithfully keep God's covenant, which they faithlessly violated. Yet this was a singlar benefit of God, that He had deigned to prefer them to the other nations, as the psalm says: "He has not dealt thus with any other nations, and has not shown them His judgments" [Psalms 147:20].

But I had good reason to say that here we must note two degrees, for in the election of a whole nation God has already shown that in His mere generosity He has not been bound by any laws but is free, so that equal apportionment of grace is not to be required of Him. The very inequality of His grace proves that it is free. For this reason, Malachi emphasizes Israel's ungratefulness, because, while not only chosen from the whole human race but also separated out of a holy house as His own people, they faithlessly and impiously despise God, their beneficent Father. "Was not Esau Jacob's brother?" He asks. "Yet I have loved Jacob, but I have hated Esau" [Mal. 1:2-3; Rom. 9:13]. For God takes it for granted that, as both had been begotten of a holy father, were successors of the covenant, and in short, were branches of a sacred root, the children of Jacob were now under extraordinary obligation, having been received into that dignity; but after the first-born, Esau, had been rejected, and their father, who was inferior by birth, had been made heir, God accuses them of being doubly thankless, and complains that they were not held by that double bond.

7. *The election of individuals as actual election*

Although it is now sufficiently clear that God by His secret plan freely chooses whom He pleases, rejecting others, still His free election has been only half explained until we come to individual persons, to whom God not only offers salvation but so assigns it that the certainty of its effect is not in suspense or doubt. These are reckoned among the unique offspring mentioned by Paul [cf. Rom. 9:8; Gal. 3:16 ff.]. The adoption was put in Abraham's hands. Nevertheless, because many of his descendants were cut off as rotten members, we must, in order that election may be effectual and truly enduring, ascend to the Head, in whom the Heavenly Father has gathered His elect together, and has joined them to Himself by an indissoluble bond. So, indeed, God's generous favor, which He has denied to others, has been displayed in the adoption of the race of Abraham; yet in the members of Christ a far more excellent power of grace appears, for, engrafted to their Head, they are never cut off from salvation. Therefore Paul skilfully argues from the passage of Malachi that I have just cited that where God has made a covenant of eternal life and calls any people to Himself, a special mode of election is employed for a part of them, so that He does not with indiscriminate grace effectually elect all [Rom. 9:13]. . . .

It is easy to explain why the general election of a people is not always firm and effectual: to those with whom God makes a covenant, He does not at once give the spirit of regeneration that would enable them to persevere in the covenant to the very end. Rather, the outward change, without the working of inner grace, which might have availed to keep them, is intermediate between the rejection of mankind and the election of a meager number of the godly. The whole people of Israel has been called "the inheritance of God" [Deut. 32:9; 1 Kings 8:51; Psalms 28:9; 33:12; etc.], yet many of them were foreigners. But because God has not pointlessly covenanted that He would become their Father and Redeemer, He sees to His freely given favor rather than to the many who treacherously desert Him. Even through them His truth was not set aside, for where He preserved some remnant for Himself, it appeared that His calling was "without repentance" [Rom. 11:29]. For the fact that God was continually gathering His church from Abraham's children rather than from profane nations had its reason in His covenant, which, when violated by that multitude, He confined to a few that it might not utterly cease. In short, that adoption of Abraham's seed in common was a visible image of the greater benefit that God bestowed on some out of the many. This is why Paul so carefully distinguishes the children of Abraham according to the flesh from the spiritual children who have been called after the example of Isaac [Gal. 4:28]. Not that it was a vain and unprofitable thing simply to be a child of Abraham; such could not be said without dishonoring the covenant! No, God's unchangeable plan, by which He predestined for Himself those whom He willed, was in fact intrinsically effectual unto salvation for these spiritual offspring alone. But I advise my readers not to take a prejudiced position on either side until, when the passages of Scripture have been adduced, it shall be clear what opinion ought to be held.

Summary survey of the doctrine of election

As Scripture, then, clearly shows, we say that God once established by His eternal and unchangeable plan those whom He long before determined once for all to receive into salvation, and those whom, on the other hand, He would devote to destruction. We assert that, with respect to the elect, this plan was founded upon His freely given mercy, without regard to human worth; but by His just and irreprehensible but incomprehensible judgment He has barred the door of life to those whom He has given over to damnation. Now among the elect we regard the call as a testimony of election. Then we hold justification another sign of its manifestation, until they come into the glory in which the fulfilment of that election lies. But as the Lord seals His elect by call and justification, so, by shutting off the reprobate from knowledge of His name or from the sanctification of His Spirit, He, as it were, reveals by these marks what sort of judgment awaits them. Here I shall pass over many fictions that stupid men have invented to overthrow predestination. They need no refutation, for as soon as they are brought forth they abundantly prove their own falsity. I shall pause only over those which either are being argued by the learned or may raise difficulty for the simple, or which impiety speciously sets forth in order to assail God's righteousness.

Chapter XXII
Confirmation of This Doctrine from Scriptural Testimonies

(*Election is not from foreknowledge of merit but is of God's sovereign purpose, 1–6*)

1. *Election vs. foreknowledge of merits*

Many persons dispute all these positions which we have set forth, especially the free election of believers; nevertheless, this cannot be shaken. For generally these persons consider that God distinguishes among men according as He foresees what the merits of each will be. Therefore, He adopts as sons those whom He foreknows will not be unworthy of His grace; He appoints to the damnation of death those whose dispositions He discerns will be inclined to evil intention and ungodliness. By thus covering election with a veil of foreknowledge, they not only obscure it but feign that it has its origin elsewhere. And this commonly accepted notion is not confined to the common folk; important authors of all periods have held it. This I frankly confess so that no one may assume that if their names be quoted against us, our case will be greatly damaged. For God's truth is here too sure to be shaken, too clear to be overwhelmed by men's authority.

But others, not versed in Scripture, and deserving no approbation, so wickedly assail this sound doctrine that their insolence is intolerable. Because God chooses some, and passes over others according to His own decision, they bring an action against Him. But if the fact itself is well known, what will it profit them to quarrel against God? We teach nothing not borne out by experience: that God has always been free to bestow His grace on whom He wills. I shall not inquire in what respect the descendants of Abraham excelled other men, except in that esteem whose cause is not found outside God. Let them answer why they are men rather than oxen or asses. Although it was in God's power to make them dogs, He formed them to His own image. Will they allow brute beasts to argue with God about their condition, as if the distinction were unjust? Surely, it is not fairer for them to possess a privilege that they have obtained without merits than for God variously to dispense His benefits according to the measure of His judgment!

If they shift the argument to individual persons where they find the inequality more objectionable, they ought at least so to tremble at the example of Christ as not to prate so irresponsibly about this lofty mystery. He is conceived a mortal man of the seed of David. By what virtues will they say that He deserved in the womb itself to be made head of the angels, only-begotten Son of God, image and glory of the Father, light, righteousness, and salvation of the world [cf. Heb. 1:2 ff.]? . . . If here anyone should ask why others were not as He was—or why all of us are separated from Him by such a long distance—why all of us are corrupt, while He is purity itself, such a questioner would display not only his madness but with it also his shamelessness. But if they wilfully strive to strip God of His free power to choose or reject, let them at the same time also take away what has been given to Christ.

Now it behooves us to pay attention to what Scripture proclaims of every person. When Paul teaches that we were chosen in Christ "before the creation of the world" [Eph. 1:4], he takes away all consideration of real worth on our part, for it is just as if he said: since among all the offspring of Adam, the heavenly Father found nothing worthy of His election, He turned His eyes upon His anointed, to choose from that body as members those whom He was to take into the fellowship of life. Let this reasoning, then, prevail among believers: we were adopted in Christ into the eternal inheritance because in ourselves we were not capable of such great excellence. . . .

2. *Election before creation and not associated with foreknowledge of merit*

That the proof may be more complete, it is worthwhile to note the individual parts of this passage [Eph. 1:4–5], which, coupled together, leave no doubt. Since he calls them "elect," it cannot be doubted that he is speaking to believers, as he also soon declares; therefore those who misinterpret the word "elect" as confined to the age when the gospel was proclaimed disfigure it with a base fabrication. By saying that they were "elect before the creation of the world" [Eph. 1:4], he takes away all regard for worth. For what basis for distinction is there among those who did not yet exist, and who were subsequently to be equals in Adam? Now if they are elect in Christ, it follows that not only is each man elected without respect to his own person but also certain ones are separated from others, since we see that not all are members of Christ. Besides, the fact that they were elected "to be holy" [Eph. 1:4] plainly refutes the error that derives election from foreknowledge since Paul declares all virtue appearing in man is the result of election. Now if a higher cause be sought, Paul answers that God has predestined it so, and that this is "according to the good pleasure of His will" [Eph. 1:5]. By these words he does away with all means of their election that men imagine in themselves. For all benefits that God bestows for the spiritual life, as Paul teaches, flow from this one source: namely, that God has chosen whom He has willed, and before their birth has laid up for them individually the grace that He willed to grant them.

3. *Elected to be holy, not because already holy*

Wherever this decision of God's holds sway, there is no consideration of works. Of course, Paul does not develop the antithesis here, but it must be understood as he himself elsewhere explains it. "He called us," Paul says, "with a holy calling, not according to our works, but according to His own purpose, and the grace that was given to us by Christ before time began" [2 Tim. 1:9]. And we have already shown that in the words that follow, "that we should be holy and spotless" [Eph. 1:4], we are freed of every doubt. Say: "Since He foresaw that we would be holy, He chose us," and you will invert Paul's order. Therefore you can safely infer the following: if He chose us that we should be holy, He did not choose us because He foresaw that we would be so. For these two notions disagree: that the godly have their holiness from election, and that they arrive at election by reason of works. The quibble to which they frequently have recourse, that the Lord does not reward preceding merits with the grace of election yet grants it to future merits, has no validity. For when it is said that believers were chosen that they might be holy, at the same time it is suggested that the holiness that was to be in them originated from election. What consistency is there in saying that the things derived from election gave cause to election?

Paul seems afterward further to confirm what he had said when he states: "According to the purpose of His will" [Eph. 1:5], "which He had purposed in Himself" [Eph. 1:9]. For to say that "God purposed in Himself" means the same thing as to say that He considered nothing outside Himself with which to be concerned in making His decree. Therefore he adds at once that the whole intent of our election is that we should be to the praise of divine grace [cf. Eph. 1:6]. Surely the grace of God deserves alone to be proclaimed in our election only if it is freely given. Now it will not be freely given if God, in choosing His own, considers what the works of each shall be. We therefore find Christ's statement to His disciples, "You did not choose me, but I chose you" [John 15:16], generally valid among all believers. There He not only rules out past merits but also indicates His disciples had nothing in themselves for which to be chosen if He had not first turned to them in his mercy. . . .

4. *Romans, chs. 9 to 11, and similar passages*

Therefore, in the letter to the Romans, where Paul both re-iterates this argument more profoundly and pursues it more at length, he states that "not all who are descendants of Israel are Israelites" [Rom. 9:6]. For even though all had been blessed by hereditary right, the succession did not pass to all equally. This discussion arose from the pride and false boasting of the Jewish people. For when they claimed for themselves the name "church," they wanted belief in the gospel to depend upon their decision. Today, in like manner, the papists with this false pretext would willingly substitute themselves for God. Paul, although he admits that, by virtue of the covenant, the offspring of Abraham are holy, still contends that many among them are outside of it. And that is not only because they degenerate from legitimate children to bastards but also because God's special election towers and rules over all, alone ratifying His adoption. If their own piety es-tablished some in the hope of salvation, and their own desertion disinherited others, it would be quite absurd for Paul to lift his readers to secret election. Now if the will of God, the cause of which neither appears nor ought to be sought outside of Himself, distinguishes some from others, so that not all the sons of Israel are true Israelites, it is vain to pretend that every man's condition begins in himself.

From the example of Jacob and Esau, Paul then develops the matter further. For although both were sons of Abraham, en-closed together in their mother's womb, the honor of the first-born was transferred to Jacob. Here was a change like a portent, which, as Paul contends, testified to the election of Jacob and the reprobation of Esau. When one asks the origin and cause, the teachers of foreknowledge would locate it in the virtues and vices of the men. Here is the sum of their facile argument: in the per-son of Jacob, God showed that He chooses those worthy of His grace; in the person of Esau, that He repudiates those whom He foresees as unworthy. So, indeed, they boldly argue. But what does Paul say? "Though they were not yet born and had done nothing either good or bad, in order that God's purpose of election might continue, not because of works but because of His call, it was said,

'The elder will serve the younger.' As it is written, 'Jacob I loved, but Esau I hated'" [Rom. 9:11-13; cf. Gen. 25:23]. If foreknowledge had any bearing upon this distinction between the brothers, the mention of time would surely have been inopportune.

Suppose we admit that Jacob was chosen because he had worth arising out of virtues to come; why should Paul say that he had not yet been born? Now it would have been rash to add that he still had done no good, for this answer will be ready: nothing is hidden from God, and so Jacob's godliness was present before Him. If works obtain grace, God's reward for them ought rightly to have been already established before Jacob's birth, just as if he had grown up. But the Apostle proceeds to resolve this difficulty, and teaches that the adoption of Jacob comes not from works but from God's call. In treating of works he does not bring in future or past time; he decidedly sets them over against God's call, wishing by establishing the one skilfully to refute the other. This is as if he said: "It is what God pleased that is to be considered, not what men brought of themselves." Finally, from the words "election" and "purpose" it is certain that all causes that men commonly devise apart from God's secret plan are remote from this cause. . . .

6. Jacob's election not to earthly blessings

But suppose someone interrupts me to say that we ought not to conclude from these inferior and slight benefits, concerning the whole of the life to come, that he who has been elevated to the honor of firstborn should accordingly be considered as adopted into the inheritance of heaven. For there are very many who do not spare even Paul from the charge that in the testimonies quoted he twisted Scripture to a foreign meaning. I reply as before that the Apostle neither slipped through thoughtlessness nor wilfully misused the testimonies of Scripture. But he saw what they cannot bear to consider: that God willed by an earthly symbol to declare Jacob's spiritual election, which otherwise lay hid in His inaccessible judgment seat. For unless we refer the right of primogeniture granted him to the age to come, it would be an empty and absurd kind of blessing, since from it he obtained nothing but manifold hardships, troubles, sad exile, many sorrows, and bitter cares. Therefore, when Paul saw without doubt that by

outward blessing God testified to the blessing, spiritual and un-
fading, that He had prepared in His kingdom for His servant, he
did not hesitate to seek in the outward blessing evidence to prove
the spiritual blessing [cf. Eph. 1:3 ff.]. We must also bear in mind
that the pledge of a heavenly dwelling place was attached to the
land of Canaan. Hence, it ought not to be doubted that Jacob was,
with the angels, engrafted into the body of Christ that he might
share the same life.

Jacob, therefore, is chosen and distinguished from the rejected
Esau by God's predestination, while not differing from him in
merits. If you ask the reason, the Apostle gives this: "For He says
to Moses, 'I will have mercy on whom I have mercy, and I will
have compassion on whom I have compassion' " [Rom. 9:15]. And
what does this mean, I ask? It is simply the Lord's clear declaration that He finds in men themselves no reason to bless them but
takes it from His mercy alone [Rom. 9:16]; therefore the salvation of His own is His own work. Inasmuch as God establishes
your salvation in Himself alone, why do you descend to yourself?
Since He appoints for you His mercy alone, why do you have
recourse to your own merits? Seeing that He confines your
thought within His mercy alone, why do you turn your attention
in part to your own works? . . .

(*Answers to opponents of this basis of election, which also is
reprobation, 7–11*)
7. *Christ's witness concerning election*
Now let the sovereign Judge and Master give utterance on the
whole question. Detecting such great hardness in His listeners
that He would be almost wasting words before the crowd, in
order to overcome this hindrance He cries out: "All that the
Father gives me will come to me" [John 6:37]. "For this is the
will of the Father, . . . that whatever He has given me, I should
lose nothing of it" [John 6:39]. Note that the Father's gift is the
beginning of our reception into the surety and protection of
Christ. Perhaps someone will here turn the argument around and
object that only those who in faith have voluntarily yielded are
considered to be the Father's own. Yet Christ insists upon this
point alone: even though the desertions of vast multitudes shake
the whole world, God's firm plan that election may never be

shaken will be more stable than the very heavens. The elect are said to have been the Father's before He gave them His only-begotten Son. They ask whether by nature. No, those who were strangers He makes His own by drawing them to Him. Christ's words are too clear to be covered up with any clouds of evasion. "No one," He says, "can come to me unless the Father . . . draws him. . . . Everyone who has heard and learned from the Father comes to me" [John 6:44–45]. If all men in general bowed the knee before Christ, election would be general; now in the fewness of believers a manifest diversity appears. Therefore, after Christ declared that the disciples who were given Him were the special possession of God the Father [John 17:6], a little later He adds: "I am not praying for the world but for those whom thou hast given me, for they are thine" [John 17:9; see also John 15:19]. Whence it comes about that the whole world does not belong to its Creator except that grace rescues from God's curse and wrath and eternal death a limited number who would otherwise perish. But the world itself is left to its own destruction, to which it has been destined. Meanwhile, although Christ interposes Himself as mediator, He claims for Himself, in common with the Father, the right to choose. "I am not speaking," He says, "of all; I know whom I have chosen" [John 13:18]. If anyone ask whence He has chosen them, He replies in another passage: "From the world" [John 15:19], which He excludes from His prayers when He commends His disciples to the Father [John 17:9]. This we must believe: when He declares that He knows whom He has chosen, He denotes in the human genus a particular species, distinguished not by the quality of its virtues but by heavenly decree.

From this we may infer that none excel by their own effort or diligence, seeing that Christ makes Himself the Author of election. He elsewhere numbers Judas among the elect, although he "is a devil" [John 6:70]. This refers only to the office of apostle, which, even though it is a clear mirror of God's favor, as Paul often acknowledges in his own person [e.g., Gal. 1:16; Eph. 3:7], still does not contain in itself the hope of eternal salvation. Judas, then, could be worse than a devil, since he faithlessly discharged the office of apostle, but Christ does not allow any of those whom He has once for all engrafted into His body to perish [John 10:28]; for in preserving their salvation He will perform what He has promised—namely, He will show forth God's power, which "is greater than all" [John 10:29]. . . . To sum up: by free adoption God makes those whom He wills to be His sons; the intrinsic cause of this is in Himself, for He is content with His own secret good pleasure. . . .

10. *The universality of God's invitation and the particularity of election*

Some object that God would be contrary to Himself if He should universally invite all men to Him but admit only a few as elect. Thus, in their view, the universality of the promises removes the distinction of special grace; and some moderate men speak thus, not so much to stifle the truth as to bar thorny questions, and to bridle the curiosity of many. A laudable intention, this, but the design is not to be approved, for evasion is never excusable. But those who insolently revile election offer a quibble too disgusting, or an error too shameful.

I have elsewhere explained how Scripture reconciles the two notions that all are called to repentance and faith by outward preaching, yet that the spirit of repentance and faith is not given to all. Soon I shall have to repeat some of this. Now I deny what they claim, since it is false in two ways. For He who threatens that while it will rain upon one city there will be drought in another [Amos 4:7], and who elsewhere announces a famine of teaching [Amos 8:11], does not bind Himself by a set law to call all men equally. And He who, forbidding Paul to speak the word in Asia [Acts 16:6], and turning him aside from Bithynia, draws him into Macedonia [Acts 16:7 ff.] thus shows that He has the right to distribute this treasure to whom He pleases. Through Isaiah He still more openly shows how He directs the promises of salvation specifically to the elect: for He proclaims that they alone, not the whole human race without distinction, are to become His disciples [Is. 8:16]. Hence it is clear that the doctrine of salvation, which is said to be reserved solely and individually for the sons of the church, is falsely debased when presented as effectually profitable to all.

Let this suffice for the present: although the voice of the gospel addresses all in general, yet the gift of faith is rare. Isaiah sets forth the cause: that "the arm of the Lord has" not "been revealed" to all [Is. 53:1]. If he had said that the gospel is mali-

ciously and wickedly despised because many stubbornly refuse to
hear it, perhaps this aspect of universal calling would have force.
But it is not the prophet's intention to extenuate men's guilt when
he teaches that the source of the blindness is that the Lord does
not deign to reveal His arm to them [Is. 53:1]. He only warns
that, because faith is a special gift, the ears are beaten upon in
vain with outward teaching. Now I should like to know from these
doctors whether preaching alone, or faith, makes God's sons.
Surely, when it is said in the first chapter of John: "All who believe in the only-begotten Son of God also become sons of God
themselves" [John 1:12], no confused mass is placed there, but
a special rank is given to believers, "who were born not of blood,
nor of the will of the flesh, nor of the will of man, but of God"
[John 1:13].

But, they say, there is a mutual agreement between faith and
the word. This is so wherever there is faith; but for seed to fall
among thorns [Matt. 13:7] or on rocky ground [Matt. 13:5] is
nothing new, not only because the greater part indeed show
themselves obstinately disobedient to God, but because not all
have been supplied with eyes and ears. How, then, shall it be consistent that God calls to Himself persons who He knows will not
come? Let Augustine answer for me: "You wish to argue with
me? Marvel with me, and exclaim, 'O depth!' Let both of us agree
in fear, lest we perish in error." Besides, if election, as Paul testifies,
is the mother of faith, I turn back upon their head the argument
that faith is not general because election is special. For from this
series of causes and effects we may readily draw this inference:
when Paul states that "we have been supplied with every spiritual
blessing . . . even as He chose us from the foundation of the
world" [Eph. 1:3-4], these riches are therefore not common to
all, for God has chosen only whom He willed. This is why Paul
in another place commends faith to the elect [Tit. 1:1]: that no
one may think that he acquires faith by his own effort but that
this glory rests with God, freely to illumine whom He previously
had chosen. . . .

We hear from the Master's own lips: "Only those see the Father
who are from God" [John 6:46]. By these words He means that
all those not reborn of God are astonished at the brightness of His
countenance. And indeed, faith is fitly joined to election, pro-

vided it takes second place. This order is elsewhere clearly expressed in Christ's words: "This is the will of my Father, that I should not lose what He has given. This is His will, that everyone who believes in the Son may not perish" [John 6:39–40, freely rendered]. If He willed all to be saved, He would set His Son over them, and would engraft all into His body with the sacred bond of faith. Now it is certain that faith is a singular pledge of the Father's love, reserved for the sons whom He has adopted. Hence Christ says in another passage: "The sheep follow the shepherd, for they know his voice. But a stranger they will not follow, . . . for they do not know the voice of strangers" [John 10:4–5]. Whence does this distinction arise but from the fact that their ears have been pierced by the Lord? For no man makes himself a sheep but is made one by heavenly grace. Whence also the Lord teaches that our salvation will be forever sure and safe, for it is guarded by God's unconquerable might [John 10:29]. Accordingly, he concludes that unbelievers are not of his sheep [John 10:26]. That is, they are not of the number of those who, as God promised through Isaiah, were to become disciples [cf. Is. 8:16; 54:13]. Now because the testimonies that I have quoted express perseverance, they at the same time attest the unvarying constancy of election.

11. *Rejection also takes place not on the basis of works but solely according to God's will*

Now a word concerning the reprobate, with whom the Apostle is at the same time there concerned. For as Jacob, deserving nothing by good works, is taken into grace, so Esau, as yet undefiled by any crime, is hated [Rom. 9:13]. If we turn our eyes to works, we wrong the Apostle, as if he did not see what is quite clear to us! Now it is proved that he did not see it, since he specifically emphasizes the point that when as yet they had done nothing good or evil, one was chosen, the other rejected. This is to prove that the foundation of divine predestination is not in works. Then when he raised the objection, whether God is unjust, he does not make use of what would have been the surest and clearest defense of his righteousness: that God recompensed Esau according to his own evil intention. Instead, he contents himself with a different solution, that the reprobate are raised up to the end that through them God's glory may be revealed.

Finally, he adds the conclusion that "God has mercy upon whomever He wills, and He hardens whomever He wills" [Rom. 9:18]. Do you see how Paul attributes both to God's decision alone? If, then, we cannot determine a reason why He vouchsafes mercy to His own, except that it so pleases Him, neither shall we have any reason for rejecting others, other than His will. For when it is said that God hardens or shows mercy to whom He wills, men are warned by this to seek no cause outside His will.

Chapter XXIII
Refutation of the false accusations with which this doctrine has always been unjustly burdened

(Reprobation the concomitant of election and an act of God's will, 1–3)

1. *Election—but no reprobation?*

Now when human understanding hears these things, its insolence is so irrepressible that it breaks forth into random and immoderate tumult as if at the blast of a battle trumpet.

Indeed many, as if they wished to avert a reproach from God, accept election in such terms as to deny that anyone is condemned. But they do this very ignorantly and childishly, since election itself could not stand except as set over against reprobation. God is said to set apart those whom He adopts into salvation; it will be highly absurd to say that others acquire by chance or obtain by their own effort what election alone confers on a few. Therefore, those whom God passes over, He condemns; and this He does for no other reason than that He wills to exclude them from the inheritance which He predestines for His own children. And men's insolence is unbearable if it refuses to be bridled by God's word, which treats of His incomprehensible plan that the angels themselves adore. However, we have by now been taught that hardening is in God's hand and will, just as much as mercy is [Rom. 9:14 ff.]. And Paul does not, as do those I have spoken of, labor anxiously to make false excuses in God's defense; he only warns that it is unlawful for the clay to quarrel with its potter [Rom. 9:20]. Now how will those who do not admit that any are condemned by God dispose of Christ's statement: "Every tree that my . . . Father has not planted will be uprooted" [Matt. 15:13]? This plainly means that all those whom the heavenly Father has not deigned to plant as sacred trees in His field are marked and intended for destruction. If they say this is no sign of reprobation, there is nothing so clear that it can be proved to them.

But if they do not stop wrangling, let sober faith be content with this admonition of Paul's: that there is no reason to quarrel with God "if desiring," on the one hand, "to show His wrath and make His power known, He has endured with much patience" and leniency "the vessels of wrath made for destruction" but, on the other hand, "makes known the riches of His glory for the vessels of mercy that he has prepared . . . for glory" [Rom. 9:22–23]. Let readers note that Paul, to cut off occasion for whispering and disparagement, gives the ultimate sovereignty to God's wrath and might, for it is wicked to subject to our determination those deep judgments which swallow up all our powers of mind. Our adversaries give a worthless answer: that God does not utterly reject those whom He tolerates in leniency but suspends judgment on them, should they perchance repent. As if Paul attributed to God patience, in which to await the conversion of those who He says have been "fashioned for destruction"! [Rom. 9:22]. Augustine rightly explains this passage: where might is joined to long-suffering, God does not permit but governs by His power. They add also that vessels of wrath are for good reason said to be "made for destruction" but that "God has prepared vessels of mercy" [Rom. 9:22]; for in this way Paul ascribes to, and claims for, God the credit for salvation, while he casts the blame for their perdition upon those who of their own will bring it upon themselves. But though I should admit to them that Paul, using a different expression, softens the harshness of the former clause, it is utterly inconsistent to transfer the preparation for destruction to anything but God's secret plan. This was also declared in a little earlier context: God aroused Pharaoh [Rom. 9:17]; then, "He hardens whom He pleases" [Rom. 9:18]. From this it follows that God's secret plan is the cause of hardening. I, at least, maintain this teaching of Augustine's: where God makes sheep out of wolves, He reforms them by a more powerful grace to subdue their hardness; accordingly, God does not convert the obstinate because He does not manifest that more powerful grace, which is not lacking if He should please to offer it.

(First objection: the doctrine of election makes God a tyrant, 2–3)
2. God's will is the rule of righteousness

To the pious and moderate and those who are mindful that they are men, these statements should be quite sufficient. Yet because these venomous dogs spew out more than one kind of venom against God, we shall answer each individually, as the matter requires.

Foolish men contend with God in many ways, as though they held Him liable to their accusations. They first ask, therefore, by what right the Lord becomes angry at His creatures who have not provoked Him by any previous offense; for to devote to destruction whomever He pleases is more like the caprice of a tyrant than the lawful sentence of a judge. It therefore seems to them that men have reason to expostulate with God if they are predestined to eternal death solely by His decision, apart from their own merit. If thoughts of this sort ever occur to pious men, they will be sufficiently armed to break their force even by the one consideration that it is very wicked merely to investigate the causes of God's will. For His will is, and rightly ought to be, the cause of all things that are. For if it has any cause, something must precede it, to which it is, as it were, bound; this is unlawful to imagine. For God's will is so much the highest rule of righteousness that whatever He wills, by the very fact that He wills it, must be considered righteous. When, therefore, one asks why God has so done, we must reply: because He has willed it. But if you proceed further to ask why He so willed, you are seeking something greater and higher than God's will, which cannot be found. Let men's rashness, then, restrain itself, and not seek what does not exist, lest perhaps it fail to find what does exist. This bridle, I say, will effectively restrain anyone who wants to ponder in reverence the secrets of his God. Against the boldness of the wicked who are not afraid to curse God openly, the Lord Himself will sufficiently defend Himself by His righteousness, without our help, when, by depriving their consciences of all evasion, He will convict them and condemn them.

And we do not advocate the fiction of "absolute might"; because this is profane, it ought rightly to be hateful to us. We fancy no lawless god who is a law unto himself. For, as Plato says, men who are troubled with lusts are in need of law; but the will of God is not only free of all fault but is the highest rule of perfection, and even the law of all laws. But we deny that He is liable to render an account; we also deny that we are competent judges to pronounce judgment in this cause according to our own understanding. Accordingly, if we attempt more than is permitted, let that threat of the psalm strike us with fear: God will be the victor whenever He is judged by mortal man [Psalms 51:4; cf. 50:6].

3. *God is just toward the reprobate*

So keeping silence, God can restrain His enemies. But lest we allow them to mock His holy name with impunity, out of His word He supplies us with weapons against them. Accordingly, if anyone approaches us with such expressions as: "Why from the beginning did God predestine some to death who, since they did not yet exist, could not yet have deserved the judgment of death?" let us, in lieu of reply, ask them, in turn, what they think God owes to man if He would judge him according to His own nature. As all of us are vitiated by sin, we can only be odious to God, and that not from tyrannical cruelty but by the fairest reckoning of justice. But if all whom the Lord predestines to death are by condition of nature subject to the judgment of death, of what injustice toward themselves may they complain?

Let all the sons of Adam come forward; let them quarrel and argue with their Creator that they were by His eternal providence bound over before their begetting to everlasting calamity. What clamor can they raise against this defense when God, on the contrary, will call them to their account before Him? If all are drawn from a corrupt mass, no wonder they are subject to condemnation! Let them not accuse God of injustice if they are destined by His eternal judgment to death, to which they feel—whether they will or not—that they are led by their own nature of itself. How perverse is their disposition to protest is apparent from the fact that they deliberately suppress the cause of condemnation, which they are compelled to recognize in themselves, in order to free themselves by blaming God. But though I should confess a hundred times that God is the author of it—which is very true—

yet they do not promptly cleanse away the guilt that, engraved upon their consciences, repeatedly meets their eyes.

(*God's justice not subject to our questioning, 4–7*)
4. *God's decree is also hidden in His justice*

Again they object: were they not previously predestined by God's ordinance to that corruption which is now claimed as the cause of condemnation? When, therefore, they perish in their corruption, they but pay the penalties of that misery in which Adam fell by predestination of God, and dragged his posterity headlong after him. Is He not, then, unjust who so cruelly deludes His creatures? Of course, I admit that in this miserable condition wherein men are now bound, all of Adam's children have fallen by God's will. And this is what I said to begin with, that we must always at last return to the sole decision of God's will, the cause of which is hidden in Him. But it does not directly follow that God is subject to this reproach. For with Paul we shall answer in this way: "Who are you, O man, to argue with God? Does the molded object say to its molder, 'Why have you fashioned me thus?' Or does the potter have no capacity to make from the same lump one vessel for honor, another for dishonor?" [Rom. 9:20–21].

They will say that God's righteousness is not truly defended thus but that we are attempting a subterfuge such as those who lack a just excuse are wont to have. For what else seems to be said here than that God has a power that cannot be prevented from doing whatever it pleases Him to do? But it is far otherwise. For what stronger reason can be adduced than when we are bidden to ponder who God is? For how could He who is the Judge of the earth allow any iniquity [cf. Gen. 18:25]? If the execution of judgment properly belongs to God's nature, then by nature He loves righteousness and abhors unrighteousness. Accordingly, the Apostle did not look for loopholes of escape as if he were embarrassed in his argument but showed that the reason of divine righteousness is higher than man's standard can measure, or than man's slender wit can comprehend. The Apostle even admits that such depth underlies God's judgments [Rom. 11:33] that all men's minds would be swallowed up if they tried to penetrate it. But he also teaches how unworthy it is to reduce

God's works to such a law that the moment we fail to understand their reason, we dare to condemn them. . . .

5. God's hidden decree is not to be searched out but obediently marveled at. . . .

I say with Paul that we ought not to seek any reason for it because in its greatness it far surpasses our understanding [cf. Rom. 9:19–23]. What marvel, this, or what absurdity? Would he wish God's might so limited as to be unable to accomplish any more than his mind can conceive? With Augustine I say: the Lord has created those whom He unquestionably foreknew would go to destruction. This has happened because He has so willed it. But why He so willed, it is not for our reason to inquire, for we cannot comprehend it. And it is not fitting that God's will should be dragged down into controversy among us, for whenever mention is made of it, under its name is designated the supreme rule of righteousness. Why raise any question of unrighteousness where righteousness clearly appears? And let us not be ashamed, following Paul's example, to stop the mouths of the wicked, and whenever they dare to rail, repeat the same thing: "Who are you, miserable men, to make accusation against God?" [Rom. 9:20]. Why do you, then, accuse Him because He does not temper the greatness of His works to your ignorance? As if these things were wicked because they are hidden from flesh! It is known to you by clear evidence that the judgments of God are beyond measure. You know that they are called a "great deep" [Psalms 36:6]. Now consider the narrowness of your mind, whether it can grasp what God has decreed with Himself. What good will it do you in your mad search to plunge into the "deep," which your own reason tells you will be your destruction? Why does not some fear at least restrain you because the history of Job as well as the prophetic books proclaim God's incomprehensible wisdom and dreadful might? . . .

It will do us no good to proceed further, for neither will it satisfy their petulance nor does the Lord need any other defense than what He used through His Spirit, who spoke through Paul's mouth; and we forget to speak well when we cease to speak with God.

6. Second objection: the doctrine of election takes guilt and responsibility away from man

Their impiety also produces another objection, which tends not so directly to accuse God as to excuse the sinner. Still, he who is condemned by God as a sinner cannot be justified without dishonoring the Judge. Therefore, profane tongues chatter thus: Why should God impute those things to men as sin, the necessity of which He has imposed by His predestination? What should they do? Should they fight against His decrees? But they would do this in vain, since they could not do it at all. Therefore they are not rightfully punished on account of those things of which the chief cause is in God's predestination. Here I shall avoid that defense to which church writers commonly have recourse: namely, that God's foreknowledge does not hinder man from being accounted a sinner; inasmuch as the evils God foresees are man's, not His own. For the quibbling would not stop here but would, rather, urge that God might have countered the evils that He foresaw if He had so willed; that, since He has not done so, by His predetermined plan He has created man to this end, that he may so conduct himself on earth. But if man was created by God's providence to this condition, that he should afterward do all that he does, then he should not be blamed for what he cannot avoid and undertakes by God's will. Therefore let us see how this difficulty ought duly to be resolved. First of all, what Solomon says ought to be agreed upon among everyone: "God has made everything for Himself, even the wicked for the evil day" [Prov. 16:4]. Behold! Since the disposition of all things is in God's hand, since the decision of salvation or of death rests in His power, He so ordains by His plan and will that among men some are born destined for certain death from the womb, who glorify His name by their own destruction. If anyone should reply that by God's providence He imposes no necessity upon them but that He has created them in this condition, since He has foreseen their wickedness to come, such a one says something but not everything. The older writers have a habit of using this solution at times but with some hesitation. But the Schoolmen rest upon it as if no objection could be made against it. Indeed, I will freely admit that foreknowledge alone imposes no necessity upon creatures, yet not all assent to this. For there are some who wish it also to be the cause of things. But it seems to me that Valla, a man not otherwise much versed in sacred matters, saw more clearly and wisely, for he showed this contention to be superfluous, since both life and death are acts of God's will more than of His foreknowledge. If God only foresaw human events, and did not also dispose and determine them by His decision, then there would be some point in raising this question: whether His foreseeing had anything to do with their necessity. But since He foresees future events only by reason of the fact that He decreed that they take place, they vainly raise a quarrel over foreknowledge, when it is clear that all things take place rather by His determination and bidding.

7. *God has also predestined the fall into sin*

They say it is not stated in so many words that God decreed that Adam should perish for his rebellion. As if, indeed, that very God, who, Scripture proclaims, "does whatever He pleases" [Psalms 115:3], would have created the noblest of His creatures to an uncertain end. They say that he had free choice that he might shape his own fortune, and that God ordained nothing except to treat man according to his own deserts. If such a barren invention is accepted, where will that omnipotence of God be whereby He regulates all things according to His secret plan, which depends solely upon itself? Yet predestination, whether they will or not, manifests itself in Adam's posterity. For it did not take place by reason of nature that, by the guilt of one parent, all were cut off from salvation. What prevents them from admitting concerning one man what they unwillingly concede concerning the whole human race? For why should they fritter away their effort in such evasions? Scripture proclaims that all mortals were bound over to eternal death in the person of one man [cf. Rom. 5:12 ff.]. Since this cannot be ascribed to nature, it is perfectly clear that it has come forth from the wonderful plan of God. It is utterly absurd that these good defenders of God's righteousness hang perplexed upon a straw yet leap over high roofs!

Again I ask: whence does it happen that Adam's fall irremediably involved so many peoples, together with their infant offspring, in eternal death unless because it so pleased God? Here their tongues, otherwise so loquacious, must become mute. The decree is dreadful indeed, I confess. Yet no one can deny that God foreknew what end man was to have before He created Him, and consequently foreknew because He so ordained by His decree. If anyone inveighs against God's foreknowledge at this point, he stumbles rashly and heedlessly. What reason is there to accuse the heavenly Judge because He was not ignorant of what was to happen? If there is any just or manifest complaint, it applies to predestination. And it ought not to seem absurd for me to say that God not only foresaw the fall of the first man, and in him the ruin of his descendants, but also meted it out in accordance with His own decision. For as it pertains to His wisdom to foreknow everything that is to happen, so it pertains to His might to rule and control everything by His hand. And Augustine also skilfully disposes of this question, as of others: "We most wholesomely confess what we most correctly believe, that the God and Lord of all things, who created all things exceedingly good [cf. Gen. 1:31], and foreknew that evil things would rise out of good, and also knew that it pertained to His most omnipotent goodness to bring good out of evil things rather than not to permit evil things to be . . . , so ordained the life of angels and men that in it He might first of all show what free will could do, and then what the blessing of His grace and the verdict of His justice could do."

(God willed, not only permitted, Adam's fall and the rejection of the reprobate, but with justice, 8–11)

8. *No distinction between God's will and God's permission!*

Here they have recourse to the distinction between will and permission. By this they would maintain that the wicked perish because God permits it, not because He so wills. But why shall we say "permission" unless it is because God so wills? Still, it is not in itself likely that man brought destruction upon himself through himself, by God's mere permission and without any ordaining. As if God did not establish the condition in which He wills the chief of His creatures to be! I shall not hesitate, then, simply to confess with Augustine that "the will of God is the necessity of things," and that what He has willed will of necessity come to pass, as those things which He has foreseen will truly come to pass. Now if either the Pelagians, or Manichees, or Anabaptists, or Epicureans (for on this issue we have to deal with these four sects) in excuse for themselves and for the wicked, raise by way of objection the necessity by which they are constrained because of divine predestination, they advance no argument applicable to the cause. For if predestination is nothing but the meting out of divine justice—secret, indeed, but blameless—because it is certain that they were not unworthy to be predestined to this condition, it is equally certain that the destruction they undergo by predestination is also most just. Besides, their perdition depends upon the predestination of God in such a way that the cause and occasion of it are found in themselves. For the first man fell because the Lord had judged it to be expedient; why He so judged is hidden from us. Yet it is certain that He so judged because He saw that thereby the glory of His name is duly revealed.

Where you hear God's glory mentioned, think of His justice. For whatever deserves praise must be just. Accordingly, man falls according as God's providence ordains, but he falls by his own fault. A little before, the Lord had declared that "everything that he had made . . . was exceedingly good" [Gen. 1:31]. Whence, then, comes that wickedness to man, that he should fall away from his God? Lest we should think it comes from creation, God had put His stamp of approval on what had come forth from Himself. By his own evil intention, then, man corrupted the pure nature he had received from the Lord; and by his fall he drew all his posterity with him into destruction. Accordingly, we should contemplate the evident cause of condemnation in the corrupt nature of humanity—which is closer to us—rather than seek a hidden and utterly incomprehensible cause in God's predestination. And let us not be ashamed to submit our understanding to God's boundless wisdom so far as to yield before its many secrets. For, of those things which it is neither given nor lawful to know, ignorance is learned; the craving to know, a kind of madness.

9. *Summary refutation of the second objection*

Perhaps someone will say that I have not yet brought forward evidence to silence this wicked excuse. But I admit this cannot be so done that impiety will not always growl and mutter. Yet it seems to me that I have said enough to banish not only all reason to gainsay but also all pretext to do so. The reprobate wish to be considered excusable in sinning, on the ground that they cannot avoid the necessity of sinning, especially since this sort of necessity is cast upon them by God's ordaining. But we deny that they are duly excused, because the ordinance of God, by which they complain that they are destined to destruction, has its own equity—unknown, indeed, to us but very sure. From this we conclude that the ills they bear are all inflicted upon them by God's most righteous judgment. Accordingly, we teach that they act perversely who to seek out the source of their condemnation turn their gaze upon the hidden sanctuary of God's plan, and wink at the corruption of nature from which it really springs. God, to prevent them from charging it against Himself, bears testimony to His creation. For even though by God's eternal providence man has been created to undergo that calamity to which he is subject, it still takes its occasion from man himself, not from God, since the only reason for his ruin is that he has degenerated from God's pure creation into vicious and impure perversity.

10. *Third objection: the doctrine of election leads to the view that God shows partiality toward persons*

Now the adversaries of God's predestination defame it with a third absurdity. Since we refer solely to the decision of the divine will the release from universal destruction of those whom He accepts as heirs of His kingdom, from this they conclude that there is with God "partiality toward persons," which Scripture everywhere denies. They further conclude either that Scripture disagrees with itself or that in God's election there is consideration of merits. First, Scripture denies that God shows partiality toward persons in another sense than that in which they judge. For it means by the word "person" not a man but those things in a man which, conspicuous to the eye, customarily either produce favor, grace, and dignity, or arouse hatred, contempt, and disgrace. Such things are riches, wealth, power, nobility, office, country, physical beauty, and the like [cf. Deut. 10:17]; also, poverty, need, baseness, vileness, contempt, and the like. Thus, Peter and Paul teach that "the Lord shows no partiality toward persons" [Acts 10:34; cf. Rom. 2:11; Gal. 2:6], for He does not distinguish between Jew and Greek [Gal. 3:28] so as to reject one but embrace the other on grounds of race alone. So James uses the same words when he wants to declare that God in His judgment has no regard for riches [James 2:5]. But Paul, in another passage, says concerning God that, in judging, a state of freedom or of bondage is not taken into consideration [Col. 3:25; Eph. 6:9]. Accordingly, no one will contradict us if we say that God chooses as sons those whom He pleases, according to the good pleasure of His will, without any regard for merit, while He casts out and condemns others.

Still, the matter can be explained to fuller satisfaction. Do they ask how it happens that of two men indistinguishable in merit, God in His election passes over one but takes the other? I, in turn, ask: "Do they think that there is anything in him who is taken that disposes God to him?" If they admit that there is nothing, as they must, it will follow that God does not consider the man but seeks from His own goodness the reason to do him good. The fact that God therefore chooses one man but rejects another arises not out of regard to the man but solely from His mercy, which ought to be free to manifest and express itself where and when He pleases. . . .

11. *God's mercy and righteousness in predestination*

Some, therefore, falsely and wickedly accuse God of biased justice because in His predestination He does not maintain the same attitude toward all. If, they say, He finds all guilty, let Him punish all equally; if innocent, let Him withhold the rigor of His judgment from all. But they so act toward Him as if either mercy were to be forbidden to Him or as if when He wills to show mercy He is compelled to renounce His judgment completely. What is it that they require? If all are guilty, that all together suffer the same punishment. We admit the common guilt, but we say that God's mercy succors some. Let it succor all, they say. But we reply that it is right for Him to show Himself a fair judge also in punishing. When they do not allow this, what do they do but either try to deprive God of His capacity to show mercy or at least allow it to Him on the condition that He give up His judgment completely?

Augustine's statements most aptly accord with this: "Since in the first man the whole mass of the race fell under condemnation, . . . those vessels of it which are made unto honor are vessels not of their own righteousness . . . but of God's mercy, but that other vessels are made unto dishonor [cf. Rom. 9:21] is to be laid not to inquiry but to judgment." Because God metes out merited penalty to those whom He condemns but distributes unmerited grace to those whom He calls, He is freed of all accusation—like a lender, who has the power of remitting payment to one, of exacting it from another. "The Lord can therefore also give grace . . . to whom He will . . . because He is merciful, and not give to all because He is a just judge. For by giving to some what they do not deserve, . . . He can show His free grace. . . . By not giving to all, He can manifest what all deserve." For when Paul writes that "God has shut up all things under sin that He may have mercy on all" [Rom. 11:32, conflated with Gal. 3:22], at the same time it should be added that He is debtor to no one, for "no one has first given to Him, that He should demand something back" [Rom. 11:35].

(Preaching of predestination not injurious but useful, 12–14)
12. Fourth objection: the doctrine of election destroys all zeal for an upright life

To overthrow predestination our opponents also raise the point that, if it stands, all carefulness and zeal for well-doing go to ruin. For who can hear, they say, that either life or death has been appointed for him by God's eternal and unchangeable decree without thinking immediately that it makes no difference how he conducts himself, since God's predestination can neither be hindered nor advanced by his effort? Thus all men will throw themselves away, and in a desperate manner rush headlong wherever lust carries them. Obviously they are not completely lying, for there are many swine that pollute the doctrine of predestination with their foul blasphemies, and by this pretext evade all admonitions and reproofs. God knows what He once for all has determined to do with us: if He has decreed salvation, He will bring us to it in His own time; if He has destined us to death, we would fight against it in vain.

But Scripture, while it requires us to consider this great mystery with so much more reverence and piety, both instructs the godly to a far different attitude and effectively refutes the criminal madness of these men. For Scripture does not speak of predestination with intent to rouse us to boldness that we may try with impious rashness to search out God's unattainable secrets. Rather, its intent is that, humbled and cast down, we may learn to tremble at His judgment and esteem His mercy. It is at this mark that believers aim. But the foul grunting of these swine is duly silenced by Paul. They say they go on unconcerned in their vices; for if they are of the number of the elect, vices will not hinder them from being at last brought into life. Yet Paul teaches that we have been chosen to this end: that we may lead a holy and blameless life [Eph. 1:4]. If election has as its goal holiness of life, it ought rather to arouse and goad us eagerly to set our mind upon it than to serve as a pretext for doing nothing. What a great difference there is between these two things: to cease well-doing because election is sufficient for salvation, and to devote ourselves to the pursuit of good as the appointed goal of election! Away, then, with such sacrileges, for they wickedly invert the whole order of election.

But they stretch their blasphemies farther when they say that he who has been condemned by God, if he endeavors through innocent and upright life to make himself approved of God [cf. 2 Tim. 2:15], will lose his labor. In this contention they are convicted of utterly shameless falsehood. Whence could such endeavor arise but from election? For whoever are of the number of the reprobate, as they are vessels made for dishonor [cf. Rom. 9:21], so they do not cease by their continual crimes to arouse God's wrath against themselves, and to confirm by clear signs that God's judgment has already been pronounced upon them —no matter how much they vainly resist it. . . .

[Church Discipline]
Chapter XII
The discipline of the church: its chief
use in censures and excommunication

(*Discussion of power of the keys in true discipline: the ends and processes of discipline, 1–7*)
1. *Necessity and nature of church discipline*
The discipline of the church, the discussion of which we have deferred to this place, must be treated briefly, that we may thereafter pass to the remaining topics. Discipline depends for the most part upon the power of the keys and upon spiritual jurisdiction. To understand it better, let us divide the church into two chief

orders: clergy and people. I call by the usual name "clergy" those who perform the public ministry in the church. We shall first speak of common discipline, to which all ought to submit; then we shall come to the clergy, who, besides the common discipline, have their own.

But because some persons, in their hatred of discipline, recoil from its very name, let them understand this: if no society, indeed, no house which has even a small family, can be kept in proper condition without discipline, it is much more necessary in the church, whose condition should be as ordered as possible. Accordingly, as the saving doctrine of Christ is the soul of the church, so does discipline serve as its sinews, through which the members of the body hold together, each in its own place. Therefore, all who desire to remove discipline or to hinder its restoration—whether they do this deliberately or out of ignorance—are surely contributing to the ultimate dissolution of the church. For what will happen if each is allowed to do what he pleases? Yet that would happen, if to the preaching of doctrine there were not added private admonitions, corrections, and other aids of the sort that sustain doctrine and do not let it remain idle. Therefore, discipline is like a bridle to restrain and tame those who rage against the doctrine of Christ; or like a spur to arouse those of little inclination; and also sometimes like a father's rod to chastise mildly and with the gentleness of Christ's Spirit those who have more seriously lapsed. When, therefore, we discern frightful devastation beginning to threaten the church because there is no concern and no means of restraining the people, necessity itself cries out that a remedy is needed. Now, this is the sole remedy that Christ has enjoined and the one that has always been used among the godly.

2. Stages of church discipline

The first foundation of discipline is to provide a place for private admonition; that is, if anyone does not perform his duty willingly, or behaves insolently, or does not live honorably, or has committed any act deserving blame—he should allow himself to be admonished; and when the situation demands it, every man should endeavor to admonish his brother. But let pastors and presbyters be especially watchful to do this, for their duty is not only to preach to the people, but to warn and exhort in every house. . . . For doctrine obtains force and authority where the minister not only explains to all together what they owe to Christ, but also has the right and means to require that it be kept by those whom he has observed are either disrespectful or languid toward his teaching.

If anyone either stubbornly rejects such admonitions or shows that he scorns them by persisting in his own vices, after having been admonished a second time in the presence of witnesses, Christ commands that he be called to the tribunal of the church, that is, the assembly of the elders, and there be more gravely admonished as by public authority, in order that, if he reverences the church, he may submit and obey. If he is not even subdued by this but perseveres in his wickedness, then Christ commands that, as a despiser of the church, he be removed from the believers' fellowship [Matt. 18:15, 17].

3. *Concealed and open sins*

But because Christ is here speaking only of secret faults, we must postulate this division: some sins are private; others, public or openly manifest. Of the former, Christ says to every individual: "Reprove him, between you and him alone" [Matt. 18:15]. Paul says to Timothy of open sins: "Rebuke them in the presence of all, so that the rest may stand in fear" [1 Tim. 5:20]. For Christ had previously said, "If your brother has sinned against you" [Matt. 18:15]. This phrase ["against you"] (unless you wish to be contentious) you cannot otherwise understand than as "with your knowledge alone, no others being aware." But what the Apostle enjoins upon Timothy concerning reproving openly those who sin openly, he himself follows in the case of Peter. For when Peter sinned to the point of public scandal, Paul did not admonish him privately but brought him into the presence of the church [Gal. 2:14].

This, then, will be the right sequence in which to act: to proceed in correcting secret sins according to the steps laid down by Christ; but in open sins, if the offense is indeed public, to proceed at once to solemn rebuke by the church.

4. *Light and grave sins*

Here is another distinction: of sins, some are faults; others,

crimes or shameful acts. To correct these latter ones, we must
not only use admonition or rebuke, but a severer remedy: as
Paul shows when he not only chastises the incestuous Corinthian
with words but punishes him with excommunication, as soon as
he has been apprised of the crime [1 Cor. 5:3 ff.]. Now, therefore, we begin to see better how the spiritual jurisdiction of the
church, which punishes sins according to the Lord's word, is the
best support of health, foundation of order, and bond of unity.
Therefore, in excluding from its fellowship manifest adulterers,
fornicators, thieves, robbers, seditious persons, perjurers, false
witnesses, and the rest of this sort, as well as the insolent (who
when duly admonished of their lighter vices mock God and His
judgment), the church claims for itself nothing unreasonable but
practices the jurisdiction conferred upon it by the Lord. Now,
that no one may despise such a judgment of the church or regard
condemnation by vote of the believers as a trivial thing, the Lord
has testified that this is nothing but the publication of His own
sentence, and what they have done on earth is ratified in heaven.
For they have the word of the Lord to condemn the perverse;
they have the word to receive the repentant unto grace [Matt.
16:19; 18:18; John 20:23]. Those who trust that without this
bond of discipline the church can long stand are, I say, mistaken;
unless, perhaps, we can with impunity go without that aid which
the Lord foresaw would be necessary for us. Truly, the variety of
uses of this discipline will better show how great the need of it is!

5. *The purpose of church discipline*

In such corrections and excommunication, the church has three
ends in view. The first is that they who lead a filthy and infamous
life may not be called Christians, to the dishonor of God, as if
His holy church [cf. Eph. 5:25–26] were a conspiracy of wicked
and abandoned men. For since the church itself is the body of
Christ [Col. 1:24], it cannot be corrupted by such foul and
decaying members without some disgrace falling upon its Head.
Therefore, that there may be no such thing in the church to
brand its most sacred name with disgrace, they from whose
wickedness infamy redounds to the Christian name must be banished from its family. And here also we must preserve the order
of the Lord's Supper, that it may not be profaned by being ad-

ministered indiscriminately. For it is very true that he to whom its distribution has been committed, if he knowingly and willingly admits an unworthy person whom he could rightfully turn away, is as guilty of sacrilege as if he had cast the Lord's body to dogs. . . . Therefore, lest this most hallowed mystery be disgraced, discretion is very much needed in its distribution. Yet this can be had only through the jurisdiction of the church.

The second purpose is that the good be not corrupted by the constant company of the wicked, as commonly happens. For (such is our tendency to wander from the way) there is nothing easier than for us to be led away by bad examples from right living. The Apostle noted this tendency when he bade the Corinthians expel the incestuous man from their company. "A little leaven," he says, "ferments the whole lump" [1 Cor. 5:6]. And he foresaw such great danger here that he prohibited all association with him. "If any brother," he says, "bears among you the name of fornicator, miser, worshiper of idols, drunkard, or reviler, I do not allow you even to take food with such a man" [1 Cor. 5:11].

The third purpose is that those overcome by shame for their baseness begin to repent. They who under gentler treatment would have become more stubborn so profit by the chastisement of their own evil as to be awakened when they feel the rod. The Apostle means this when he speaks as follows: "If anyone does not obey our teaching, note that man; and do not mingle with him, that he may be ashamed" [2 Thess. 3:14]. . . .

6. *The handling of church discipline in the various cases*

With these purposes enumerated, it remains for us to see how the church carries out this part of discipline which falls within its jurisdiction.

To begin with, let us keep the division set forth above: that some sins are public; others, private or somewhat secret. Public sins are those witnessed not by one or two persons, but committed openly and to the offense of the entire church. I call secret sins, not those completely hidden from men, as are those of hypocrites (for these do not fall under the judgment of the church), but those of an intermediate sort, which are not unwitnessed, yet not public.

The first kind does not require the steps which Christ lists [Matt. 18:15-17]; but when any such sin appears, the church ought to do its duty in summoning the sinner and correcting him according to his fault.

In the second kind, according to that rule of Christ, the case does not come before the church until the sinner becomes obstinate. When it has come before the church, then the other division between crimes and faults is to be observed. For such great severity is not to be used in lighter sins, but verbal chastisement is enough—and that mild and fatherly—which should not harden or confuse the sinner, but bring him back to himself, that he may rejoice rather than be sad that he has been corrected. But shameful acts need to be chastised with a harsher remedy. Nor is it enough if he, who by setting a bad example through his misdeed has gravely injured the church, be chastised only with words; but he ought for a time to be deprived of the communion of the Supper until he gives assurance of his repentance. For Paul not only rebuked the Corinthian in words but banished him from the church, and chided the Corinthians for bearing with him so long [1 Cor. 5:1-7].

The ancient and better church kept this procedure while lawful government flourished. For if anyone had committed a crime that caused offense, he was ordered first to abstain from partaking of the Sacred Supper, then to humble himself before God and witness his repentance before the church. There were, moreover, solemn rites customarily enjoined as marks of repentance upon those who had lapsed. When these had been performed to the satisfaction of the church, the penitent was received into grace with laying on of hands, a reception that Cyprian often calls "peace."

7. *In the ancient church, discipline applied to all offenders alike*

As no one was exempt from this discipline, both princes and common people submitted to it. And rightly! For it was established by Christ, to whom it is fitting that all royal scepters and crowns submit. Thus Theodosius, when he was deprived of the right of communion by Ambrose because of the slaughter committed at Thessalonica, threw down all his royal trappings; in church he publicly wept over his sin, which had overtaken him through others' deceit, and begged pardon with groaning and tears. For great kings ought not to count it any dishonor to prostrate themselves as suppliants before Christ, the King of Kings; nor ought they to be displeased that they are judged by the church. For inasmuch as they hear almost nothing but mere flatteries in their courts, it is all the more necessary for them to be rebuked by the Lord through the mouth of priests. Rather, they ought to desire not to be spared by the priests, that God may spare them.

In this place I say nothing about those persons through whom this jurisdiction is to be exercised; for I have discussed this elsewhere. I add only this: Paul's course of action for excommunicating a man is the lawful one, provided the elders do not do it by themselves alone, but with the knowledge and approval of the church; in this way the multitude of the people does not decide the action but observes as witness and guardian so that nothing may be done according to the whim of a few. Indeed, the whole sequence of the action, besides the calling on God's name, ought to have that gravity which bespeaks the presence of Christ in order that there may be no doubt that He Himself presides at His own tribunal. . . .

(*Moderation in discipline enjoined, and rigorists confuted, 8–13*)
8. *Severity and mildness in church discipline*

But we ought not to pass over the fact that such severity as is joined with a "spirit of gentleness" [Gal. 6:1] befits the church. For we must always, as Paul bids us, take particular care that he who is punished be not overwhelmed with sorrow [2 Cor. 2:7]. Thus a remedy would become destruction. But, from the purpose intended it would be better to take a rule of moderation. For, in excommunication the intent is to lead the sinner to repentance and to remove bad examples from the midst, lest either Christ's name be maligned or others be provoked to imitate them. If, then, we look to these things, it will be easy for us to judge how far severity ought to go and where it ought to stop. Therefore, when a sinner gives testimony of his repentance to the church, and by this testimony wipes out the offense as far as he can, he is not to be urged any further. If he is so urged, the rigor will now exceed due measure.

In this respect we cannot at all excuse the excessive severity of the ancients, which both completely departed from the Lord's injunction and was also terribly dangerous. For when they imposed solemn penance and deprivation from Holy Communion sometimes for seven, sometimes for four, sometimes for three, years, and sometimes for life, what could be the result but either great hypocrisy or utter despair? Likewise, it was not profitable or consonant with reason that one who had fallen again should not be admitted to a second repentance, but should be cast out of the church to the end of his life. Whoever will weigh the matter with sound judgment will recognize their lack of prudence in this. . . .

9. *The limits of our judgment according to church discipline*

This gentleness is required in the whole body of the church, that it should deal mildly with the lapsed and should not punish with extreme rigor, but rather, according to Paul's injunction, confirm its love toward them [2 Cor. 2:8]. Similarly, each layman ought to temper himself to this mildness and gentleness. It is, therefore, not our task to erase from the number of the elect those who have been expelled from the church, or to despair as if they were already lost. It is lawful to regard them as estranged from the church, and thus, from Christ—but only for such time as they remain separated. However, if they also display more stubbornness than gentleness, we should still commend them to the Lord's judgment, hoping for better things of them in the future than we see in the present. Nor should we on this account cease to call upon God in their behalf. And (to put it in one word) let us not condemn to death the very person who is in the hand and judgment of God alone; rather, let us only judge of the character of each man's works by the law of the Lord. While we follow this rule, we rather take our stand upon the divine judgment than put forward our own. Let us not claim for ourselves more license in judgment, unless we wish to limit God's power and confine His mercy by law. For God, whenever it pleases Him, changes the worst men into the best, engrafts the alien, and adopts the stranger into the church. And the Lord does this to frustrate men's opinion and restrain their rashness—which, unless it is checked, ventures to assume for itself a greater right of judgment than it deserves.

10. *Excommunication is corrective*

For when Christ promises that what His people "bind on earth shall be bound in heaven" [Matt. 18:18], He limits the force of binding to ecclesiastical censure. By this those who are excommunicated are not cast into everlasting ruin and damnation, but in hearing that their life and morals are condemned, they are assured of their everlasting condemnation unless they repent. Excommunication differs from anathema in that the latter, taking away all pardon, condemns and consigns a man to eternal destruction; the former, rather, avenges and chastens his moral conduct. And although excommunication also punishes the man, it does so in such a way that, by forewarning him of his future condemnation, it may call him back to salvation. But if that be obtained, reconciliation and restoration to communion await him. Moreover, anathema is very rarely or never used. Accordingly, though ecclesiastical discipline does not permit us to live familiarly or have intimate contact with excommunicated persons, we ought nevertheless to strive by whatever means we can in order that they may turn to a more virtuous life and may return to the society and unity of the church. So the Apostle also teaches: "Do not look upon them as enemies, but warn them as brothers" [2 Thess. 3:15]. Unless this gentleness is maintained in both private and public censures, there is danger lest we soon slide down from discipline to butchery.

11. *Against wilful excess in demanding church discipline*

This is also a prime requisite for the moderation of discipline, as Augustine argues against the Donatists: that individual laymen, if they see vices not diligently enough corrected by the council of elders, should not therefore at once depart from the church; and that the pastors themselves, if they cannot cleanse all that needs correction according to their hearts' desire, should not for that reason resign their ministry or disturb the entire church with unaccustomed rigor. For what Augustine writes is very true: "Whoever either corrects what he can by reproof, or excludes, without breaking the bond of peace, what he cannot correct—disapproving with fairness, bearing with firmness—this man is free and loosed from the curse."

⊔⊔⊔⊔⊔⊔⊔⊔⊔⊔⊔⊔⊔⊔⊔⊔⊔⊔⊔⊔⊔⊔⊔⊔⊔⊔

18. Philip Mornay: *A Defence of Liberty Against Tyrants* (1579)*

Calvin's thought underwent a variety of changes as it spread through-out Europe and was expounded by his disciples. Perhaps Calvin him-self would not have found acceptance among the Calvinists of a later time. The excerpts below come from a document of French Calvinism of the second half of the sixteenth century; while reminis-cent of Calvin's writings, this document is distinctly different. France was then embroiled in bitter wars of religion. In a way these wars were a contest between rival factions of nobility, and the crown was almost a bystander. Then with the Massacre of St. Bartholomew in 1572 the crown became dramatically involved. This led the French Calvinists to reexamine their attitude toward governmental authority and the monarchy.

Philip Mornay, the probable author of the *Vindiciae contra Tyran-nos*, or *A Defence of Liberty Against Tyrants*, was one of the most prominent of the Calvinist "monarchomachists," who on legal as well as biblical grounds repudiated the notion of an absolute monarchy. A sovereign who violated the laws of the land had to be opposed—an important political theory which a century later exerted considerable influence upon the rise of the notion of representative government.

A Defence of Liberty Against Tyrants was published in 1579, though it had been written some five years earlier under the impact of the Massacre of St. Bartholomew. Originally written in Latin, a French edition came out in 1581, and an English edition, interestingly enough, in 1689, the year of the Glorious Revolution. Of the four questions dealt with in the book, reprinted here are a section from the second question ("Whether it be lawful to resist a Prince which does infringe the law of God or ruine the church, by whom and how, and how far is it lawful?") and all of the third.

* H. J. Laski (ed.), *A Defence of Liberty Against Tyrants. A Translation of the* Vindiciae contra Tyrannos (Gloucester, Mass., 1963), pp. 113 ff.

LITERATURE
G. L. Hunt (ed.), *Calvinism and the Political Order* (Philadelphia, 1965).

Whether it be lawful to take arms for religion

FURTHERMORE, to take away all scruple, we must necessarily answer those who esteem, or else would that others should think they hold that opinion, that the church ought not to be defended by arms. They say withal that it was not without a great mystery that God did forbid in the law, that the altar should be made or adorned with the help of any tool of iron; in like manner, that at the building of the temple of Solomon, there was not heard any noise of axe or hammer, or other tools of iron; from whence they collect the church which is the lively temple of the Lord, ought not to be reformed by arms; yea, as if the stones of the altar, and of the temple were hewed and taken out of the quarries without any instrument of iron, which the text of the holy scripture doth sufficiently clear.

But if we oppose to this goodly allegory, that which is written in the fourth chapter of the Book of Nehemiah, that one part of the people carried mortar, and another part stood ready with their weapons, that some held in one hand their swords, and with the other carried the materials to the workmen, for the rebuilding of the temple; to the end, by this means, to prevent their enemies from ruining their work; we say also, that the church is neither advanced nor edified by these material weapons; but by these arms it is warranted and preserved from the violence of the enemies, which will not by any means endure the increase of it. Briefly, there has been an infinite number of good kings and princes (as histories do testify) which by arms have maintained and defended the service of God against pagans. They reply readily to this, that wars in this manner were allowable under the law; but since the time that grace has been offered by Jesus Christ, who would not enter into Jerusalem mounted on a brave horse, but meekly sitting on an ass, this manner of proceeding has had an end. I answer first, that all agree with me in this, that our Savior Christ, during all the time that He conversed in this world, took not on Him the office of a judge or king; but rather of a private person, and a delinquent by imputation of our transgressions; so that it is an allegation besides the purpose, to say that He hath not managed arms.

But I would willingly demand of such exceptionalists, whether that they think by the coming of Jesus Christ in the flesh, that magistrates have lost their right in the sword of authority? If they say so, Saint Paul contradicts them, who says that the magistrates carry not the sword in vain, and did not refuse their assistance and power against the violence of those who had conspired his death. And if they consent to the saying of the Apostle, to what purpose should the magistrates bear the sword, if it be not to serve God, who has committed it to them, to defend the good and punish the bad? Can they do better service than to preserve the church from the violence of the wicked, and to deliver the flock of Christ from the swords of murderers? I would demand of them, yet, whether they think that all use of arms is forbidden to Christians? If this be their opinion, then would I know of them, wherefore Christ did grant to the centurion his request? Wherefore did He give so excellent a testimony of him? Wherefore does St. John Baptist command the men at arms to content themselves with their pay, and not to use any extortion, and does not rather persuade them to leave their calling? Wherefore did St. Peter baptize Cornelius the Centurion, who was the first fruits of the Gentiles? From whence comes it that he did not in any sort whatsoever counsel him to leave his charge?

Now, if to bear arms and to make war be a thing lawful, can there possibly be found any war more just than that which is taken in hand by the command of the superior, for the defense of the church, and the preservation of the faithful? Is there any greater tyranny than that which is exercised over the soul? Can there be imagined a war more commendable than that which suppresses such a tyranny? For the last point, I would willingly know of these men, whether it be absolutely prohibited Christians to make war upon any occasion whatsoever? If they say that it is forbidden them, from whence comes it then that the men at arms, captains and centurions, who had no other employment, but the managing of arms, were always received into the church? Wherefore do the ancient Fathers, and Christian historians make so horrible mention of certain legions composed wholly of Christian soldiers, and amongst others of that of Malta, so renowned for the victory which they obtained, and of that of Thebes, of the which St. Mauritius was general, who suffered martyrdom, together with all his troops, for the confessing of the name of Jesus Christ? And if it be permitted to make war (as it may be they will confess) to keep the limits and towns of a country, and to repulse an invading enemy, is it not yet a thing much more reasonable to take arms to preserve and defend honest men, to suppress the wicked, and to keep and defend the limits and bounds of the church, which is the kingdom of Jesus Christ? If it were otherwise, to what purpose should St. John have foretold that the whore of Babylon shall be finally ruined by the ten kings, whom she has bewitched? Furthermore, if we hold a contrary opinion, what shall we say of the wars of Constantine, against Maxentius, and Licimius, celebrated by so many public orations, and approved by the testimony of an infinite number of learned men? What opinion should we hold of the many voyages made by Christian princes against the Turks and Saracens to conquer the Holy Land, who had not, or at the least, ought not to have had, any other end in their designs, but to hinder the enemy from ruining the temple of the land, and to restore the integrity of His service into those countries?

Although then the church be not increased by arms, notwithstanding it may be justly preserved by the means of arms. I say further, that those that die in so holy a war are no less the martyrs of Jesus Christ than their brethren who were put to death for religion; nay, they who die in that war seem to have this disadvantage, that with a free will and knowing sufficiently hazard, into which they cast themselves, notwithstanding, do courageously expose their lives to death and danger, whereas the other do only not refuse death, when it behoveth them to suffer. The Turks strive to advance their opinion by the means of arms, and if they do subdue a country, they presently bring in by force the impieties of Mohamet, who in his Alcoran, hath so recommended arms, as they are not ashamed to say it is the ready way to heaven, yet do the Turks constrain no man in matter of conscience. But he who is a much greater adversary to Christ and true religion, with all those kings whom he has enchanted, opposes fire and faggots, to the light of the gospel, tortures the word of God, compelling by wracking and torments, as much as in him lies, all men to become idolaters, and finally is not ashamed to advance and maintain their faith and law by perfidious disloyalty, and their traditions by continual treasons.

Now on the contrary, those good princes and magistrates are said properly to defend themselves, who environ and fortify by all their means and industry the vine of Christ, already planted, to be planted in places where it has not yet been, lest the wild boar of the forest should spoil or devour it. They do this (I say) in covering with their buckler, and defending with their sword, those who by the preaching of the gospel have been converted to true religion, and in fortifying with their best ability, by ravelins, ditches, and rampers the temple of God built with lively stones, until it have attained the full height, in despite of all the furious assaults of the enemies thereof. We have lengthened out this discourse thus far, to the end we might take away all scruple concerning this question. Set, then, the estates, and all the officers of a kingdom, or the greatest part of them, every one established in authority by the people: know, that if they contain not within his bounds (or at the least, employ not the utmost of their endeavors thereto) a king who seeks to corrupt the law of God, or hinders the reestablishment thereof, that they offend grievously against the Lord, with whom they have contracted covenants upon those conditions. Those of a town, or of a province, making a portion of a kingdom, let them know also, that they draw upon themselves the judgment of God if they drive not impiety out of their walls and confines if the king seek to bring it in, or if they be wanting to preserve by all means, the pure doctrine of the gospel, although for the defense thereof, they suffer for a time banishment, or any other misery. Finally, more private men must be all advertised, that nothing can excuse them, if they obey any in that which offends God, and that yet they have no right nor warrant, neither may in any sort by their private authority take arms, if it appear not most evidently, that they have extraordinary vocation thereunto, all which our discourse will suppose we have confirmed by pregnant testimonies drawn from holy writ.

The Third Question

Whether it be lawful to resist a prince who doth oppress or ruin a public state, and how far such resistance may be extended: by whom, how, and by what right or law it is permitted

FOR so much as we must here dispute of the lawful authority of a lawful prince, I am confident that this question will be the less acceptable to tyrants and wicked princes; for it is no marvel if those who receive no law, but what their own will and fancy dictate unto them, be deaf unto the voice of that law which is grounded upon reason. But I persuade myself that good princes will willingly entertain this discourse, insomuch as they sufficiently know that all magistrates, be they of never so high a rank, are but an inanimated and speaking law. Neither though anything be pressed home against the bad, can it fall within any inference against the good kings or princes, as also good and bad princes are in a direct diameter opposite and contrary: therefore, that which shall be urged against tyrants, is so far from detracting anything from kings, as on the contrary, the more tyrants are laid open in their proper colors, the more glorious does the true worth and dignity of kings appear; neither can the vicious imperfections of the one be laid open, but it gives addition of perfections and respect to the honor of the other.

But for tyrants let them say and think what they please, that shall be the least of my care; for it is not to them, but against them that I write; for kings I believe that they will readily consent to that which is propounded, for by true proportion of reason they ought as much to hate tyrants and wicked governors, as shepherds hate wolves, physicians, poisoners, true prophets, false doctors; for it must necessarily occur that reason infuses into good kings as much hatred against tyrants, as nature imprints in dogs against wolves, for as the one lives by rapine and spoil, so the other is born or bred to redress and prevent all such outrages. It may be the flatterers of tyrants will cast a supercilious aspect on these lines; but if they were not past all grace they would rather blush for shame. I very well know that the friends and faithful servants of kings will not only approve and lovingly entertain this discourse, but also, with their best abilities, defend the contents thereof. Accordingly as the reader shall find himself moved either with content or dislike in the reading hereof, let him know that by that he shall plainly discover either the affection or hatred that he bears to tyrants. Let us now enter into the matter.

Kings are made by the people

We have showed before that it is God that does appoint kings, who chooses them, who gives the kingdom to them: now we say that the people establish kings, put the scepter into their hands, and who with their suffrages, approves the election. God would have it done in this manner, to the end that the kings should acknowledge, that after God they hold their power and sovereignty from the people, and that it might the rather induce them, to apply and address the utmost of their care and thoughts for the profit of the people, without being puffed with any vain imagination, that they were formed of any matter more excellent than other men, for which they were raised so high above others; as if they were to command our flocks of sheep, or herds of cattle. But let them remember and know, that they are of the same mold and condition as others, raised from the earth by the voice and acclamations, now as it were upon the shoulders of the people unto their thrones, that they might afterwards bear on their own shoulders the greatest burdens of the commonwealth. Divers ages before that, the people of Israel demanded a king. God gave and appointed the law of royal government contained in the seventeenth chapter, verse fourteen of Deuteronomy, when, says Moses, "thou art come unto the land which the Lord thy God giveth thee, and shalt possess it, and shalt dwell therein, and shalt say, I will set a king over me like as all the nations that are about me, thou shalt in any wise set him whom the Lord thy God shall choose from amongst thy brethren, etc." You see here, that the election of the king is attributed to God, the establishment to the people: now when the practice of this law came in use, see in what manner they proceeded.

The elders of Israel, who presented the whole body of the people (under this name of elders are comprehended the captains, the centurions, commanders over fifties and tens, judges, provosts, but principally the chiefest of tribes) came to meet Samuel in Ramah, and not being willing longer to endure the government of the sons of Samuel, whose ill carriage had justly drawn on them the people's dislike, and withal persuading themselves that they had found the means to make their wars hereafter with more advantage, they demanded a king of Samuel, who asking counsel of the Lord, he made known that He had chosen Saul for the governor of His people. . . .

And for David, by the commandment of God, and in a manner more evident than the former, after the rejection of Saul, Samuel anointed for king over Israel, David, chosen by the Lord, which being done, the Spirit of the Lord presently left Saul, and wrought in a special manner in David. But David, notwithstanding, reigns not, but was compelled to save himself in deserts and rocks, oftentimes falling upon the very brim of destruction, and never reigned as king until after the death of Saul: for then by the suffrages of all the people of Judah he was first chosen king of Judah, and seven years after by the consent of all Israel, he was inaugurated king of Israel in Hebron. So, then, he is anointed first by the prophet at the commandment of God, as a token he was chosen. Secondly, by the commandment of the people when he was established king. And that to the end that kings may always remember that it is from God, but by the people, and for the people's sake that they do reign, and that in their glory they say not (as is their custom) they hold their kingdom only of God and their sword, but withal add that it was the people who first girt them with that sword. The same order offered in Solomon. Although he was the king's son, God had chosen Solomon to sit upon the throne of his kingdom, and by express words had promised David to be with him and assist him as a father his son. David had with his own mouth designed Solomon to be successor to his crown in the presence of some of the principal of his court.

But this was not enough, and therefore David assembled at

Jerusalem the princes of Israel, the heads of the tribes, the captains of the soldiers, and ordinance officers of the kings, the centurions and other magistrates of towns, together with his sons, the noblemen and worthiest personages of the kingdom, to consult and resolve upon the election. In this assembly, after they had called upon the name of God, Solomon, by the consent of the whole congregation, was proclaimed and anointed for king, and sat (so says the text) upon the throne of Israel; then, and not before, the princes, the noblemen, his brothers themselves do him homage, and take the oath of allegiance. And to the end, that it may not be said that that was only done to avoid occasion of difference, which might arise amongst the brothers and sons of David about the succession, we read that the other following kings have, in the same manner, been established in their places. It is said, that after the death of Solomon, the people assembled to create his son Rehoboam king. After that Amaziah was killed, Ozias, his only son, was chosen king by all the people, Ochosias after Joram, Joachim, the son of Josias, after the decease of his father, whose piety might well seem to require that without any other solemnity, notwithstanding, both he and the other were chosen and invested into the royal throne, by the suffrages of the people. . . .

It may be collected from this, that the kingdom of Israel was not hereditary, if we consider David and the promise made to him, and that it was wholly elective, if we regard the particular persons. But to what purpose is this, but to make it apparent that the election is only mentioned, that the kings might have always in their remembrance that they were raised to their dignities by the people, and therefore they should never forget during life in what a strict bound of observance they are tied to those from whom they have received all their greatness. We read that the kings of the heathen have been established also by the people; for as when they had either troubles at home, or wars abroad, someone, in whose ready valor and discreet integrity the people did principally rely and repose their greatest confidence, him they presently, with a universal consent, constituted king.

Cicero says, that among the Medes, Diocles, from a judge of private controversies, was, for his uprighteness, by the whole people elected king, and in the same manner were the first kings chosen among the Romans. . . .

Briefly, for so much as none were ever born with crowns on their heads, and scepters in their hands, and that no man can be a king by himself, nor reign without people, whereas on the contrary, the people may subsist of themselves, and were, long before they had any kings, it must of necessity follow, that kings were at the first constituted by the people; and although the sons and dependents of such kings, inheriting their fathers' virtues, may in a sort seem to have rendered their kingdoms hereditary to their offsprings, and that in some kingdoms and countries, the right of free election seems in a sort buried; yet, notwithstanding, in all well-ordered kingdoms, this custom is yet remaining. The sons do not succeed the fathers, before the people have first, as it were, anew established them by their new approbation: neither were they acknowledged in quality, as inheriting it from the dead; but approved and accounted kings then only, when they were invested with the kingdom, by receiving the scepter and diadem from the hands of those who represent the majesty of the people. One may see most evident marks of this in Christian kingdoms, which are at this day esteemed hereditary; for the French king, he of Spain and England, and others, are commonly sacred, and, as it were, put into possession of their authority by the peers, lords of the kingdom, and officers of the crown, who represent the body of the people; no more nor less than the emperors of Germany are chosen by the electors, and the kings of Polonia, by the yawodes and palatines of the kingdom, where the right of election is yet in force. . . .

But not to wander from France, the long continuance and power of which kingdom may in some sort plead for a ruling authority, and where succession seems to have obtained most reputation. We read that Pharamond was chosen in the year 419, Pepin in the year 751, Charles the Great, and Charlemain, the son of Pepin, in the year 768, without having any respect to their fathers' former estate. Charlemain dying in the year 772, his portion fell not presently into the possession of his brother Charles the Great, as it ordinarily happens in the succession of inheritances, but by the ordinance of the people and the estates of the kingdom he is invested with it; the same author witnesses, that in the year 812, Louis the Courteous, although he was the son of Charles the Great, was also elected; and in the testament of Charlemain, inserted into the history written by Nauclere, Charlemain does entreat the people to choose, by a general assembly of the estates of the kingdom, which of his grandchildren or nephews the people pleased, and commanding the uncles to observe and obey the ordinance of the people, by means whereof, Charles the Bold, nephew to Louis the Courteous and Judith, declares himself to be chosen king, as Aimonius the French historian recites.

To conclude in a word, all kings at the first were altogether elected, and those who at this day seem to have their crowns and royal authority by inheritance, have or should have, first and principally their confirmation from the people. Briefly, although the people of some countries have been accustomed to choose their kings of such a lineage, which for some notable merits have worthily deserved it, yet we must believe that they choose the stock itself, and not every branch that proceeds from it; neither are they so tied to that election, as if the successor degenerate, they may not choose another more worthy, neither those who come and are the next of that stock, are born kings, but created such, nor called kings, but princes of the blood royal.

The whole body of the people is above the king

Now, seeing that the people choose and establish their kings, it follows that the whole body of the people is above the king; for it is a thing most evident, that he who is established by another, is accounted under him who has established him, and he who receives his authority from another, is less than he from whom he derives his power. Potiphar the Egyptian sets Joseph over all his house; Nebuchadnezzar, Daniel over the province of Babylon; Darius the six score governors over the kingdom. It is commonly said that masters establish their servants, kings their officers. In like manner, also, the people establish the king as administrator of the commonwealth. Good kings have not disdained this title; yea, the bad ones themselves have affected it; insomuch, as for the space of divers ages, no Roman emperor (if it were not some absolute tyrant, as Nero, Domitian, Caligula) would suffer himself to be called lord. Furthermore, it must necessarily be, that kings were instituted for the people's sake, neither can it be, that for the pleasure of some hundreds of men, and without doubt more foolish and worse than many of the other, all the rest were made, but much rather that these hundred were made for the use and service of all the other, and reason requires that he be preferred above the other, who was made only to and for his occasion: so it is, that for the ship's sail, the owner appoints a pilot over her, who sits at the helm, and looks that she keep her course, nor run not upon any dangerous shelf; the pilot doing his duty, is obeyed by the mariners; yea, and of himself who is owner of the vessel, notwithstanding, the pilot is a servant as well as the least in the ship, from whom he only differs in this, that he serves in a better place than they do.

In a commonwealth, commonly compared to a ship, the king holds the place of pilot, the people in general are owners of the vessel, obeying the pilot, while he is careful of the public good; as though this pilot neither is nor ought to be esteemed other than servant to the public; as a judge or general in war differs little from other officers, but that he is bound to bear greater burdens, and expose himself to more dangers. By the same reason also which the king gains by acquist of arms, be it that he possesses himself of frontier places in warring on the enemy, or that which he gets by escheats or confiscations, he gets it to the kingdom, and not to himself, to wit, to the people, of whom the kingdom is composed, no more nor less than the servant does for his master; neither may one contract or oblige themselves to him, but by and with reference to the authority derived from the people. Furthermore, there is an infinite sort of people who live without a king, but we cannot imagine a king without people. And those who have been raised to the royal dignity were not advanced because they excelled other men in beauty and comeliness, nor in some excellency of nature to govern them as shepherds do their flocks, but rather being made out of the same mass with the rest of the people, they should acknowledge that for them, they, as it were, borrow their power and authority.

The ancient custom of the French represents that exceeding well, for they used to lift up on a buckler, and salute him king whom they had chosen. And wherefore is it said, I pray you, that kings have an infinite number of eyes, a million of ears, with extreme long hands, and feet exceeding swift? Is it because they are like to Argos, Gerien, Midas, and divers others so celebrated by the poets? No, truly, but it is said in regard of all the people, whom the business principally concerns, who lend to the king for the good of the commonwealth, their eyes, their ears, their means, their faculties. Let the people forsake the king, he presently falls to the ground, although before, his hearing and sight seemed most excellent, and that he was strong and in the best disposition that might be; yea, that he seemed to triumph in all magnificence, yet in an instant he will become most vile and contemptible: to be brief, instead of those divine honors wherewith all men adore him, he shall be compelled to become a pedant, and whip children in the school at Corinth. Take away but the basis to this giant, and like the Rhodian Colossus, he presently tumbles on the ground and falls into pieces. Seeing then that the king is established in this degree by the people, and for their sake, and that he cannot subsist without them, who can think it strange, then, for us to conclude that the people are above the king?

Now that which we speak of all the people universally, ought also to be understood, as has been delivered in the second question, of those who in every kingdom or town do lawfully represent the body of the people, and who ordinarily (or at least should be) called the officers of the kingdom, or of the crown, and not of the king; for the officers of the king, it is he who places and displaces them at his pleasure, yea, after his death they have no more power, and are accounted as dead. On the contrary, the officers of the kingdom receive their authority from the people in the general assembly of the states (or, at the least were accustomed so anciently to have done) and cannot be disauthorized but by them, so then the one depends of the king, the other of the kingdom, those of the sovereign officer of the kingdom, who is the king himself, those of the sovereignty itself, that is of the people, of which sovereignty, both the king and all his officers of the kingdom ought to depend, the charge of the one has proper relation to the care of the king's person; that of the other, to look that the commonwealth receive no damage; the first ought to serve and assist the king, as all domestic servants are bound to do to their masters; the other to preserve the rights and privileges of the people, and to carefully hinder the prince, that he neither omit the things that may advantage the state, nor commit anything that may endamage the public.

Briefly, the one are servants and domestics of the king, and received into their places to obey his person; the other, on the contrary, are as associates to the king, in the administration of justice, participating of the royal power and authority, being bound to the utmost of their power to be assisting in the managing of the affairs of state, as well as the king, who is, as it were, president among them, and principal only in order and degree.

Therefore, as all the whole people is above the king, and likewise taken in one entire body, are in authority before him, yet being considered one by one, they are all of them under the king. It is easy to know how far the power of the first kings extended, in that Ephron, king of the Hittites, could not grant Abraham the sepulcher but in the presence, and with the consent of the people: neither could Hemor the Hevite, king of Sichem, contract an alliance with Jacob without the people's assent and confirmation thereof; because it was then the custom to refer the most important affairs to be dispensed and resolved in the general assemblies of the people. This might easily be practiced in those kingdoms which were then almost confined within the circuit of one town.

But since the kings began to extend their limits, and that it was impossible for the people to assemble together all into one place because of their great numbers, which would have occasioned confusion, the officers of the kingdom were established, who should ordinarily preserve the rights of the people, in such sort notwithstanding, as when extraordinary occasion required, the people might be assembled, or at the least such an abridgment as might by the most principal members be a representation of the whole body. We see this order established in the kingdom of Israel, which (in the judgment of the wisest politicians) was excellently ordered. The king had his cupbearers, his carvers, his chamberlains and stewards. The kingdom had her officers, to wit, the seventy-one elders, and the heads and chief chosen out of all the tribes, who had the care of the public faith in peace and war.

Furthermore, the kingdom had in every town magistrates, who had the particular government of them, as the former were for the whole kingdom. At such times as affairs of consequence were to be treated of, they assembled together, but nothing that concerned the public state could receive any solid determination. David assembled the officers of his kingdom when he desired to invest his son Solomon with the royal dignity; when he would have examined and approved that manner of policy, and managing of affairs, that he had revived and restored, and when there was no question of removing the ark of the covenant.

And because they represented the whole people, it is said in the history, that all the people assembled. These were the same officers who delivered Jonathan from death, condemned by the sentence of the king, by which it appears, that there might be an appeal from the king to the people.

After that the kingdom was divided through the pride of Rehoboam. The council at Jerusalem composed of seventy-one ancients, seems to have such authority, that they might judge the king as well as the king might judge every one of them in particular. . . .

We read in another place, that Zedechias held in such reverence the authority of this council, that he was so far from delivering of Jeremy from the dungeon, whereunto the seventy-one had cast him, that he dare scarce remove him into a less rigorous prison. They persuading him to give his consent to the putting to death the prophet Jeremy, he answered, that he was in their hands, and that he might not oppose them in anything. The same king, fearing lest they might make information against him, to bring him to an account for certain speeches he had used to the prophet Jeremy, was glad to feign an untrue excuse. It appears by this, that in the kingdom of Judah this council was above the king, in this kingdom, I say, not fashioned or established by Plato or Aristotle, but by the Lord God Himself, being author of all their order, and supreme moderator in that monarchy. Such were the seven magi or sages in the Persian empire, who had almost a paralleled dignity with the king, and were termed the ears and eyes of the king, who also never dissented from the judgment of those sages. . . .

In the times of the emperors, there was the senate, the consuls, the praetors, the great provosts of the empire, the governors of provinces, attributed to the senate and the people, all which were called the magistrates and officers of the people of Rome. And therefore, when that by the decree of the senate, the emperor

Maximus was declared enemy of the commonwealth, and that Maximus and Albinus were created emperors by the senate, the men of war were sworn to be faithful and obedient to the people of Rome, the senate, and the emperors. Now for the empires and public states of these times (except those of Turkey, Muscovy and such like, which are rather a rhapsody of robbers, and barbarous intruders, than any lawful empires), there is not one, which is not, or hath not heretofore been governed in the manner we have described. And if through the conveniency and sloth of the principal officers, the successors have found the business in a worse condition, those who have for the present the public authority in their hands, are notwithstanding bound as much as in them lies to reduce things into their primary estate and condition.

In the empire of Germany, which is conferred by election, there are the electors and the princes, both secular and ecclesiastical, the counts, barons, and deputies of the imperial cities, and as all these in their proper places are solicitors for the public good, likewise in the Diets do they represent the majesty of the empire, being obliged to advise, and carefully foresee, that neither by the emperor's partiality, hate nor affection, the public state do suffer or be interested. And for this reason, the empire has its chancellor, as well as the emperor his, both the one and the other have their peculiar officers and treasurers apart. And it is a thing so notorious, that the empire is preferred before the emperor, that it is a common saying, "That emperor does homage to the empire." . . .

The kingdom of France heretofore preferred before all other, both in regard of the excellency of their laws and majesty of their estate, may pass with most as a ruling case. Now, although that those who have the public commands in their hands do not discharge their duties as were to be desired, it follows not though that they are not bound to do it. The king has his high steward of his household, his chamberlains, his masters of his games, cupbearers, and others, whose offices were wont so to depend on the person of the king: after that the death of their master, their offices were void. And indeed at the funeral of the king, the lord high steward in the presence of all the officers and servants of the household, breaks his staff of office, and says, "Our master is dead, let every one provide for himself." On the other side, the kingdom has her officers, to wit, the mayor of the palace, who since has been called the constable, the marshals, the admiral, the chancellor, or great referendary, the secretaries, the treasurers and others, who heretofore were created in the assembly of the three estates, the clergy, the nobility, and the people.

Since that the Parliament of Paris was made sedentary, they are not thought to be established in their places before they have been first received and approved by that course of Parliament, and may not be dismissed nor disposed, but by the authority and consent of the same. Now all these officers take their oath to the kingdom, which is as much as to say, to the people in the first place, then to the king who is protector of the kingdom, the which appears by the tenure of the oath. Above all, the constable, who, receiving the sword from the king, has it girded unto him with this charge, that he maintain and defend the commonwealth, as appears by the words that the king then pronounces.

Besides, the kingdom of France has the peers (so called either for that they are the king's companions, or because they are the fathers of the commonwealth) taking their denominations from the several provinces of the kingdom, in whose hands the king at his inauguration takes his oath as if all the people of the kingdom were in them present, which shows that these twelve peers are above the king. They on the other side swear, "That they will preserve not the king, but the crown, that they will assist the commonwealth with their counsel, and therefore will be present with their best abilities to counsel the prince both in peace and war," as appears plainly in the patentee of their peership. . . .

We may also know, that those peers of France did often discuss suits and differences between the king and his subjects. Insomuch, that when Charles the Sixth would have given sentence against the Duke of Brittany they opposed it, alleging that the discussing of that business belonged properly to the peers and not to the king, who might not in any sort derogate from their authority.

Therefore it is that yet at this day the Parliament of Paris is called the court of peers, being in some sort constituted judge between the king and the people; yea, between the king and every private person, and is bound and ought to maintain the meanest in the kingdom against the king's attorney, if he undertake anything contrary to law.

Furthermore, if the king ordain anything in his council, if he treat any agreement with the princes his neighbors, if he begin a war, or make peace, as lately with Charles the Fifth the emperor, the Parliament ought to interpose their authority, and all that which concerns the public state must be therein registered; neither is there anything firm and stable which the Parliament does not first approve. And to the end that the counselors of that Parliament should not fear the king, formerly they attained not to that place, but by the nomination of the whole body of the court; neither could they be dismissed for any lawful cause, but by the authority of the said body.

Furthermore, if the letters of the king be not subsigned by a secretary of the kingdom, at this day called a secretary of state, and if the letters patent be not sealed by the chancellor, who has power also to cancel them, they are of no force or value. There are also dukes, marquesses, earls, viscounts, barons, seneschals, and, in the cities and good towns, mayors, bailiffs, lieutenants, capitols, consuls, syndics, sheriffs and others, who have special authority, through the circuit of some countries or towns to preserve the people of their jurisdiction. Time it is that at this day some of these dignities are become hereditary. Thus much concerning the ordinary magistrates.

V . *The English Reformation*

LΠΓLΠΓLΠΓLΠΓLΠΓLΠΓLΠΓLΠΓLΠΓLΠΓLΠΓLΠΓLΠΓLΠΓL

19. William Tyndale: The New Testament in English (1525)*

One consequence of the Protestant Reformation was that the Scriptures were made available in the vernacular. In England the publication and use of the English Bible was encouraged by Henry VIII despite his own conservative views in theology. William Tyndale ranks first among the names to be mentioned in connection with the English Bible. On his translation all subsequent ones have been based, including the King James version of 1611. Tyndale had a passion for translating Scripture and when he failed to receive official encouragement in London he proceeded on his own. Afterward he traveled to the Continent, where he absorbed Luther's theology in addition to getting his translation into the press. His New Testament came out in 1525. Published in Germany, it was quickly shipped across the Channel and was received with official hostility and public enthusiasm.

Tyndale did not hesitate to render certain Greek terms in an anti-Catholic sense, but he did so because he was convinced that the text made this necessary. Like Luther, he was a brilliant stylist, as the following selections tellingly convey.

LITERATURE
J. F. Mozley, *William Tyndale* (London, 1937).

The. v. Chapter
[The Gospel of St. Matthew].

WHEN he sawe the people, he went vp into a mountayne, and when he was set, his disciples came to hym, and he opened hys

---

* *The New Testament Translated by William Tyndale, 1534* (Cambridge, 1938), pp. 31–35.

mouthe, and taught them sayinge: Blessed are the povre in sprete: for theirs is the kyngdome of heven. Blessed are they that morne: for they shalbe conforted. Blessed are the meke: for they shall inheret the erth. Blessed are they which honger and thurst for rightewesnes: for they shalbe filled. Blessed are the mercifull: for they shall obteyne mercy. Blessed are the pure in herte: for they shall se God. Blessed are the peacemakers: for they shalbe called the chyldren of God. Blessed are they which suffre persecucion for rightwesnes sake: for theirs ys the kyngdome of heuen. Blessed are ye when men reuyle you, and persecute you, and shall falsly say all manner of yvell saynges agaynst you for my sake. Reioyce, and be glad, for greate is youre rewarde in heven. For so persecuted they the Prophetes which were before youre dayes.

ye are the salt of the erthe: but and yf the salt have lost hir saltnes, what can be salted therwith? It is thence forthe good for nothynge, but to be cast oute, and tobe troaden vnder fote of men. ye are the light of the worlde. A cite that is set on an hill, cannot be hid, nether do men lyght a candell and put it vnder a busshell, but on a candelstick, and it lighteth all that are in the house. Let youre light so shyne before men, that they maye se your good workes, and glorify youre father which is in heven.

Thinke not that I am come to destroye the lawe, or the Prophets: no I am nott come to destroyethem, but to fulfyll them. For truely I saye vnto you, till heven and erth perisshe, one iott or one tytle of the lawe shall not scape, tyll all be fulfilled.

Whosoever breaketh one of these lest commaundmentes, and teacheth men so, he shalbe called the leest in the kyngdome of heven. But whosoever obserueth and teacheth, the same shal be called greate in the kyngdome of heven.

For I saye vnto you, except youre rightewesnes excede, the righetewesnes of the Scribes and Pharises, ye cannot entre into the kyngdome of heven.

ye have herde howe it was sayd vnto them of the olde tyme: Thou shalt not kyll. For who soever kylleth, shall be in daunger of iudgement. But I say vnto you, whosoever is angre with hys brother, shalbe in daunger of iudgement. Whosoeuer sayeth vnto his brother Racha, shalbe in daunger of a counsell. But whosoeuer sayeth thou fole, shalbe in daunger of hell fyre.

Therfore when thou offrest thy gifte at the altare, and their remembrest that thy brother hath ought agaynst the: leue there thyne offrynge before the altre, and go thy waye first and be reconcyled to thy brother, and then come and offre thy gyfte.

Agre with thyne adversary quicklye, whyles thou arte in the waye with hym, lest that adversary deliver the to the iudge, and the iudge delivre the to the minister, and then thou be cast into preson. I say vnto the verely: thou shalt not come out thence till thou have payed the utmost farthinge.

ye haue hearde howe it was sayde to them of olde tyme: Thou shalt not committ advoutrie. But I say vnto you, that whosoeuer looketh on a wyfe, lustynge after her, hathe committed advoutrie with hir alredy in his hert.

Wherfore yf thy right eye offende the, plucke hym out, and caste him from the. Better it is for the that one of thy membres perrisshe, then that thy hole bodye shuld be cast into hell. Also if thy right honde offend the, cut hym of and caste hym from the. Better yt ys that one of thy membres perisshe, then that all thy body shulde be caste into hell.

It ys sayd, whosoever put awaye his wyfe, let hym geve her a testymonyall also of the devorcement. But I say vnto you: whosoever put awaye his wyfe, (except it be for fornicacion) causeth her to breake matrymony. And whosoever maryeth her that is devorsed, breaketh wedlocke.

Agayne ye haue hearde how it was sayd to them of olde tyme, thou shalt not forswere thy selfe, but shalt performe thyne othe to God. But I saye vnto you, swere not at all: nether by heuen, for it ys Goddes seate: nor yet by the erth, for it is his fote stole: nether by Ierusalem, for it ys the cyte of that greate kynge: nether shalt thou sweare by thy heed, because thou canst not make wone white heer, or blacke: But your communicacion shalbe, ye, ye: nay, nay. For what soeuer is more then that, commeth of yvell.

ye have hearde how it ys sayd, an eye for an eye: a tothe for a tothe. But I saye to you, that ye resist not wronge. But whosoever geve the a blowe on thy right cheke, tourne to him the other. And yf eny man will sue the at the lawe, and take away thy coote, let hym have thy cloocke also. And whosoever wyll compell the to goo a myle, goo wyth him twayne. Geve to him that axeth, and from him that wolde borowe tourne not awaye.

ye have hearde how it is sayde: thou shalt love thyne neghbour, and hate thine enimy. But I saye vnto you, love youre enimies. Blesse them that coursse you. Do good to them that hate you. Praye for them which doo you wronge and persecute you, that ye maye be the chyldern of youre father that is in heauen: for he maketh his sunne to aryse on the yvell, and on the good, and sendeth his reyn on the iuste and vniuste. For yf ye love them, which love you: what rewarde shall ye have? Doo not the Publicans euen so? And yf ye be frendly to youre brethren onlye: what singuler thynge doo ye? Do not the Publicans lyke wyse? ye shal therfore be perfecte, even as youre father which is in heauen, is perfecte.

The. vi. Chapter.

Take hede to youre almes. That ye geve it not in the syght of men, to the intent that ye wolde be sene of them. Or els ye get no rewarde of youre father which is in heven. When soever therfore thou gevest thine almes, thou shalt not make a trompet to be blowen before the, as the ypocrites do in the synagogis and in the stretis, for to be preysed of men. Verely I say vnto you, they have their rewarde. But when thou doest thine almes, let not thy lyfte hand knowe, what thy righte hand doth, that thine almes may be secret: and thy father which seith in secret, shall rewarde the openly.

And when thou prayest, thou shalt not be as the ypocrites are. For they love to stond and praye in the synagoges, and in the corners of the stretes, because they wolde be sene of men. Verely I saye vnto you, they haue their rewarde. But when thou prayest, entre into thy chamber, and shut thy dore to the, and praye to thy father which ys in secrete: and thy father which seith in secret, shall rewarde the openly.

And when ye praye, bable not moche, as the hethen do: for they thincke that they shalbe herde, for their moche bablynges sake. Be ye not lyke them therfore. For youre father knoweth wherof ye haue neade, before ye axe of him. After thys maner therfore praye ye.

O oure father which arte in heven, halowed be thy name. Let thy kyngdome come. Thy wyll be fulfilled, as well in erth, as it ys in heven. Geve vs thisdaye oure dayly breede. And forgeve vs

oure treaspases, even as we forgeve oure trespacers. And leade vs
not into temptacion: but delyver vs from evell. For thyne is the
kyngedome and the power, and the glorye for ever. Amen. For
and yf ye shall forgeve other men their treaspases, youre hevenly
father shall also forgeve you. But and ye wyll not forgeve men
their trespases, nomore shall youre father forgeve youre treaspases.

Moreoure when ye faste, be not sad as the ypocrytes are. For
they disfigure their faces, that they myght besene of men how
they faste. Verely I say vnto you, they have their rewarde. But
thou, when thou fastest, annoynte thyne heed, and washe thy
face, that it appere not vnto men howe that thou fastest: but vnto
thy father which is in secrete: and thy father which seeth in
secret, shall rewarde the openly.

Se that ye gaddre you not treasure vpon the erth, where rust
and mothes corrupte, and where theves breake through and steale.
But gaddre ye treasure togeder in heven, where nether rust nor
mothes corrupte, and where theves nether breake vp nor yet
steale. For where soever youre treasure ys, there will youre hertes
be also.

The light of the body is thyne eye. Wherfore yf thyne eye
besyngle, all thy body shalbe full of light. But and if thyne eye
be wycked then all thy body shalbe full of derckenes. Wherefore
yf the light that is in the, be darckenes: how greate is that darckenes.

No man can serve two masters. For ether he shall hate the one
and love the other: or els he shall lene to the one and despise the
other: ye can not serve God and mammon. Therfore I saye vnto
you, be not carefull for your lyfe, what ye shall eate, or what ye
shall drincke, nor yet for youre body, what ye shall put on. ys not
the lyfe more worth then meate, and the body more of value then
raymeut? Beholde the foules of the ayer: for they sowe not,
nether reepe, nor yet cary in to the barnes: and yet youre hevenly
father fedeth them. Are ye not moche better then they?

Which of you (though he toke thought therfore) coulde put
one cubit vnto his stature? And why care ye then for rayment?
Considre the lylies of the felde, how they growe. They labour
not nether spynne. And yet for all that I saye vnto you, that euen
Salomon in all his royalte was not arayed lyke vnto one of these.

Wherfore yf God so clothe the grasse, which ys to daye in

the felde, and to morowe shalbe caste into the fournace: shall he
not moche more do the same vnto you, o ye of lytle fayth?

Therfore take no thought sayinge: what shall we eate, or what
shall we drincke, or wherwith shall we be clothed? After all
these thynges seke the gentyls. For youre hevenly father knoweth
that ye have neade of all these thynges. But rather seke yefyrst the
kyngdome of heuen and the rightwisnes therof, and all these
thynges shalbe ministred vnto you.

Care not then for the morow, but let the morow care for it
selfe: for the daye present hath ever ynough of his awne trouble.

The. vii. Chapter.

Ivdge not, that ye be not iudged. For as ye iudge so shall ye be
iudged. And with what mesure ye mete, with the same shall it be
mesured to you agayne. Why seist thou a moote in thy brothers
eye, and perceavest not the beame that ys yn thyne awne eye. Or
why sayest thou to thy brother: suffre me to plucke oute the
moote oute of thyne eye, and behold a beame is in thyne awne eye.
ypocryte, fyrst cast oute the beame oute of thyne awne eye, and
then shalte thou se clearly to plucke oute the moote out of thy
brothers eye.

Geve not that which is holy, to dogges, nether cast ye youre
pearles before swyne, lest they treade them vnder their fete, and
the other tourne agayne and all to rent you.

Axe and it shalbe geven you. Seke and ye shall fynd. knocke
and it shalbe opened vnto you. For whosoever axeth receaveth and
he that seketh fyndeth, and to hym that knocketh, it shalbe
opened. Ys there eny man amonge you which if his sonne axed
hym bread, wolde offer him astone? Or if he axed fysshe, wolde
he proffer hym a serpent? yf ye then which are evyll, cane geve
to youre chyldren good gyftes: how moche moore shall youre
father which is in heven, geve good thynges to them that axe
hym?

Therfore whatsoever ye wolde that men shulde do to you,
even so do ye to them. This ys the lawe and the Prophettes.

Enter in at the strayte gate: for wyde is the gate, and broade
is the waye that leadeth to destruccion: and many ther be which
goo yn therat. But strayte is the gate, and narowe ys the waye
which leadeth vnto lyfe: and feawe there be that fynde it.

Beware of false Prophetes, which come to you in shepes clothinge, but inwardly they are ravenynge wolves. Ye shall knowe them by their frutes. Do men gaddre grapes of thornes? or figges of bryres? Euen soo every good tree bryngeth forthe good frute. But a corrupte tree, bryngethe forthe evyll frute. A good tree cannot bryngeforthe bad frute: nor yet a bad tree can bringe forthe good frute. Every tree that bryngethe not forthe good frute, shalbe hewen doune, and cast into the fyre. Wherfore by their frutes ye shall knowethem.

Not all they that saye vnto me, Master, Master, shall enter in to the kyngdome of heven: but he that dothe my fathers will which ys in heven. Many will saye to me in that daye, Master, master, have we not in thy name prophesied? And in thy name have caste oute devyls? And in thy name have done many miracles? And then will I knowlege vnto them, that I never knewe them. Departe from me, ye workers of iniquite.

Whosoever heareth of me these sayinges and doethe the same, I wyll lyken hym vnto a wyse man which bylt hys housse on a rocke: and aboundance of rayne descended, and the fluddes came, and the wyndes blewe and bet vpon that same housse, and it fell not, because it was grounded on the rocke. And whosoever heareth of me these sayinges and does them not, shalbe lykened vnto a folysh man which bilt hys housse apon the sonde: and aboundaunce of rayne descended, and the fluddes came, and the wyndes blewe and beet vpon that housse, and it fell, and great was the fall of it.

And it came to passe, that when Iesus had ended these saynges, the people were astonnyed at hys doctryne. For he taught them as one havynge power, and not as the Scribes. . . .

The. xiii. Chapter. [1 Corinthians]

Though I spake with the tonges of men and angels, and yet had no love, I were even as soundinge brasse: or as a tynklynge Cymball. And though I coulde prophesy, and vnderstode all secretes, and all knowledge: yee, yf I had all fayth so that I coulde move mountayns oute of ther places, and yet had no love, I were nothynge. And though I bestowed all my gooddes to fede the poore, and though I gave my body even that I burned, and yet had no love, it profeteth me nothinge.

Love suffreth longe, and is corteous. Love envieth not. Love doth not frowardly, swelleth not dealeth not dishonestly, seketh not her awne, is not provoked to anger, thynketh not evyll, reioyseth not in iniquite: but reioyseth in the trueth, suffreth all thynge, beleveth all thynges, hopeth all thynges, endureth in all thynges. Though that prophesyinge fayle, other tonges shall cease, or knowledge vanysshe awaye, yet love falleth never awaye.

For oure knowledge is vnparfect, and oure prophesyinge is vnperfet. But when that which is parfect is come, then that which is vnparfet shall bedone awaye. When I was a chylde, I spake as a chylde, I vnderstode as a childe, I ymagened as a chylde. But assone as I was a man, I put awaye childesshnes. Now we se in a glasse even in a darke speakynge: but then shall we se face to face. Now I knowe vnparfectly: but then shall I knowe even as I am knowen. Now abideth fayth, hope, and love, even these thre: but the chefe of these is love.

20. John Jewel: *An Apology of the Church of England* (1562)*

John Jewel, appointed bishop of Salisbury in 1559, was a scholar and the perfect choice to prepare a defense of the Elizabethan settlement of religion against Catholic charges in 1561. Jewel offered both a defense against the Catholic accusations and a positive statement of the faith of the English church. The Catholic charges had been those of schism, heresy, and immorality; Jewel argued that they could be leveled against the Catholics as well. Moreover, he emphatically asserted that the Catholic church had departed from the biblical and apostolic norm. The Council of Trent was in session when Jewel's work was published, and it must also be seen as a defense of the English refusal to attend its deliberations and accept its decisions.

The work appeared in 1562 in both Latin and English, the latter under the title *An Apologia, or Answer in Defence of the Church of*

* John Jewel, *An Apology of the Church of England*, ed. J. E. Booty (Ithaca, New York, 1963), pp. 7–21.

England, Concerning the State of Religion Used in the Same. Numerous editions followed, an indication that Jewel had offered an incisive, if perhaps colorless, defense of the Anglican settlement.

The section reprinted here is a major portion of the first of the seven "parts" of the treatise.

LITERATURE

W. M. Southgate, *John Jewel and the Problem of Doctrinal Authority.* Cambridge, Mass., 1962.

Part 1

IT hath been an old complaint, even from the first time of the patriarchs and prophets, and confirmed by the writings and testimonies of every age, that the truth wandereth here and there as a stranger in the world and doth readily find enemies and slanderers amongst those that know her not. Albeit perchance this may seem unto some a thing hard to be believed, I mean to such as have scant well and narrowly taken heed thereunto, specially seeing all mankind of nature's very motion without a teacher doth covet the truth of their own accord; and seeing our Savior Christ himself, when He was on earth, would be called "the truth," as by a name most fit to express all His divine power; yet we—which have been exercised in the holy Scriptures, and which have both read and seen what hath happened to all godly men commonly at all times; what to the prophets, to the apostles, to the holy martyrs, and what to Christ Himself; with what rebukes, revilings, and despites they were continually vexed while they here lived, and that only for the truth's sake—we (I say) do see that this is not only no new thing or hard to be believed, but that it is a thing already received and commonly used from age to age. Nay, truly, this might seem much rather a marvel and beyond all belief, if the devil, who is "the father of lies" and enemy to all truth, would now upon a sudden change his nature and hope that truth might otherwise be suppressed than by belying it, or that he would begin to establish his own kingdom by using now any other practices than the same which he hath ever used from the beginning. For since any man's remembrance we can scant find one time, either when religion did first grow, or when it was settled, or when it did afresh spring up again, wherein truth and innocency were not by all unworthy means and most despitefully entreated. Doubtless the devil well seeth that so long as truth is in good safety, himself cannot be safe nor yet maintain his own estate.

For, letting pass the ancient patriarchs and prophets, who, as we said, had no part of their life free from contumelies and slanders, we know there were certain in times past which said and commonly preached that the old ancient Jews (of whom we make no doubt but they were the worshipers of the only and true God) did worship either a sow or an ass in God's stead, and that all the same religion was nothing else but a sacrilege and a plain contempt of all godliness. We know also that the Son of God, our Savior Jesus Christ, when He taught the truth, was counted a juggler and an enchanter, a Samaritan, Beelzebub, a deceiver of the people, a drunkard, and a glutton. Again, who wotteth not what words were spoken against St. Paul, the most earnest and vehement preacher and maintainer of the truth? Sometime, that he was a seditious and busy man, a raiser of tumults, a causer of rebellion; sometime again, that he was an heretic; sometime, that he was mad. Sometime, that only upon strife and stomach he was both a blasphemer of God's law and a despiser of the fathers' ordinances. . . .

Or who is ignorant that in times past there were some which reproved the holy Scriptures of falsehood, saying they contained things both contrary and quite one against another, and how that the apostles of Christ did severally disagree betwixt themselves and that St. Paul did vary from them all? And, not to make rehearsal of all, for that were an endless labor, who knoweth not after what sort our fathers were railed upon in times past, which first began to acknowledge and profess the name of Christ, how they made private conspiracies, devised secret counsels against the commonwealth, and to that end made early and privy meetings in the dark, killed young babes, fed themselves with men's flesh, and, like savage and brute beasts, did drink their blood? In conclusion, how that, after they had put out the candles, they committed adultery between themselves, and without regard wrought incest one with another, that brethren lay with their sisters, sons with their mothers, without any reverence of nature or kin, without shame, without difference; and that they were wicked men without all care of religion and without any opinion of God, being the very enemies of mankind, unworthy to be suffered in the world and unworthy of life?

All these things were spoken in those days against the people of God, against Christ Jesus, against Paul, against Stephen, and against all them, whosoever they were, which at the first beginning embraced the truth of the gospel and were contented to be called by the name of Christians, which was then an hateful name among the common people. And, although the things which they said were not true, yet the devil thought it should be sufficient for him if at the least he could bring it so to pass as they might be believed for true, and that the Christians might be brought into a common hatred of everybody and have their death and destruction sought of all sorts. . . .

Wherefore we ought to bear it more quietly, which have taken upon us to profess the gospel of Christ, if we for the same cause be handled after the same sort; and if we, as our forefathers were long ago, be likewise at this day tormented and baited with railings, with spiteful dealings, and with lies; and that for no desert of our own but only because we teach and acknowledge the truth.

They cry out upon us at this present everywhere that we are all heretics and have with new persuasions and wicked learning utterly dissolved the concord of the church; that we renew, and, as it were, fetch again from hell the old and many-a-day condemned heresies; that we sow abroad new sects and such broils as never erst were heard of; also that we are already divided into contrary parts and opinions and could yet by no means agree well among ourselves; that we be cursed creatures and like the giants do war against God Himself and live clean without any regard or worshiping of God; that we despise all good deeds; that we use no discipline of virtue, no laws, no customs; that we esteem neither right, nor order, nor equity, nor justice; that we give the bridle to all naughtiness and provoke the people to all licentiousness and lust; that we labor and seek to overthrow the state of monarchies and kingdoms and to bring all things under the rule of the rash inconstant people and unlearned multitude;

that we have seditiously fallen from the Catholic church and by a wicked schism and division have shaken the whole world and troubled the common peace and universal quiet of the church; and that, as Dathan and Abiram conspired in times past against Moses and Aaron, even so we at this day have renounced the bishop of Rome without any cause reasonable; that we set nought by the authority of the ancient Fathers and councils of old time; that we have rashly and presumptuously disannulled the old ceremonies, which have been well allowed by our fathers and forefathers many hundred years past, both by good customs and also in ages of more purity; and that we have by our own private head, without the authority of any sacred and general council, brought new traditions into the church; and have done all these things not for religion's sake but only upon a desire of contention and strife: but that they for their part have changed no manner of thing but have held and kept still such a number of years to this very day all things as they were delivered from the apostles and well approved by the most ancient fathers.

And that this matter should not seem to be done but upon privy slander, and to be tossed to and fro in a corner, only to spite us, there have been besides wilily procured by the bishop of Rome certain persons of eloquence enough, and not unlearned neither, which should put their help to this cause, now almost despaired of, and should polish and set forth the same, both in books and with long tales, to the end that when the matter was trimly and eloquently handled ignorant and unskilful persons might suspect there was some great thing in it. Indeed they perceived that their own cause did everywhere go to wrack; that their sleights were now espied and less esteemed; and that their helps did daily fail them; and that their matter stood altogether in great need of a cunning spokesman.

Now, as for those things which by them have been laid against us, in part they be manifestly false, and condemned so by their own judgments which spake them; partly again, though they be as false too indeed, yet bear they a certain show and color of truth, so as the reader (if he take not good heed) may easily be tripped and brought into error by them, especially when their fine and cunning tale is added thereunto; and part of them be of such sort as we ought not to shun them as crimes or faults but to acknowledge and profess them as things well done and upon very good reason.

For, shortly to say the truth, these folk falsely accuse and slander all our doings, yea, the same things which they themselves cannot deny but to be rightly and orderly done, and for malice do so misconstrue and deprave all our sayings and doings, as though it were impossible that any thing could be rightly spoken or done by us. They should more plainly and sincerely have gone to work if they would have dealt truly. But now they neither truly, nor sincerely, nor yet Christianly, but darkly and craftily, charge and batter us with lies and do abuse the blindness and fondness of the people, together with the ignorance of princes, to cause us to be hated and the truth to be suppressed. . . .

Now therefore, if it be leefull for these folks to be eloquent and fine-tongued in speaking evil, surely it becometh not us in our cause, being so very good, to be dumb in answering truly. For men to be careless what is spoken by them and their own matter, be it never so falsely and slanderously spoken (especially when it is such that the majesty of God and the cause of religion may thereby be damaged), is the part doubtless of dissolute and reckless persons and of them which wickedly wink at the injuries done unto the name of God. For, although other wrongs, yea, oftentimes great, may be borne and dissembled of a mild and Christian man; yet he that goeth smoothly away and dissembleth the matter when he is noted of heresy, Rufinus was wont to deny that man to be a Christian. We therefore will do the same thing, which all laws, which nature's own voice, doth command to be done, and which Christ Himself did in like case, when He was checked and reviled; to the intent we may put off from us these men's slanderous accusations and may defend soberly and truly our own cause and innocency. . . .

But we, truly, seeing that so many thousands of our brethren in these last twenty years have borne witness unto the truth in the midst of most painful torments that could be devised; and when princes, desirous to restrain the gospel, sought many ways, but prevailed nothing; and that now almost the whole world doth begin to open their eyes to behold the light; we take it that our cause hath already been sufficiently declared and defended, and think it not needful to make many words, since the very matter saith enough for itself. For, if the popes would, or else if they could, weigh with their own selves the whole matter, and also the beginning and proceedings of our religion, how in a manner all their travail hath come to nought, nobody driving it forward, and without any worldly help; and how, on the other side, our cause, against the will of emperors from the beginning, against the wills of so many kings, in spite of the popes, and almost mauger the head of all men, hath taken increase, and by little and little spread over into all countries, and is come at length even into kings' courts and palaces. These same things, methinketh, might be tokens great enough to them that God Himself doth strongly fight in our quarrel and doth from heaven laugh at their enterprises; and that the force of the truth is such as neither man's power nor yet hell gates are able to root it out. For they be not all mad at this day, so many free cities, so many kings, so many princes, which have fallen away from the seat of Rome and have rather joined themselves to the gospel of Christ.

And, although the popes have never hitherunto leisure to consider diligently and earnestly of these matters, or though some other cares do now let them and diverse ways pull them, or though they count these to be but common and trifling studies and nothing to appertain to the pope's worthiness, this maketh not why our matter ought to seem the worse. Or if they perchance will not see that which they see indeed, but rather will withstand the known truth, ought we therefore by and by to be counted heretics, because we obey not their will and pleasure? If so be that Pope Pius were the man (we say not, which he would so gladly be called), but if he were indeed a man that either would account us for his brethren, or at least would take us to be men, he would first diligently have examined our reasons and would have seen what might be said with us, what against us, and would not in his bull, whereby he lately pretended a council, so rashly have condemned so great a part of the world, so many learned and godly men, so many commonwealths, so many kings, and so many princes, only upon his own blind prejudices and foredeterminations, and that without hearing of them speak, or without showing cause why.

But because he hath already so noted us openly, lest by holding our peace we should seem to grant a fault, and especially because we can by no means have audience in the public assembly of the general council, wherein he would no creature should have power to give his voice or declare his opinion except he were sworn and straitly bound to maintain his authority—for we have had experience hereof in the last conference at the Council of Trent, where the ambassadors and divines of the princes of Germany and of the free cities were quite shut out from their company; neither can we yet forget how Julius the Third, above ten years past, provided warily by his writ that none of our sort should be suffered to speak in the Council (except that there were some man peradventure that would recant and change his opinion)—for this cause chiefly we thought it good to yield up an account of our faith in writing and truly and openly to make answer to those things wherewith we have been openly charged; to the end the world may see the parts and foundations of that doctrine in the behalf whereof so many good men have little regarded their own lives; and that all men may understand what manner of people they be, and what opinion they have of God and of religion, whom the bishop of Rome, before they were called to tell their tale, hath condemned for heretics, without any good consideration, without any example, and utterly without law or right, only because he heard tell that they did dissent from him and his in some point of religion. . . .

Further, if we do show it plain that God's holy gospel, the ancient bishops, and the primitive church do make on our side, and that we have not without just cause left these men, and rather have returned to the apostles and old Catholic Fathers; and if we shall be found to do the same not colorably or craftily but in good faith before God, truly, honestly, clearly, and plainly; and if they themselves which fly our doctrine and would be called Catholics shall manifestly see how all these titles of antiquity, whereof they boast so much, are quite shaken out of their hands, and that there is more pith in this our cause than they thought for; we then hope and trust that none of them will be so negligent and careless of his own salvation but he will at length study and bethink himself to whether part he were best to join him. Undoubtedly, except one will altogether harden his heart and refuse to hear, he shall not repent him to give good heed to this our defense, and to mark well what we say and how truly and justly it agreeth with Christian religion.

For where they call us heretics, it is a crime so heinous, that, unless it may be seen, unless it may be felt, and in manner may be holden with hands and fingers, it ought not lightly to be judged or believed, when it is laid to the charge of any Christian man. For heresy is a forsaking of salvation, a renouncing of God's grace, a departing from the body and spirit of Christ. But this was ever an old and solemn property with them and their forefathers, if any did complain of their errors and faults and desired to have true religion restored, straightway to condemn such ones for heretics, as men newfangled and factious. Christ for no other cause was called a Samaritan but only for that He was thought to have fallen to a certain new religion and to be the author of a new sect. And Paul, the Apostle of Christ, was called before the judges to make answer to a matter of heresy, and therefore he said: "According to this way, which they call heresy, I do worship the God of my fathers; believing all things which be written in the law and in the prophets."

Shortly to speak, this universal religion, which Christian men profess at this day, was called first of the heathen people a sect and heresy. With these terms did they always fill princes' ears, to the intent when they had once hated us with a foredetermined opinion and had counted all that we said to be faction and heresy, they might be so led away from the truth and right understanding of the cause. But the more sore and outrageous a crime heresy is, the more it ought to be proved by plain and strong arguments, especially in this time, when men begin to give less credit to their words and to make more diligent search of their doctrine than they were wont to do. For the people of God are otherwise instructed now than they were in times past, when all the bishop of Rome's sayings were allowed for gospel, and when all religion did depend only upon their authority. Nowadays the holy Scripture is abroad, the writings of the apostles and prophets are in print, whereby all truth and catholic doctrine may be proved and all heresy may be disproved and confuted.

Sithence, then, they bring forth none of these for themselves, and call us nevertheless heretics which have neither fallen from Christ, nor from the apostles, nor yet from the prophets, this is an injurious and a very spiteful dealing. With this sword did Christ put off the devil when He was tempted of him; with these weapons ought all presumption, which doth advance itself against God, to be overthrown and conquered. "For all Scripture," saith St. Paul, "that cometh by the inspiration of God, is profitable to teach, to confute, to instruct, and to reprove; that the man of God may be perfect, and thoroughly framed to every good work." Thus did the holy Fathers always fight against the heretics with none other force than with the holy Scriptures. . . . For at that time made the Catholic Fathers and bishops no doubt but that our religion might be proved out of the holy Scriptures. Neither were they ever so hardy to take any for an heretic whose error they could not evidently and apparently reprove by the selfsame Scriptures. And we verily do make answer on this wise, as St. Paul did, "According to this way which they call heresy we do worship God and the Father of our Lord Jesus Christ, and do allow all things which have been written either in the law, or in the prophets," or in the apostles' works.

Wherefore, if we be heretics, and they (as they would fain be called) be Catholics, why do they not as they see the Fathers, which were Catholic men, have always done? Why do they not convince and master us by the divine Scriptures? Why do they not call us again to be tried by them? Why do they not lay before us how we have gone away from Christ, from the prophets, from the apostles, and from the holy Fathers? Why stick they to do it? Why are they afraid of it? It is God's cause: why are they doubtful to commit it to the trial of God's word? If we be heretics, which refer all our controversies unto the holy Scriptures and report us to the selfsame words which we know were sealed by God Himself, and in comparison of them set little by all other things, whatsoever may be devised by men; how shall we say to these folk, I pray you, what manner of men be they, and how is it meet to call them, which fear the judgment of the holy Scriptures, that is to say, the judgment of God Himself, and do prefer before them their own dreams and full cold inventions; and, to maintain their own traditions, have defaced and corrupted, now these many hundred years, the ordinances of Christ and of the apostles?

⎍⎍⎍⎍⎍⎍⎍⎍⎍⎍⎍⎍⎍⎍⎍⎍⎍⎍⎍⎍⎍⎍⎍⎍⎍⎍

21. John Field and Thomas Wilcox:
An Admonition to the Parliament
(1572)*

The Elizabethan settlement of religion was from the very beginning bitterly assailed by those who thought it a compromise with popery. One of the most spectacular expressions of discontent came in June, 1572 with the publication of a tract entitled *An Admonition to the Parliament.* Vehemently denouncing the settlement, this *Admonition* was "one of the boldest adventures, surely, of the whole Elizabethan age." It sought to counter Queen Elizabeth's influence upon the course of ecclesiastical affairs. The queen had recently ordered that bills affecting religion had to be approved by the church before they could be introduced in Parliament. The temper of Parliament was congenial to additional ecclesiastical reform while the hierarchy on the other hand was not likely to approve comprehensive reform measures. Thus the queen's order seemed to block effectively any further ecclesiastical change.

The *Admonition* not only rejected the queen's interference; it also spelled out the kind of religious settlement considered biblical, and thus acceptable, by the Puritan reformers. Thus the document constitutes an excellent source for early "Puritan" sentiment. Its two authors, John Field and Thomas Wilcox, paid for the publication with a prison sentence. The source of many of the ideas in the document was Thomas Cartwright, formerly Lady Margaret Professor of divinity at Cambridge. He subsequently became embroiled with John Whitgift in a literary controversy over the *Admonition.*

A condensed version (with ellipses indicated) of the entire *Admonition* is reprinted below.

* W. H. Frere & C. E. Douglas (eds.), *Puritan Manifestoes* (London, 1954), pp. 8–19.

LITERATURE
D. J. McGinn, *The Admonition Controversy* (New Brunswick, 1949).

An Admonition to the Parliament

SEEING that nothyng in this mortal life is more diligently to be soght for, and carefully to be loked unto than the restitution of true religion and reformation of Gods church: it shall be your partes (dearly beloved) in this present Parliament assembled, as much as in you lyeth to promote the same, and to employ your whole labour and studie; not onely in abandoning al popish remnants both in ceremonies and regiment, but also in bringing in and placing in Gods church those things only, which the Lord himself in his word commandeth. Because it is not enough to take paynes in takyng away evil, but also to be occupied in placing good in the stead thereof. Now because many men see not al things, and the world in this respect is marvelously blynded, it hath ben thought good to proferre to your godly considerations, a true platforme of a church reformed, to the end that it beyng layd before your eyes, to beholde the great unlikenes betwixt it & this our english church: you may learne either with perfect hatred to detest the one, and with singular love to embrace, and carefull endevoir to plant the other: or els to be without excuse before the majestie of our God, who (for the discharge of our conscience, and manifestation of his truth) hath by us revealed unto you at this present, the sinceritie and simplicitie of his Gospel. Not that you should either wilfully withstand, or ungraciously tread the same under your feete, for God doth not disclose his wil to any such end, but that you should yet now at the length with all your mayne and might, endevoir that Christ (whose easie yoke and light burthen we have of long time caste of from us) might rule and raygne in his church by the scepter of his worde onely. . . . We in England are so fare of, from having a church rightly reformed, accordyng to the prescript of Gods worde, that as yet we are not come to the outwarde face of the same. For to speake of that wherin al consent, & whereupon al writers accorde. The outwarde markes wherby a true christian church is knowne, are preaching of the worde purely, ministring of the sacraments sincerely, and ecclesiastical discipline which consisteth in admonition and correction of faults severelie. Touching the fyrst, namely the ministerie of the worde, although it must be confessed that the substance of doctrine by many delivered is sound and good, yet here in it faileth, that neither the ministers thereof are accordyng to Gods worde proved, elected, called, or ordayned: nor the function in such sorte so narrowly loked unto, as of right it ought, and is of necessitie required. For whereas in the olde church a trial was had both of their abilitie to instruct, and of their godly conversation also: now, by the letters commendatorie of some one man, noble or other, tag and rag, learned and unlearned, of the basest sorte of the people (to the sclander of the Gospell in the mouthes of the adversaries) are freely receaved. In those daies no idolatrous sacrificers or heathnish priests were apointed to be preachers of the Gospel: but we allow, and like wel of popish masse mongers, men for all seasons, Kyng Henries priests, Kyng Edwards priests, Queene Maries priestes, who of a truth (yf Gods worde were precisely folowed) should from the same be utterly removed. Then thei taught others, now they must be instructed themselves, and therefore lyke young children they must learne cathechismes. Then election was made by the common consent of the whole church: now every one picketh out for himself some notable good benefice, he obtaineth the next advouson, by money or by favour, and so thinketh hymself to be sufficiently chosen. Then the congregation had authoritie to cal ministers: in stead thereof now, they runne, they ryde, and by unlawful sute & buying, prevent other suters also. Then no minister placed in any congregation, but by the consent of the people, now, that authoritie is geven into the hands of the byshop alone, who by his sole authoritie thrusteth upon them such, as they many times aswel for unhonest life, as also for lacke of learning, may, & doe justly dislike. Then, none admitted to the ministerie, but a place was voyde before hand, to which he should be called: but nowe, bishops (to whom the right of ordering ministers doth at no hand appertaine) do make 60, 80, or a 100 at a clap, & send them abroad into the cuntry lyke masterles men. Then, after just tryal and vocation they were admitted to their function, by laying on of the hands of the company of the eldership onely: now ther is (neither of these being loked unto) required an albe, a surplesse, a vestiment, a pastoral staffe, beside that ridiculus, and (as they use it to their newe creatures) blasphemous saying, receave the holy gost. Then every pastor had his flocke, and every flocke his shepheard, or els shepheards: Now they doe not onely run fyskyng from place to place (a miserable disorder in Gods church) but covetously joine living to living, making shipwracke of their owne consciences, and being but one shepherd (nay, wold to God they were shepheards and not wolves) have many flockes. Then the ministers wer preachers: now bare readers. And yf any be so well disposed to preach in their owne charges, they may not, without my Lords licence. In those dayes knowne by voice, learning and doctrine: now they must be discerned from other by popish and Antichristian apparel, as cap, gowne, tippet, etc. Then, as God gave utterance they preached the worde onely: now they read homilies, articles, injunctions, etc. Then it was paineful: now gaineful. Then poore and ignominious: now rich & glorious. And therfore titles, livings, and offices by Antichrist devised are geven to them, as Metropolitane, Archbishoppe, Lordes grace, Lorde Bishop, Suffragan, Deane, Archdeacon, Prelate of the garter, Earle, Countie Palatine, Honor, High commissioners, Justices of peace and Quorum, etc. All which, together with their offices, as they are strange & unheard of in Chrystes church, nay playnely in Gods word forbidden: So are they utterlie with speed out of the same to be removed. Then ministers were not tyed to any forme of prayers invented by man, but as the spirit moved them, so they powred forth hartie supplications to the Lorde. Now they are bound of necessitie to a prescript order of service, and booke of common prayer in which a great number of things contrary to Gods word are contained, as baptism by women, private Communions, Jewish purifyings, observing of holydayes, etc, patched (if not all together, yet the greatest peece) out of the Popes portuis. Then feedyng the flocke diligently: now teaching quarterly. Then preaching in season and out of season: now once in a month is thoght sufficient, if twice, it is judged a worke of supererogation. Then nothing taught but Gods word, Now Princes pleasures, mennes devices, popish ceremonies, and Antichristian rites in publique pulpits defended. Then they sought them, now they seeke theirs.

These, and a great meanie other abuses ar in the ministerie

remainyng, which unlesse they be removed and the truth brought in, not onely Gods justice shal be powred forth, but also Gods church in this realme shall never be builded. For if they which seeme to be workemen, are no workemen in deede, but in name, or els worke not so diligently & in such order as the workemaster commaundeth, it is not onely unlikely that the buildyng shall go forwarde, but altogether impossible that ever it shal be perfited. The way therfore to avoid these inconveniences, and to reforme these deformities is this: Your wisedomes have to remove Advousons, Patronages, Impropriations, and bishoppes authoritie, claiming to themselves therby right to ordayne ministers, and to bryng in that old and true election, which was accustomed to be made by the congregation. You must displace those ignorant and unable ministers already placed, & in their rowmes appoint such as both can, and will by Gods asistance feed the flock. . . . Appoint to every congregation a learned & diligent preacher. Remove homilies, articles, injunctions, a prescript order of service made out of the masse booke. Take away the Lordship, the loyteryng, the pompe, the idlenes, and livinges of Bishops, but yet employ them to such ends as they were in the olde churche apointed for. . . .

Now to the second point, which concerneth ministration of Sacraments. In the olde time, the worde was preached, before they were ministred: now it is supposed to be sufficient, if it be read. Then, they wer ministred in publique assemblies, now in private houses. Then by ministers only, now by midwives, and Deacons, equally. But because in treating of both the sacraments together, we should deale confusedly: we wyll therefore speake of them severallie. And fyrst for the Lordes supper, or holy communion.

They had no introite, for Celestinus a pope broght it in, aboute the yeare 430. But we have borrowed a peece of one out of the masse booke. They read no fragments of the Epistle and Gospell: we use both. The Nicene crede was not read in their Communion: we have it in oures. Ther was then, accustumed to be an examination of the communicants, which now is neglected. Then they ministred the Sacrament with common and usual bread: now with wafer cakes, brought in by Pope Alexander, being in forme, fashion and substance, lyke their god of the alter. They receaved it sitting:

we kneelyng, accordyng to Honorius Decree. Then it was delivered generally, & in definitely, Take ye and eat ye: we perticu-
lerly, and singulerly, Take thou, and eat thou. They used no other
wordes but such as Chryste lefte: We borrowe from papistes, The
body of our Lorde Jesus Chryst which was geven for thee, &c.
They had no Gloria in excelsis in the ministerie of the Sacrament
then, for it was put to afterward. We have now. They toke it with
conscience. We with custume. They shut men by reasen of their
sinnes, from the Lords Supper. We thrust them in their sinne to
the Lordes Supper. They ministred the Sacrament plainely. We
pompously, with singing, pypyng, surplesse and cope wearyng.
They simply as they receeved it from the Lorde. We, sinfullye,
mixed with mannes inventions and devises. And as for Baptisme, it
was enough with them, if they had water, and the partie to be
baptised faith, and the minister to preach the word and minister
the sacraments.

Nowe, we must have surplesses devised by Pope Adrian, inter-
rogatories ministred to the infant, godfathers and Godmothers,
brought in by Higinus, holy fonts invented by Pope Pius, crossing
and suche like peces of poperie, which the church of God in the
Apostles times never knew (and therfore not to be used) nay
(which we are sure of) were and are mannes devises, broght in
long after the puritie of the primative church. To redresse these,
your wisedomes have to remove (as before) ignorant ministers,
to take awai private communions and baptismes, to enjoyne Deacons and Midwives not to meddle in ministers matters, if they doe,
to see them sharpelie punished. To joyne assistance of Elders, and
other officers, that seing men wyl not examine themselves, they
may be examined, and brought to render a reason of their hope.
That the statute against waffer cakes may more prevaile then an
Injunction. That people be apointed to receave the Sacrament,
rather sitting, for avoydyng of superstition, than kneelyng, havyng
in it the outwarde shewe of evyl, from which we must abstaine.
That Excommunication be restored to his olde former force. That
papists nor other, neither constrainedly nor customably, communicate in the misteries of salvation. That both the Sacrament of
the Lordes supper and Baptisme also, may be ministred according
to the ancient puritie & simplicitie. That the parties to be baptised,
if they be of the yeares of discretion, by themselves & in their owne

persons, or if they be infants, by their parents (in whose rowme
if upon necessarye occasions & businesses they be absent, some of
the congregation knowing the good behaviour and sound faith of
the parents) may both make rehearsal of their faith, And also if
their faith be sound, and agreable to holie scriptures, desire to be
in the same baptised. And finally, that nothing be don in this or
ani other thing, but that which you have the expresse warrant of
Gods worde for.

Let us come now to the third parte, which concerneth ecclesiastical discipline. The officers that have to deale in this charge,
are chiefly three ministers preachers or pastors of whom before.
Seniors or Elders, and Deacons. Concerning Seniors, not onely
their office but their name also is out of this english church utterly
removed. Their office was to governe the church with the rest of
the ministers, to consulte, to admonish, to correct, and to order
all thinges apperteigning to the state of the congregation. In steed
of these Seniors in every church, the pope hath brought in and
we yet maintaine, the Lordship of one man over many churches,
yea over sundrie Shieres. These Seniors then, because their charge
was not overmuch, did execute their offices in their owne persones
without substitutes. Our Lords bishops have their under officers,
as Suffraganes, Chancelours, Archdeacons, Officialles, Commissaries, and such lyke. Touchyng Deacons, though their names be
remaining, yet is the office fowlie perverted and turned upside
downe, for their dutie in the primative church, was to gather the
almes diligently, and to distribute it faithfully, also for the sicke
and impotent persones to provide painefully, having ever a diligent
care, that the charitie of godly men, wer not wasted upon loiterers
and idle vagabounds. Now it is the first step to the ministerie, nay,
rather a mere order of priesthode. For they may baptise in the
presence of a bishop or priest, or in their absence (if necessitie so
require) minister the other Sacrament, likewise read the holy
Scriptures and homilies in the congregation, instructe the youth in
the Cathechisme, and also preach, if he be commanded by the
bishop. Agayne, in the olde church every congregation had their
Deacons. Now they are tied to Cathedrall churches onely, and
what doe they there? gather the almes and distribute to the poore?
nay, that is the least peece or rather no parte of their function.
What then? to sing a gospel when the bishop ministreth the Com-

munion. If this be not a pervertyng of this office and charge, let every one judge. And yet least the reformers of our time should seeme utterly to take out of Gods Church this necessarie function, they appoint somewhat to it concerning the poore, and that is, to search for the sicke, needy, and impotent people of the parish, and to intimate their estates, names, and places where they dwell to the Curate, that by his exhortation they may be relieved by the parysh, or other convenient almes. And this as you see, is the nighest parte of his office, and yet you must understand it to be in suche places where there is a Curate and a Deacon: every parish can not be at that cost to have both, nay, no parish so farre as can be gathered, at this present hath. Now then, if you wyl restore the church to his ancient officers, this you must doe. In stead of an Archbishop or Lord bishop, you must make equalitie of ministers. In stead of Chancelours, Archdeacons, Officialles, Commissaries, Proctours, Doctors, Summoners, Churchwardens, and such like: you have to plant in every congregation a lawful and godly seignorie. The Deaconship must not be confounded with the ministerie, nor the Collectours for the poore, maye not usurpe the Deacons office: But he that hath an office, must looke to his office, and every man muste kepe himselfe within the boundes and limmits of his owne vocation. And to these three jointly, that is, the Ministers, Seniors, and deacons, is the whole regiment of the church to be committed. This regiment consisteth especially in ecclesiastical discipline, which is an order left by God unto his church, wherby men learne to frame their wylles and doyngs accordyng to the law of God, by instructing and admonishing one another, yea and by correcting and punishing all wylfull persones, and contemners of the same. Of this discipline there is two kyndes, one private, wherwith we wyl not deale because it is impertinent to our purpose, an other publique, which although it hathe bene long banished, yet if it might now at the length be restored, wolde be very necessarie and profitable for the building up of Gods house. The final end of this discipline, is the reforming of the disordered, and to bryng them to repentance, and to bridle such as wold offend. The chieffest parte and last punishment of this discipline is excommunication, by the consent of the church determined, if the offender be obstinate, which how miserably it hath ben by the Popes

proctours, and is by our new Canonists abused, who seeth not?
In the primative church it was in many mennes handes: now one
alone excommunicateth. In those days it was the last censure of
the church, and never went forth but for notorious crimes: Now
it is pronounced for every light trifle. Then excommunication was
greatly regarded and feared. Now because it is a money matter,
no whit at al estemed. Then for great sinnes, severe punishment,
and for smal offences, little censures. Now great sinnes eyther not
at al punished, as blasphemy, usury, etc, or else sleightly passed
over with pricking in a blanket, or pinning in a sheet, as adulterie,
whoredome, drunkennes, etc. Againe, suche as are no sinnes (as
if a man conforme not himself to popysh orders and ceremonies,
if he come not at the whistle of him, who hath by Gods worde
no authoritie to cal, we meane Chancelors, Officials, Doctors, and
all that rable) are grevously punished, not only by excommunication, suspention, deprivation and other (as they terme it) spiritual
coertion, but also by banishyng, imprisonyng, revyling, taunting,
and what not? Then the sentence was tempered accordyng to the
notoriousnes of the facte. Now on the one side either hatred
against some persones, caryeth men headlong into rash and cruell
judgement: or els favoure, affection, or money, mitigaeth the rig-
our of the same, and al this cometh to passe, because the regiment
lefte of Christ to his church, is committed into one mannes hands,
whom alone it shal be more easie for the wicked by bribing to
pervert, than to overthrow the faith and pietie of a zealous and
godlie companie, for such manner of men in deede shoulde the
Seigniors be. Then it was said tell the church: now it is spoken,
complaine to my Lords grace, primate and Metropolitane of al
England, or to his inferiour, my Lord Bishop of the diocesse, if
not to him, shew the Chancelor or Officiall, or Commissarie or
Doctor. Againe, whereas the excommunicate were never receaved
tyll they had publikely confessed their offence. Now for paying
the fees of the court, they shal by master Officiall, or Chancelour,
easely be absolved in som private place. Then the congregation,
by the wickednes of the offendour grieved, was by his publique
penance satisfied. Now absolution shal be pronounced, though
that be not accomplished. Then the partie offendyng should in
his owne person, heare the sentence of Absolution pronounced.

Now, Bishops, Archdeacons, Chancelors, Officials, Commissaries and such lyke, absolve one man for another. And this is that order of ecclesiastical discipline which all godly wish to be restored, to the end that every one by the same, may be kept within the limmits of his vocation, and a great number be brought to live in godly conversation. Not that we meane to take away the authoretie of the civill Magistrate and chief governour, to whome we wish all blessednes, and for the encreace of whose godlines we dayly pray: but that Christ being restored into his kyngdome, to rule in the same by the scepter of his worde, and severe discipline: the Prince may be better obeyed, the realme more florish in godlines, and the Lord himself more sincerely and purely according to his revealed wil served then heretofore he hath ben, or yet at this present is. Amend therfore these horrible abuses, and reforme Gods church, and the Lorde is on your right hand, you shall not be removed for ever. For he wyl deliver and defend you from all your enemies, either at home or abroad, as he did faithfull Jacob & good Jehosaphat. Let these things alone, and God is a righteous judge, he wyl one day cal you to your reckonyng. Is a reformation good for France? and can it be evyl for England? Is discipline meete for Scotland? and is it unprofitable for this Realme? Surely God hath set these examples before your eyes to encourage you to go foreward to a thorow and a speedy reformation. You may not do as heretofore you have done, patch and peece, nay rather goe backeward, and never labour or contend to perfection. But altogether remove whole Antichrist, both head body and branch, and perfectly plant that puritie of the word, that simplicitie of the sacraments, and severitie of discipline, which Christ hath commanded, and commended to his church. . . .

The God of all glorie so open your eyes to see his truth, that you may not onely be inflamed with a love thereof, but with a continuall care seeke to promote, plant, and place the same amongst us, that we the English people, and our posteritie, enjoyeng the sinceritie of Gods gospel for ever, may say alwayes: The Lorde be praysed. To whome with Chryst Jesus his sonne our onely saviour, & the Holy gost our alone comfortor, be honour, prayse, and glorie, for ever and ever. Amen.

ⅬⅬⅬⅬⅬⅬⅬⅬⅬⅬⅬⅬⅬⅬⅬⅬⅬⅬⅬⅬⅬⅬⅬⅬⅬⅬⅬ

22. Richard Hooker: *The Laws of Ecclesiastical Polity* (1593 ff.)*

Richard Hooker (1554–1600) was the most important systematic theologian of the Church of England in the sixteenth century and his *magnum opus*, the *Laws of Ecclesiastical Polity*, has been said to mark "the beginning of what we now call Anglicanism." Such praise is well deserved, though it is one of the ironies of Hooker's life that he was a modest cleric who never occupied a position of ecclesiastical responsibility or academic eminence.

The *Laws of Ecclesiastical Polity* grew out of Hooker's controversy with Walter Travers, a staunchy Puritan divine who lost no opportunity to attack the Anglican settlement for its supposedly unbiblical character. Hooker's *Laws* was intended to counter the Puritan claims, and not the least of the accomplishments of its eight books was a fair summary of the Puritan position. Hooker emphatically repudiated this position and set down his own theological principles, making a lasting theological contribution to the Anglican communion. The harmonious sweep of the work is impressive; each argument occupies its logical position, and Hooker's literary style is masterly. His basic contention was that beyond the trifles that accounted for so much of the controversy between the Puritans and their Anglican opponents stood basic issues that caused a wide rift between the two sides.

The first four books of the *Laws* appeared in 1593; the fifth book four years later; the sixth and eighth in 1648, and the seventh not until 1661. This protracted publication suggests that works of theological erudition—then as now—are not necessarily best sellers. The sections reprinted here are from the first book, which deals with "laws and their several kinds in general."

LITERATURE

J. S. Marshall, *Hooker and the Anglican Tradition* (Sewanee, 1963).

* *The Works of That Learned and Judicious Divine, Mr. Richard Hooker: [The Laws of Ecclesiastical Polity]*. Arranged by John Keble (Oxford, 1888), pp. 199–204; 215–62.

For as much help whereof as may be in this case, I have endeavored throughout the body of this whole discourse, that every former part might give strength unto all that follow, and every later bring some light unto all before. So that if the judgments of men do but hold themselves in suspense as touching these first more general meditations, till in order they have perused the rest that ensue; what may seem dark at the first will afterward be found more plain, even as the later particular decisions will appear I doubt not more strong, when the other have been read before.

(3) The laws of the church, whereby for so many ages together we have been guided in the exercise of Christian religion and the service of the true God, our rites, customs, and orders of ecclesiastical government, are called in question: we are accused as men that will not have Christ Jesus to rule over them, but have wilfully cast His statutes behind their backs, hating to be reformed and made subject unto the scepter of His discipline. Behold therefore we offer the laws whereby we live unto the general trial and judgment of the whole world; heartily beseeching almighty God, whom we desire to serve according to His own will, that both we and others (all kind of partial affection being clean laid aside) may have eyes to see and hearts to embrace the things that in His sight are most acceptable.

And because the point about which we strive is the quality of our laws, our first entrance hereinto cannot better be made, than with consideration of the nature of law in general, and of that law which giveth life unto all the rest, which are commendable, just, and good; namely the law whereby the Eternal Himself doth work. Proceeding from hence to the law, first of Nature, then of Scripture, we shall have the easier access unto those things which come after to be debated, concerning the particular cause and question which we have in hand.

II

All things that are, have some operation not violent or casual. Neither doth any thing ever begin to exercise the same, without some fore-conceived end for which it worketh. And the end which it worketh for is not obtained, unless the work be also fit to obtain it by. For unto every end every operation will not serve. That which doth assign unto each thing the kind, that which doth moderate the force and power, that which doth appoint the form and measure, of working, the same we term a *law*. So that no certain end could ever be attained, unless the actions whereby it is attained were regular; that is to say, made suitable, fit and correspondent unto their end, by some canon, rule or law. Which thing doth first take place in the works even of God Himself.

(2) All things therefore do work after a sort, according to law: all other things according to a law, whereof some superior, unto whom they are subject, is author; only the works and operations of God have Him both for their worker, and for the law whereby they are wrought. The being of God is a kind of law to His working: for that perfection which God is, giveth perfection to that He doth. Those natural, necessary, and internal operations of God, the Generation of the Son, the Proceeding of the Spirit, are without the compass of my present intent: which is to touch only such operations as have their beginning and being by a voluntary purpose, wherewith God hath eternally decreed when and how they should be. Which eternal decree is that we term an eternal law.

Dangerous it were for the feeble brain of man to wade far into the doings of the Most High; whom although to know be life, and joy to make mention of His name; yet our soundest knowledge is to know that we know Him not as indeed He is, neither can know Him: and our safest eloquence concerning Him is our silence, when we confess without confession that His glory is inexplicable, His greatness above our capacity and reach. He is above, and we upon earth; therefore it behoveth our words to be wary and few.

Our God is one, or rather very *Oneness*, and mere unity, having nothing but itself in itself, and not consisting (as all things do besides God) of many things. In which essential Unity of God a Trinity personal nevertheless subsisteth, after a manner far exceeding the possibility of man's conceit. The works which outwardly are of God, they are in such sort of Him being one, that each Person hath in them somewhat peculiar and proper. For being Three, and they all subsisting in the essence of one Deity; from the Father, by the Son, through the Spirit, all things are. That which the Son doth hear of the Father, and which the Spirit doth receive of the Father and the Son, the same we have at the hands of the Spirit as being the last, and therefore the nearest unto us in order, although in power the same with the second and the first.

(3) The wise and learned among the very heathens themselves have all acknowledged some First Cause, whereupon originally the being of all things dependeth. Neither have they otherwise spoken of that cause than as an Agent, which knowing *what* and *why* it worketh, observeth in working a most exact *order* or *law.* . . . They all confess therefore in the working of that first cause, that counsel is used, reason followed, a way observed; that is to say, constant order and law is kept; whereof itself must needs be author unto itself. Otherwise it should have some worthier and higher to direct it, and so could not itself be the first. Being the first, it can have no other than itself to be the author of that law which it willingly worketh by.

God therefore is a law both to Himself, and to all other things besides. To Himself He is a law in all those things, whereof our Savior speaketh, saying, "My Father worketh as yet, so I." God worketh nothing without cause. All those things which are done by Him have some end for which they are done; and the end for which they are done is a reason of His will to do them. His will had not inclined to create woman, but that He saw it could not be well if she were not created. *Non est bonum,* "It is not good man should be alone; therefore let us make a helper for him." That and nothing else is done by God, which to leave undone were not so good.

If therefore it be demanded, why God having power and ability infinite, the effects notwithstanding of that power are all so limited as we see they are: the reason hereof is the end which He hath proposed, and the law whereby His wisdom hath stinted the effects of His power in such sort, that it doth not work infinitely, but correspondently unto that end for which it worketh . . . in most decent and comely sort," all things in "measure, number, and weight."

(4) The general end of God's external working is the exercise of His most glorious and most abundant virtue. Which abundance doth show itself in variety, and for that cause this variety is often-

times in Scripture expressed by the name of *riches*. "The Lord hath made all things for His own sake." Not that any thing is made to be beneficial unto Him, but all things for Him to show beneficence and grace in them.

The particular drift of every act proceeding externally from God we are not able to discern, and therefore cannot always give the proper and certain reason of His works. Howbeit undoubtedly a proper and certain reason there is of every finite work of God, inasmuch as there is a law imposed upon it; which if there were not, it should be infinite, even as the worker Himself is.

(5) They err therefore who think that of the will of God to do this or that there is no reason besides His will. Many times no reason known to us; but that there is no reason thereof I judge it most unreasonable to imagine. . . . And whatsoever is done with counsel or wise resolution hath of necessity some reason why it should be done, albeit that reason be to us in some things so secret, that it forceth the wit of man to stand, as the blessed Apostle himself doth, amazed thereat: "O the depth of the riches both of the wisdom and knowledge of God! how unsearchable are His judgments," &c. That law eternal which God Himself hath made to Himself, and thereby worketh all things whereof He is the cause and author; that law in the admirable frame whereof shineth with most perfect beauty the countenance of that wisdom which hath testified concerning herself, "The Lord possessed me in the beginning of His way, even before His works of old I was set up"; that law, which hath been the pattern to make, and is the card to guide the world by; that law which hath been of God and with God everlastingly; that law, the author and observer whereof is one only God to be blessed for ever: how should either men or angels be able perfectly to behold? The book of this law we are neither able nor worthy to open and look into. That little thereof which we darkly apprehend we admire, the rest with religious ignorance we humbly and meekly adore.

(6) . . . The law whereby He worketh is eternal, and therefore can have no show or color of mutability: for which cause, a part of that law being opened in the promises which God hath made (because His promises are nothing else but declarations what God will do for the good of men) touching those promises the Apostle hath witnessed, that God may as possibly "deny Himself"

and not be God, as fail to perform them. And concerning the counsel of God, he termeth it likewise a thing "unchangeable"; the counsel of God, and that law of God whereof now we speak, being one.

Nor is the freedom of the will of God any whit abated, let or hindered, by means of this; because the imposition of this law upon Himself is His own free and voluntary act.

This law therefore we may name eternal, being "that order which God before all ages hath set down with Himself, for Himself to do all things by."

III

I am not ignorant that by "law eternal" the learned for the most part do understand the order, not which God hath eternally purposed Himself in all His works to observe, but rather that which with Himself He hath set down as expedient to be kept by all His creatures, according to the several condition wherewith He hath endued them. They who thus are accustomed to speak apply the name of law unto that only rule of working which superior authority imposeth; whereas we somewhat more enlarging the sense thereof term any kind of rule or canon, whereby actions are framed, a law. Now that law which, as it is laid up in the bosom of God, they call *eternal*, receiveth according unto the different kinds of things which are subject unto it different and sundry kinds of names. That part of it which ordereth natural agents we call usually *nature's* law; that which angels do clearly behold and without any swerving observe is a law *celestial* and heavenly; the law of *reason*, that which bindeth creatures reasonable in this world, and with which by reason they may most plainly perceive themselves bound; that which bindeth them, and is not known but by special revelation from God, *divine* law; *human* law, that which out of the law either of reason or of God men probably gathering to be expedient, they make it a law. All things therefore, which are as they ought to be, are conformed unto *this second law eternal;* and even those things which to this eternal law are not conformable are notwithstanding in some sort ordered by *the first eternal law.* For what good or evil is there under the sun, what action correspondent or repugnant unto the law which God hath imposed upon His creatures, but in or upon it God doth work according to the law which Himself hath eternally purposed to keep; that is to say, the *first law eternal?* So that a twofold law eternal being thus made, it is not hard to conceive how they both take place in all things. . . .

V

God alone excepted, who actually and everlastingly is whatsoever He may be, and which cannot hereafter be that which now He is not; all other things besides are somewhat in possibility, which as yet they are not in act. And for this cause there is in all things an appetite or desire, whereby they incline to something which they may be; and when they are it, they shall be perfecter than now they are. All which perfections are contained under the general name of goodness. And because there is not in the world any thing whereby another may not some way be made the perfecter, therefore all things that are, are good.

(2) Again, sith there can be no goodness desired which proceedeth not from God Himself, as from the supreme cause of all things; and every effect doth after a sort contain, at leastwise resemble, the cause from which it proceedeth: all things in the world are said in some sort to seek the highest, and to covet more or less the participation of God Himself. Yet this doth no where so much appear as it doth in man, because there are so many kinds of perfections which man seeketh. The first degree of goodness is that general perfection which all things do seek, in desiring the continuance of their being. All things therefore coveting as much as may be to be like unto God in being ever, that which cannot hereunto attain personally doth seek to continue itself another way, that is by offspring and propagation. The next degree of goodness is that which each thing coveteth by affecting resemblance with God in the constancy and excellency of those operations which belong unto their kind. The immutability of God they strive unto, by working either always or for the most part after one and the same manner; His absolute exactness they imitate, by tending unto that which is most exquisite in every particular. Hence have risen a number of axioms in philosophy, showing how "the works of nature do always aim at that which cannot be bettered."

(3) These two kinds of goodness rehearsed are so nearly united to the things themselves which desire them, that we scarcely perceive the appetite to stir in reaching forth her hand toward them.

But the desire of those perfections which grow externally is more apparent; especially of such as are not expressly desired unless they be first known, or such as are not for any other cause than for knowledge itself desired. Concerning perfections in this kind; that by proceeding in the knowledge of truth, and by growing in the exercise of virtue, man amongst the creatures of this inferior world aspireth to the greatest conformity with God; this is not only known unto us, whom He Himself hath so instructed, but even they do acknowledge, who amongst men are not judged the nearest unto Him. . . .

VI

In the matter of knowledge, there is between the angels of God and the children of men this difference: angels already have full and complete knowledge in the highest degree that can be imparted unto them; men, if we view them in their spring, are at the first without understanding or knowledge at all. Nevertheless from this utter vacuity they grow by degrees, till they come at length to be even as the angels themselves are. That which agreeth to the one now, the other shall attain unto in the end; they are not so far disjoined and severed, but that they come at length to meet. The soul of man being therefore at the first as a book, wherein nothing is and yet all things may be imprinted; we are to search by what steps and degrees it riseth unto perfection of knowledge.

(2) Unto that which hath been already set down concerning natural agents this we must add, that albeit therein we have comprised as well creatures living as void of life, if they be in degree of nature beneath men; nevertheless a difference we must observe between those natural agents that work altogether unwittingly, and those which have though weak yet some understanding what they do, as fishes, fowls, and beasts have. Beasts are in sensible capacity as ripe even as men themselves, perhaps more ripe. For as stones, though in dignity of nature inferior unto plants, yet exceed them in firmness of strength or durability of being; and plants, though beneath the excellency of creatures endued with sense, yet exceed them in the faculty of vegetation and of fertility: so beasts, though otherwise behind men, may notwithstanding in actions of sense and fancy go beyond them; because the endeavors of nature, when it hath a higher perfection to seek, are in lower

the more remiss, not esteeming thereof so much as those things do, which have no better proposed unto them.

(3) The soul of man therefore being capable of a more divine perfection, hath (besides the faculties of growing unto sensible knowledge which is common unto us with beasts) a further ability, whereof in them there is no show at all, the ability of reaching higher than unto sensible things. Till we grow to some ripeness of years, the soul of man doth only store itself with conceits of things of inferior and more open quality, which afterwards do serve as instruments unto that which is greater; in the meanwhile above the reach of meaner creatures it ascendeth not. When once it comprehendeth any thing above this, as the differences of time, affirmations, negations, and contradictions in speech, we then count it to have some use of natural reason. Whereunto if afterwards there might be added the right helps of true art and learning (which helps, I must plainly confess, this age of the world, carrying the name of a learned age, doth neither much know nor greatly regard), there would undoubtedly be almost as great difference in maturity of judgment between men therewith inured, and that which now men are, as between men that are now and innocents. Which speech if any condemn, as being over hyperbolical, let them consider but this one thing. No art is at the first finding out so perfect as industry may after make it. . . .

(5) Education and instruction are the means, the one by use, the other by precept, to make our natural faculty of reason both the better and the sooner able to judge rightly between truth and error, good and evil. But at what time a man may be said to have attained so far forth the use of reason, as sufficeth to make him capable of those laws, whereby he is then bound to guide his actions; this is a great deal more easy for common sense to discern, than for any man by skill and learning to determine; even as it is not in philosophers, who best know the nature both of fire and of gold, to teach what degree of the one will serve to purify the other, so well as the artisan, who doth this by fire, discerneth by sense when the fire hath that degree of heat which sufficeth for his purpose.

VII

By reason man attaineth unto the knowledge of things that are and are not sensible. It resteth therefore that we search how man

attaineth unto the knowledge of such things unsensible as are to
be known that they may be done. Seeing then that nothing can
move unless there be some end, the desire whereof provoketh unto
motion; how should that divine power of the soul, that "spirit of
our mind," as the Apostle termeth it, ever stir itself unto action,
unless it have also the like spur? The end for which we are moved
to work, is sometimes the goodness which we conceive of the very
working itself, without any further respect at all; and the cause
that procureth action is the mere desire of action, no other good
besides being thereby intended. Of certain turbulent wits it is said,
"Illis quieta movere magna merces videbatur": they thought the
very disturbance of things established an hire sufficient to set them
on work. Sometimes that which we do is referred to a further end,
without the desire whereof we would leave the same undone; as in
their actions that gave alms to purchase thereby the praise of men.

(2) Man in perfection of nature being made according to the
likeness of his Maker resembleth Him also in the manner of working: so that whatsoever we work as men, the same we do wittingly
work and freely; neither are we according to the manner of natural
agents any way so tied, but that it is in our power to leave the
things we do undone. The good which either is gotten by doing,
or which consisteth in the very doing itself, causeth not action,
unless apprehending it as good we so like and desire it: that we do
unto any such end, the same we choose and prefer before the
leaving of it undone. Choice there is not, unless the thing which
we take be so in our power that we might have refused and left
it. If fire consume the stubble, it chooseth not so to do, because
the nature thereof is such that it can do no other. To choose is to
will one thing before another. And to will is to bend our souls
to the having or doing of that which they see to be good. Goodness is seen with the eye of the understanding. And the light of
that eye, is reason. So that two principal fountains there are of
human action, knowledge and will; which will, in things tending
toward any end, is termed choice. Concerning knowledge, "Behold, (saith Moses,) I have set before you this day good and evil,
life and death." Concerning will, he addeth immediately, "Choose
life"; that is to say, the things that tend unto life, them choose.

(3) But of one thing we must have special care, as being a matter
of no small moment; and that is, how the will, properly and strictly

taken, as it is of things which are referred unto the end that man desireth, differeth greatly from that inferior natural desire which we call appetite. The object of appetite is whatsoever sensible good may be wished for; the object of will is that good which reason doth lead us to seek. Affections, as joy, and grief, and fear, and anger, with such like, being as it were the sundry fashions and forms of appetite, can neither rise at the conceit of a thing indifferent, nor yet choose but rise at the sight of some things. Wherefore it is not altogether in our power, whether we will be stirred with affections or no: whereas actions which issue from the disposition of the will are in the power thereof to be performed or stayed. Finally, appetite is the will's solicitor, and the will is appetite's controller; what we covet according to the one by the other we often reject; neither is any other desire termed properly will, but that where reason and understanding, or the show of reason, prescribeth the thing desired.

It may be therefore a question, whether those operations of men are to be counted voluntary, wherein that good which is sensible provoketh appetite, and appetite causeth action, reason being never called to counsel; as when we eat or drink, and betake ourselves unto rest, and such like. The truth is, that such actions in men having attained to the use of reason are voluntary. For as the authority of higher powers hath force even in those things, which are done without their privity, and are of so mean reckoning that to acquaint them therewith it needeth not; in like sort, voluntarily we are said to do that also, which the will if it listed might hinder from being done, although about the doing thereof we do not expressly use our reason or understanding, and so immediately apply our wills thereunto. In cases therefore of such facility, the will doth yield her assent as it were with a kind of silence, by not dissenting; in which respect her force is not so apparent as in express mandates or prohibitions, especially upon advice and consultation going before.

(4) Where understanding therefore needeth, in those things reason is the director of man's will by discovering in action what is good. For the laws of well-doing are the dictates of right reason. Children, which are not as yet come unto those years whereat they may have; again, innocents, which are excluded by natural defect from ever having; thirdly, madmen, which for the

present cannot possibly have the use of right reason to guide
themselves, have for their guide the reason that guideth other
men, which are tutors over them to seek and to procure their good
for them. In the rest there is that light of reason, whereby good
may be known from evil, and which discovering the same rightly
is termed right.

(5) The will notwithstanding doth not incline to have or do
that which reason teacheth to be good, unless the same do also
teach it to be possible. For albeit the appetite, being more general,
may wish any thing which seemeth good, be it never so impossible;
yet for such things the reasonable will of man doth never seek.
Let reason teach impossibility in any thing, and the will of man
doth let it go; a thing impossible it doth not affect, the impossibility
thereof being manifest.

(6) There is in the will of man naturally that freedom, whereby
it is apt to take or refuse any particular object whatsoever being
presented unto it. Whereupon it followeth, that there is no particular object so good, but it may have the show of some difficulty
or unpleasant quality annexed to it, in respect whereof the will
may shrink and decline it; contrariwise (for so things are blended)
there is no particular evil which hath not some appearance of
goodness whereby to insinuate itself. For evil as evil cannot be
desired: if that be desired which is evil, the cause is the goodness
which is or seemeth to be joined with it. Goodness doth not move
by being, but by being apparent; and therefore many things are
neglected which are most precious, only because the value of
them lieth hid. Sensible goodness is most apparent, near, and
present; which causeth the appetite to be therewith strongly provoked. Now pursuit and refusal in the will do follow, the one the
affirmation the other the negation of goodness, which the understanding apprehendeth, grounding itself upon sense, unless some
higher reason do chance to teach the contrary. And if reason have
taught it rightly to be good, yet not so apparently that the mind
receiveth it with utter impossibility of being otherwise, still there
is place left for the will to take or leave. Whereas therefore
amongst so many things as are to be done, there are so few, the
goodness whereof reason in such sort doth or easily can discover,
we are not to marvel at the choice of evil even then when the
contrary is probably known. Hereby it cometh to pass that custom

inuring the mind by long practice, and so leaving there a sensible impression, prevaileth more than reasonable persuasion what way soever. Reason therefore may rightly discern the thing which is good, and yet the will of man not incline itself thereunto, as oft as the prejudice of sensible experience doth oversway. . . .

VIII

Wherefore to return to our former intent of discovering the natural way, whereby rules have been found out concerning that goodness wherewith the will of man ought to be moved in human actions; as every thing naturally and necessarily doth desire the utmost good and greatest perfection whereof nature hath made it capable, even so man. Our felicity therefore being the object and accomplishment of our desire, we cannot choose but wish and covet it. All particular things which are subject unto action, the will doth so far forth incline unto, as reason judgeth them the better for us, and consequently the more available to our bliss. If reason err, we fall into evil, and are so far forth deprived of the general perfection we seek. Seeing therefore that for the framing of men's actions the knowledge of good from evil is necessary, it only resteth that we search how this may be had. Neither must we suppose that there needeth one rule to know the good and another the evil by. For he that knoweth what is straight doth even thereby discern what is crooked, because the absence of straightness in bodies capable thereof is crookedness. Goodness in actions is like unto straightness; wherefore that which is done well we term *right*. For as the straight way is most acceptable to him that travelleth, because by it he cometh soonest to his journey's end; so in action, that which doth lie the evenest between us and the end we desire must needs be the fittest for our use. Besides which fitness for use, there is also in rectitude, beauty; as contrariwise in obliquity, deformity. And that which is good in the actions of men, doth not only delight as profitable, but as amiable also. In which consideration the Grecians most divinely have given to the active perfection of men a name expressing both beauty and goodness, because goodness in ordinary speech is for the most part applied only to that which is beneficial. But we in the name of goodness do here imply both. . . .

(3) Signs and tokens to know good by are of sundry kinds;

some more certain and some less. The most certain token of evident goodness is, if the general persuasion of all men do so account it. And therefore a common received error is never utterly overthrown, till such time as we go from signs unto causes, and show some manifest root or fountain thereof common unto all, whereby it may clearly appear how it hath come to pass that so many have been overseen. In which case surmises and slight probabilities will not serve, because the universal consent of men is the perfectest and strongest in this kind, which comprehendeth only the signs and tokens of goodness. Things casual do vary, and that which a man doth but chance to think well of cannot still have the like hap. Wherefore although we know not the cause, yet thus much we may know; that some necessary cause there is, whensoever the judgments of all men generally or for the most part run one and the same way, especially in matters of natural discourse. For of things necessarily and naturally done there is no more affirmed but this, "They keep either always or for the most part one tenure." The general and perpetual voice of men is as the sentence of God Himself. For that which all men have at all times learned, Nature herself must needs have taught; and God being the author of Nature, her voice is but his instrument. . . .

(4) A law therefore generally taken, is a directive rule unto goodness of operation. The rule of divine operations outward, is the definitive appointment of God's own wisdom set down within Himself. The rule of natural agents that work by simple necessity, is the determination of the wisdom of God, known to God Himself the principal director of them, but not unto them that are directed to execute the same. The rule of natural agents which work after a sort of their own accord, as the beasts do, is the judgment of common sense or fancy concerning the sensible goodness of those objects wherewith they are moved. The rule of ghostly or immaterial natures, as spirits and angels, is their intuitive intellectual judgment concerning the amiable beauty and high goodness of that object, which with unspeakable joy and delight doth set them on work. The rule of voluntary agents on earth is the sentence that reason giveth concerning the goodness of those things which they are to do. And the sentences which reason giveth are some more some less general, before it come to define in particular actions what is good.

(5) The main principles of reason are in themselves apparent. For to make nothing evident of itself unto man's understanding were to take away all possibility of knowing any thing. And herein that of Theophrastus is true, "They that seek a reason of all things do utterly overthrow reason." In every kind of knowledge some such grounds there are, as that being proposed the mind doth presently embrace them as free from all possibility of error, clear and manifest without proof. In which kind axioms or principles more general are such as this, "that the greater good is to be chosen before the less." If therefore it should be demanded what reason there is, why the will of man, which doth necessarily shun harm and covet whatsoever is pleasant and sweet, should be commanded to count the pleasures of sin gall, and notwithstanding the bitter accidents wherewith virtuous actions are compassed, yet still to rejoice and delight in them: surely this could never stand with Reason, but that wisdom thus prescribing groundeth her laws upon an infallible rule of comparison; which is, "That small difficulties, when exceeding great good is sure to ensue, and on the other side momentary benefits, when the hurt which they draw after them is unspeakable, are not at all to be respected." This rule is the ground whereupon the wisdom of the Apostle buildeth a law, enjoining patience unto himself; "The present lightness of our affliction worketh unto us even with abundance upon abundance an eternal weight of glory; while we look not on the things which are seen, but on the things which are not seen: for the things which are seen are temporal, but the things which are not seen are eternal": therefore Christianity to be embraced, whatsoever calamities in those times it was accompanied withal. Upon the same ground our Savior proveth the law most reasonable, that doth forbid those crimes which men for gain's sake fall into. "For a man to win the world if it be with the loss of his soul, what benefit or good is it?" Axioms less general, yet so manifest that they need no further proof, are such as these, "God to be worshipped"; "parents to be honored"; "others to be used by us as we ourselves would by them." Such things, as soon as they are alleged, all men acknowledge to be good; they require no proof or further discourse to be assured of their goodness.

Notwithstanding whatsoever such principle there is, it was at the first found out by discourse, and drawn from out of the very bowels of heaven and earth. For we are to note, that things in the world are to us discernible, not only so far forth as serveth for our vital preservation, but further also in a twofold higher respect. For first if all other uses were utterly taken away, yet the mind of man being by nature speculative and delighted with contemplation in itself, they were to be known even for mere knowledge and understanding's sake. Yea further besides this, the knowledge of every the least thing in the whole world hath in it a second peculiar benefit unto us, inasmuch as it serveth to minister rules, canons, and laws, for men to direct those actions by, which we properly term human. This did the very heathens themselves obscurely insinuate, by making *Themis*, which we call *Fus*, or Right, to be the daughter of heaven and earth. . . .

(7) Touching the several grand mandates, which being imposed by the understanding faculty of the mind must be obeyed by the will of man, they are by the same method found out, whether they import our duty toward God or toward man.

Touching the one, I may not here stand to open, by what degrees of discourse the minds even of mere natural men have attained to know, not only that there is a God, but also what power, force, wisdom, and other properties that God hath, and how all things depend on him. This being therefore presupposed, from that known relation which God hath unto us as unto children, and unto all good things as unto effects whereof Himself is the principal cause, these axioms and laws natural concerning our duty have arisen, "that in all things we go about His aid is by prayer to be craved": "that He cannot have sufficient honor done unto Him, but the utmost of that we can do to honor Him we must"; which is in effect the same that we read, "Thou shalt love the Lord thy God with all thy heart, with all thy soul, and with all thy mind": which law our Savior doth term "The first and the great commandment."

Touching the next, which as our Savior addeth is "like unto this," (he meaneth in amplitude and largeness, inasmuch as it is the root out of which all laws of duty to men-ward have grown, as out of the former all offices of religion toward God) the like natural inducement hath brought men to know that it is their duty no less to love others than themselves. For seeing those things which are equal must needs all have one measure; if I cannot but wish to receive all good, even as much at every man's hand as any man can wish unto his own soul, how should I look to have any part of my desire herein satisfied, unless myself be careful to satisfy the like desire which is undoubtedly in other men, we all being of one and the same nature? To have any thing offered them repugnant to this desire must needs in all respects grieve them as much as me: so that if I do harm I must look to suffer; there being no reason that others should show greater measure of love to me than they have by me showed unto them. My desire therefore to be loved of my equals in nature as much as possible may be, imposeth upon me a natural duty of bearing to them-ward fully the like affection. From which relation of equality between ourselves and them that are as ourselves, what several rules and canons natural reason hath drawn for direction of life no man is ignorant; as namely, "That because we would take no harm, we must therefore do none"; "That sith we would not be in any thing extremely dealt with, we must ourselves avoid all extremity in our dealings"; "That from all violence and wrong we are utterly to abstain"; with such like; which further to wade in would be tedious, and to our present purpose not altogether so necessary, seeing that on these two general heads already mentioned all other specialities are dependent.

(8) Wherefore the natural measure whereby to judge our doings, is the sentence of reason, determining and setting down what is good to be done. . . .

(9) Laws of reason have these marks to be known by. Such as keep them resemble most lively in their voluntary actions that very manner of working which Nature herself doth necessarily observe in the course of the whole world. The works of Nature are all behoveful, beautiful, without superfluity or defect; even so theirs, if they be framed according to that which the law of reason teacheth. Secondly, those laws are investigable by reason, without the help of revelation supernatural and divine. Finally, in such sort they are investigable, that the knowledge of them is general, the world hath always been acquainted with them; according to that which one in Sophocles observeth concerning a branch of this law, "It is no child of today's or yesterday's birth, but hath been no man knoweth how long sithence." It is not agreed upon by one, or two, or few, but by all. Which we may

not so understand, as if every particular man in the whole world did know and confess whatsoever the law of reason doth contain; but this law is such that being proposed no man can reject it as unreasonable and unjust. Again, there is nothing in it but any man (having natural perfection of wit and ripeness of judgment) may by labor and travail find out. And to conclude, the general principles thereof are such, as it is not easy to find men ignorant of them, law rational therefore, which men commonly use to call the law of nature, meaning thereby the law which human nature knoweth itself in reason universally bound unto, which also for that cause may be termed most fitly the law of reason; this law, I say, comprehendeth all those things which men by the light of their natural understanding evidently know, or at leastwise may know, to be beseeming or unbeseeming, virtuous or vicious, good or evil for them to do. . . .

IX

Now the due observation of this law which reason teacheth us cannot but be effectual unto their great good that observe the same. For we see the whole world and each part thereof so compacted, that as long as each thing performeth only that work which is natural unto it, it thereby preserveth both other things and also itself. Contrariwise, let any principal thing, as the sun, the moon, any one of the heavens or elements, but once cease or fail, or swerve, and who doth not easily conceive that the sequel thereof would be ruin both to itself and whatsoever dependeth on it? And is it possible, that man being not only the noblest creature in the world, but even a very world in himself, his transgressing the law of his nature should draw no manner of harm after it? Yes, "tribulation and anguish unto every soul that doeth evil." Good doth follow unto all things by observing the course of their nature, and on the contrary side evil by not observing it; but not unto natural agents that good which we call reward, not that evil which we properly term punishment. The reason whereof is, because amongst creatures in this world, only man's observation of the law of his nature is righteousness, only man's transgression sin. And the reason of this is the difference in his manner of observing or transgressing the law of his nature. He doth not otherwise than voluntarily the one or the other. What we do

against our wills, or constrainedly, we are not properly said to
do it, because the motive cause of doing it is not in ourselves, but
carrieth us, as if the wind should drive a feather in the air, we no
whit furthering that whereby we are driven. In such cases therefore the evil which is done moveth compassion; men are pitied for
it, as being rather miserable in such respect than culpable. Some
things are likewise done by man, though not through outward
force and impulsion, though not against, yet without their wills;
as in alienation of mind, or any the like inevitable utter absence
of wit and judgment. For which cause, no man did ever think the
hurtful actions of furious men and innocents to be punishable.
Again, some things we do neither against nor without, and yet
not simply and merely with our wills, but with our wills in such
sort moved, that albeit there be no impossibility but that we
might, nevertheless we are not so easily able to do otherwise. In
this consideration one evil deed is made more pardonable than another. Finally, that which we do being evil, is notwithstanding by
so much more pardonable, by how much the exigence of so doing
or the difficulty of doing otherwise is greater; unless this necessity
or difficulty have originally risen from ourselves. It is no excuse
therefore unto him, who being drunk committeth incest, and
allegeth that his wits were not his own; inasmuch as himself might
have chosen whether his wits should by that means have been
taken from him. Now rewards and punishments do always pre-
suppose something willingly done well or ill; without which respect though we may sometimes receive good or harm, yet then
the one is only a benefit and not a reward, the other simply an
hurt not a punishment. From the sundry dispositions of man's
will, which is the root of all his actions, there groweth variety in
the sequel of rewards and punishments, which are by these and
the like rules measured: "Take away the will, and all acts are
equal: That which we do not, and would do, is commonly accepted as done." By these and the like rules men's actions are
determined of and judged, whether they be in their own nature
rewardable or punishable. . . .

X

That which hitherto we have set down is (I hope) sufficient to
show their brutishness, which imagine that religion and virtue are

only as men will account of them; that we might make as much
account, if we would, of the contrary, without any harm unto
ourselves, and that in nature they are as indifferent one as the
other. We see then how nature itself teacheth laws and statutes to
live by. The laws which have been hitherto mentioned do bind
men absolutely even as they are men, although they have never
any settled fellowship, never any solemn agreement amongst
themselves what to do or not to do. But forasmuch as we are not
by ourselves sufficient to furnish ourselves with competent store
of things needful for such a life as our nature doth desire, a life fit
for the dignity of man; therefore to supply those defects and imperfections which are in us living single and solely by ourselves,
we are naturally induced to seek communion and fellowship with
others. This was the cause of men's uniting themselves at the first
in politic societies, which societies could not be without government, nor government without a distinct kind of law from that
which hath been already declared. Two foundations there are
which bear up public societies; the one, a natural inclination,
whereby all men desire sociable life and fellowship; the other, an
order expressly or secretly agreed upon touching the manner of
their union in living together. The latter is that which we call the
law of a commonweal, the very soul of a politic body, the parts
whereof are by law animated, held together, and set on work in
such actions, as the common good requireth. Laws politic, ordained for external order and regiment amongst men, are never
framed as they should be, unless presuming the will of man to be
inwardly obstinate, rebellious, and averse from all obedience unto
the sacred laws of his nature; in a word, unless presuming man to
be in regard of his depraved mind little better than a wild beast,
they do accordingly provide notwithstanding so to frame his outward actions, that they be no hindrance unto the common good
for which societies are instituted: unless they do this, they are not
perfect. It resteth therefore that we consider how nature findeth
out such laws of government as serve to direct even nature depraved to a right end.

(2) All men desire to lead in this world a happy life. That life
is led most happily, wherein all virtue is exercised without impediment or let. The Apostle, in exhorting men to contentment
although they have in this world no more than very bare food

and raiment, giveth us thereby to understand that those are even the lowest of things necessary; that if we should be stripped of all those things without which we might possibly be, yet these must be left; that destitution in these is such an impediment, as till it be removed suffereth not the mind of man to admit any other care. For this cause, first God assigned Adam maintenance of life, and then appointed him a law to observe. For this cause, after men began to grow to a number, the first thing we read they gave themselves unto was the tilling of the earth and the feeding of cattle. Having by this mean whereon to live, the principal actions of their life afterward are noted by the exercise of their religion. True it is, that the kingdom of God must be the first thing in our purposes and desires. But inasmuch as righteous life presupposeth life; inasmuch as to live virtuously it is impossible except we live; therefore the first impediment, which naturally we endeavor to remove, is penury and want of things without which we cannot live. Unto life many implements are necessary; more, if we seek (as all men naturally do) such a life as hath in it joy, comfort, delight, and pleasure. To this end we see how quickly sundry arts mechanical were found out, in the very prime of the world. As things of greatest necessity are always first provided for, so things of greatest dignity are most accounted of by all such as judge rightly. Although therefore riches be a thing which every man wisheth, yet no man of judgment can esteem it better to be rich, than wise, virtuous, and religious. If we be both or either of these, it is not because we are so born. For into the world we come as empty of the one as of the other, as naked in mind as we are in body. Both which necessities of man had at the first no other helps and supplies than only domestical; such as that which the prophet implieth, saying, "Can a mother forget her child?" such as that which the Apostle mentioneth, saying, "He that careth not for his own is worse than an infidel"; such as that concerning Abraham, "Abraham will command his sons and his household after him, that they keep the way of the Lord."

(3) But neither that which we learn of ourselves nor that which others teach us can prevail, where wickedness and malice have taken deep root. If therefore when there was but as yet one only family in the world, no means of instruction human or divine could prevent effusion of blood; how could it be chosen but that

when families were multiplied and increased upon earth, after
separation each providing for itself, envy, strife, contention and
violence must grow amongst them? For hath not nature furnished
man with wit and valor, as it were with armor, which may be
used as well unto extreme evil as good? Yea, were they not used
by the rest of the world unto evil; unto the contrary only by
Seth, Enoch, and those few the rest in that line? We all make
complaint of the iniquity of our times: not unjustly; for the days
are evil. But compare them with those times wherein there were
no civil societies, with those times wherein there was as yet no
manner of public regiment established, with those times wherein
there were not above eight persons righteous living upon the
face of the earth; and we have surely good cause to think that
God hath blessed us exceedingly, and hath made us behold most
happy days.

(4) To take away all such mutual grievances, injuries, and
wrongs, there was no way but only by growing unto composition
and agreement amongst themselves, by ordaining some kind of
government public, and by yielding themselves subject thereunto; that unto whom they granted authority to rule and govern,
by them the peace, tranquillity, and happy estate of the rest might
be procured. Men always knew that when force and injury was
offered they might be defenders of themselves; they knew that
howsoever men may seek their own commodity, yet if this were
done with injury unto others it was not to be suffered, but by all
men and by all good means to be withstood; finally they knew that
no man might in reason take upon him to determine his own
right, and according to his own determination proceed in maintenance thereof, inasmuch as every man is toward himself and
them whom he greatly affecteth partial; and therefore that strifes
and troubles would be endless, except they gave their common
consent all to be ordered by some whom they should agree upon:
without which consent there were no reason that one man should
take upon him to be lord or judge over another; because, although
there be according to the opinion of some very great and judicious
men a kind of natural right in the noble, wise, and virtuous, to
govern them which are of servile disposition; nevertheless for
manifestation of this their right, and men's more peaceable con-

tentment on both sides, the assent of them who are to be governed seemeth necessary.

To fathers within their private families Nature hath given a supreme power; for which cause we see throughout the world even from the foundation thereof, all men have ever been taken as lords and lawful kings in their own houses. Howbeit over a whole grand multitude having no such dependency upon any one, and consisting of so many families as every politic society in the world doth, impossible it is that any should have complete lawful power, but by consent of men, or immediate appointment of God; because not having the natural superiority of fathers, their power must needs be either usurped, and then unlawful; or, if lawful, then either granted or consented unto by them over whom they exercise the same, or else given extraordinarily from God, unto whom all the world is subject. It is no improbable opinion therefore which the arch-philosopher was of, that as the chiefest person in every household was always as it were a king, so when numbers of households joined themselves in civil society together, kings were the first kind of governors amongst them. Which is also (as it seemeth) the reason why the name of Father continued still in them, who of fathers were made rulers; as also the ancient custom of governors to do as Melchisedec, and being kings to exercise the office of priests, which fathers did at the first, grew perhaps by the same occasion.

Howbeit not this the only kind of regiment that hath been received in the world. The inconveniences of one kind have caused sundry other to be devised. So that in a word all public regiment of what kind soever seemeth evidently to have risen from deliberate advice, consultation, and composition between men, judging it convenient and behoveful; there being no impossibility in nature considered by itself, but that men might have lived without any public regiment. Howbeit, the corruption of our nature being presupposed, we may not deny but that the law of Nature doth now require of necessity some kind of regiment, so that to bring things unto the first course they were in, and utterly to take away all kind of public government in the world, were apparently to overturn the whole world.

(5) The case of man's nature standing therefore as it doth, some

kind of regiment the law of Nature doth require; yet the kinds thereof being many, Nature tieth not to any one, but leaveth the choice as a thing arbitrary. At the first when some certain kind of regiment was once approved, it may be that nothing was then further thought upon for the manner of governing, but all permitted unto their wisdom and discretion which were to rule; till by experience they found this for all parts very inconvenient, so as the thing which they had devised for a remedy did indeed but increase the sore which it should have cured. They saw that to live by one man's will became the cause of all men's misery. This constrained them to come unto laws, wherein all men might see their duties beforehand, and know the penalties of transgressing them. If things be simply good or evil, and withal universally so acknowledged, there needs no new law to be made for such things. The first kind therefore of things appointed by laws human containeth whatsoever being in itself naturally good or evil, is notwithstanding more secret than that it can be discerned by every man's present conceit, without some deeper discourse and judgment. In which discourse because there is difficulty and possibility many ways to err, unless such things were set down by laws, many would be ignorant of their duties which now are not, and many that know what they should do would nevertheless dissemble it, and to excuse themselves pretend ignorance and simplicity, which now they cannot.

DATE DUE

JAN 3 0 '70			
MAY 2 4 '82			
DEC 1 8 1989			
JAN 1 3 1994			
2/4/94			
MAR 0 9 1994			
MAR 2 2 1994			
MAR 1 5 1996			
MAR 1 1 1998			
3/25/98			
GAYLORD			PRINTED IN U.S.A.